THE ECONOMIC DEVELOPMENT OF NICARAGUA

REPUBLIC OF NICARAGUA

DEPARTMENTS

1 JINOTEGA
2 NUEVA SEGOVIA
3 MADRIZ
4 ESTELI
5 CHINANDEGA
6 LEON
7 MANAGUA
8 MASAYA
9 GRANADA

10 CARAZO
11 RIVAS
12 RIO SAN JUAN
13 CHONTALES
14 BOACO
15 MATAGALPA
16 ZELAYA
17 COMARCA DE EL CABO

— ·· — ·· — INTERNATIONAL BOUNDARIES
· · · · · · · · DEPARTMENTAL BOUNDARIES
——— RIVERS
● NATIONAL CAPITAL
◉ DEPARTMENTAL CAPITALS
⚒ GOLD MINES

20   40   60
MILES

HONDURAS

PUERTO CABO
GRACIAS A DIOS

R. COCO

R. NUESO

17

R. HUAHUA

16

PUERTO
CABEZAS

⚒ BONANZA

R. CUCALAYA

OCOTAL
SOMOTO
COCO
2
3
○ SIUNA
4
SAN RAFAEL DEL NORTE
5
ESTELI
EL SAUCE
JINOTEGA
R. TUMA
15
R. TUMA
PRINZAPOLCA
PUERTO MORAZAN
REAL
MATAGALPA
R. GRANDE
6
EL LIMON
R. GRANDE
RIO GRANDE
CHINANDEGA
DARIO
R. CURINHUAS
CORINTO
LEON
14
NAGAROTE
BOACO
R. SIQUIA
13
LAKE MANAGUA
R. MICO
RAMA
MANAGUA
7
JUIGALPA
R. ESCONDIDO
BLUEFIELDS
8
MASAYA
9
GRANADA
DIRIAMBA
JINOTEPE
10
11
EL MORRITO
PUNTA GORDA
ISLE OF OMETEPE
12
RIVAS
SAN CARLOS
SAN JUAN DEL SUR
LAKE NICARAGUA
R. SAN JUAN
SAN JUAN DEL NORTE
MASACHAPA

N

COSTA   RICA

AREA COVERED BY MAP

THE
ECONOMIC DEVELOPMENT OF
NICARAGUA

REPORT OF A MISSION ORGANIZED BY THE
INTERNATIONAL BANK FOR RECONSTRUCTION AND DEVELOPMENT
AT THE REQUEST OF THE GOVERNMENT OF NICARAGUA

PUBLISHED FOR THE INTERNATIONAL
BANK FOR RECONSTRUCTION AND DEVELOPMENT
BY THE JOHNS HOPKINS PRESS • BALTIMORE, U.S.A.

The Mission

E. HARRISON CLARK	*Special Representative*
WALTER J. ARMSTRONG	*Engineering Adviser*

GEORGE GARVY	*Adviser on Public Finance*
ALVARO MARFAN	*Adviser on Development Organization and Planning*
JOHN F. V. PHILLIPS	*Adviser on Agriculture and Forestry*
ARTHUR WUBNIG	*Adviser on Transportation and Communications*

SUZANNE LESSARD	*Secretary*

v

INTERNATIONAL BANK FOR
RECONSTRUCTION AND DEVELOPMENT
WASHINGTON 25, D. C.

OFFICE OF THE PRESIDENT

September 10, 1952

His Excellency
General Anastasio Somoza
President of the Republic of Nicaragua
Managua, Nicaragua

My Dear Mr. President:

It is with pleasure that I transmit to you the Report of the Special Mission which was stationed in Nicaragua during the past year by the International Bank for Reconstruction and Development at the request of your Government.

The Bank has followed with interest the measures already taken by your Government, in cooperation with the mission, to prepare the way for the development of the country. It is the Bank's hope that the impartial analysis contained in the mission's Report, and the five-year investment program formulated by the mission in cooperation with your Government, will provide a firm basis for the further progress of Nicaragua.

You will understand, of course, that since the Executive Directors and management of the Bank have not had the opportunity to review the mission's recommendations in detail, they are transmitted to you as the views of the mission. We believe, however, that the Report provides a concrete and workable program for the development of Nicaragua, and that it is deserving of the fullest consideration by the Government and people of Nicaragua.

The Bank will continue to follow with interest the actions taken by your Government in connection with the Report. The Bank is prepared, at any appropriate time, to discuss with the Government measures by which the Bank can assist in the execution of the investment program.

It is my sincere hope that the Report will give great impetus to the economic development of your country.

Sincerely yours,

Eugene R Black

INTERNATIONAL BANK FOR
RECONSTRUCTION AND DEVELOPMENT
1818 H STREET, N. W.
WASHINGTON 25, D. C.

September 10, 1952

Mr. Eugene R. Black
President
International Bank for Reconstruction and Development
Washington 25, D. C.

Dear Mr. Black:

I take pleasure in submitting herewith the Report of the Special Mission of the International Bank for Reconstruction and Development, which was stationed in Nicaragua from July 1951 through May 1952 at the request of the Government of Nicaragua. The report contains the final recommendations of the mission, including a five-year program for the development of the country's resources.

The investment program has been formulated in close association with the Government over the past year. This association, together with the work of the experts attached to the mission, has been, I believe, productive of results which should form a solid basis for the rapid progress of the country.

I should like to express the mission's great appreciation for the interest in, and encouragement given to, the work of the mission by His Excellency, General Anastasio Somoza, President of the Republic.

In addition, I should like to express our thanks for the friendly and close collaboration of the National Economic Council, including its Chairman, Dr. Enrique Delgado, Minister of Economy, its members, Don Rafael Huezo, Minister of Finance, Don Constantino Lacayo Fiallos, Minister of Fomento, Don Enrique Sanchez, Minister of Agriculture, and Dr. Leon DeBayle, General

viii

Manager of the National Bank, and its Executive Secretary, Dr. Jorge A. Montealegre.

It is the expectation and hope of the mission that, in carrying out a five-year development program, Nicaragua's efforts will achieve the rising standard of living its people so richly deserve.

Sincerely,

E. Harrison Clark

Preface

This is a report of a special mission of the International Bank for Reconstruction and Development, which was stationed in Nicaragua from July, 1951 to May, 1952, at the request of the Government of Nicaragua.

On January 31, 1951, the Government asked the Bank to send a general survey mission to the country to assist it in formulating an over-all development plan. In response to the request, the Bank suggested that, instead of sending a development mission for a relatively short stay, it would station a Special Representative and an Engineering Adviser in the country for a period up to one year. The former, as chief of mission, would assist the Government in arranging for visits by such special experts as would be needed.

Under the proposal, as accepted by the Government, the mission had three objectives:

(a) to assist the government in the preparation of an over-all long-range development program;

(b) to advise the government on current economic policies as well as improvements in the existing administrative and financial structure to prepare the groundwork for such a development program;

(c) to coordinate the work of specialized experts from the Bank and other international agencies and to assist the government in carrying out their recommendations.

In accordance with an agreed program, specialists in various fields came to Nicaragua during the period of the mission. The *Corporacion de Fomento* of Chile provided an expert on the proposed development institute, the Federal Reserve Bank of New York, an expert on public finance, and the Food and Agricultural

Organization, an expert on tropical agriculture. An expert on transportation and communications was provided by the International Bank. In addition, the International Monetary Fund sent a mission on banking and credit.

The Bank mission also drew on the specialized experience and knowledge of United States "Point Four" representatives in power, education, agriculture and public health, who were in the country during the mission's stay.

The mission worked in close cooperation with the National Economic Council, under the chairmanship of the Minister of Economy. Associated with the Minister of Economy on the Council are the Ministers of Public Works, Finance, Agriculture, and the General Manager of the National Bank. The Executive Secretary, Dr. Jorge A. Montealegre, acted as liaison officer.

The mission, with the specialized experts, traveled more than 10,000 miles within the country. Its field trips took it over every mile of rail and air transport and almost every mile of road and water route in the country. The trips covered every department and almost every town over 1,000 population. They included all the principal agricultural and forestry regions, and most of the major industries and mines.

The report of the mission consists of five parts. Part I is the main report which contains the proposed five-year development program as well as a summary of the principal recommendations of the mission. Part II covers industries, power and mining; Part III, transportation and communications; Part IV, agriculture and forestry; and Part V, the fiscal system of Nicaragua. A report on the banking system is being made by the International Monetary Fund.

Contents

CONTENTS

CONTENTS

CONTENTS

Contents

Contents

Tables

TABLES

TABLES

Maps

EXCHANGE RATES

(Nicaragua at present has multiple exchange rates. For the purposes of this report a rate of seven cordobas to the U. S. dollar has been used.)

7 cordobas	=	1 U. S. dollar
1 cordoba	=	14.3 U. S. cents
1 million cordobas	=	143,000 U. S. dollars

UNITS OF MEASUREMENT

1 manzana	=	1.74 acres
1 quintal	=	101.4 U. S. pounds
1 kilometer	=	.6214 U. S. mile

Introduction

This section, a brief description of the economy, has been added to the formal report presented to the Government of Nicaragua, as background for readers not familiar with the country.

THE STRUCTURE OF THE ECONOMY

I. *Geography and Climate*

Nicaragua is the largest of the Central American republics. Its area is usually given as 57,000 square miles, an approximate figure until the current geodetic survey is completed. The country lies entirely within the tropics; it borders Costa Rica in the south and Honduras in the north and extends from the Caribbean to the Pacific Ocean. Its climate is typical of such areas. In the coastal plains and valleys it is hot and humid most of the year; as the elevation rises, the temperature falls, and above 3,000 feet there is a cool and bracing climate.

Certain characteristics of the country are worth noting. There is, first, the heavy concentration of population. Some 60% of all inhabitants live in a narrow belt along the Pacific, two hundred miles long but only twelve to sixty miles in width. A second belt, averaging sixty miles further inland, contains another 32% of the population. The remaining land area, embracing more than half the total, contains only 8% of the whole population.

A second feature is the low over-all density of population which is less than six per square mile, or a little over half that of Costa Rica and perhaps a fifth that of El Salvador. There is a high ratio of arable land not in cultivation to population. Since there have been no thorough land-use surveys, no accurate figure is available, but it is conservatively estimated that no more than a fourth of the country's arable land is under cultivation or grazing. This factor, among others, indicates both the degree of underdevelopment and the potential of the country.

A final characteristic is the richness of the volcanic soils. Even after centuries of exploitation which have brought serious erosion in the developed areas and acute damage to the forest cover, the soils are fertile, although their continued fertility will depend on soil conservation measures.

There are four main regions. In describing them, it is convenient to use the classification employed in the report of a recent FAO mission to Nicaragua.* They are:

(a) *The Western Plains of the Pacific Coast*—volcanic plains ranging from sea level to an elevation of several hundred feet, with rainy and dry seasons of approximately six months each. The volcanic ash soils are of high fertility. Main crops include corn, sorghum, sesame, rice, beans, cotton, sugar and livestock.

(b) *The Managua-Carazo Uplands*—a comparatively small sierra and upland plateau ranging in height from about 1,300 to 4,000 feet. The region has a dry season of five to six months. The environment is cooler than the western plains because of the elevation.

Although staple crops are grown, and there is some livestock, the region is predominantly coffee country.

(c) *The Central Montane Region (Matagalpa-Jinotega)*—situated in the range of mountains forming the Continental Divide, with an elevation ranging from 1,500 feet to about 5,500 feet. The topography is rugged with comparatively restricted lowland valleys and plateaus. The climate is cool, with little seasonal change but marked diurnal range. This is predominantly coffee country, but there are areas at the lower elevations suitable for mixed farming and livestock. It is also a region of pine lumber.

(d) *The Eastern Plains Region*—comprises over half the total area of the country. It is made up of slopes of low relief and the

---

*Food and Agriculture Organization, Rome, 1950.

low-lying plains of the Atlantic and has a wide range of soils. The rainfall is heavier than in the rest of the country, extending over nine to twelve months of the year. The prevailing vegetation is tropical evergreen hardwood forest of mixed composition, but the northeast has an extensive area of pine flats. Mahogany and pine are exploited in the area. Some staple crops are produced and there is a small livestock industry. The major gold mines of the country are located here.

II. The Population

The 1950 national census, the most thorough in the country's history, indicated a population of 1,053,000. While two thirds of the population is considered rural and one third urban, there is no sharp distinction between these groups as there is in more developed countries. The urban lawyer or businessman is often a part-time farmer; the city worker, a seasonal crop picker.

The inhabitants are largely of a distinct *mestizo* type, predominantly Indian but with an admixture of European, mainly Spanish, blood. Probably some 75% are mestizo, another 15% white or predominantly white, and the remainder pure Indians, Negroes or mulattoes. The latter group live, for the most part, on the east coast.

The present working population is estimated at 324,000, of whom 274,000 are men. Nicaraguan labor, on the whole, is willing and, when properly trained, fully capable of highly skilled work. During the harvests of 1952 there were local shortages of unskilled labor. The growing labor shortage on the west coast will necessitate increased mechanization in agriculture and more efficient techniques in industry. Only on the east coast is there surplus labor, as a result of structural changes in the east coast economy, particularly the loss of the banana trade.

Although a few people enjoy high incomes and a standard of living comparable to the higher levels of Latin America, Europe and the United States, the general standard of living is low. The basic diet of corn, beans, bananas or plantains, and rice, supplemented by sugar and some meat, is sufficient to fill the stomach but it is neither balanced nor energy-producing. Drinking water is not safe even in the major towns and sanitation is inadequate everywhere. Even in the capital only half the population has electricity and many of the streets need paving. The oxcart and horse are still the usual means of transport, although these are giving way to trucks and busses on the main highways. The literacy rate is probably no more than 30%. High disease rates, especially of malaria and dysentery, induce low labor productivity. Infant mortality is high.

Nevertheless, the mission gained the impression that over the past few years there had been a slight improvement in general standards of living. Although statistically reliable data on the point are unavailable, some evidence of improvement exists. The DDT campaign has had an impact on the malaria rate, real wages have increased slightly in the past two years, and there has been a basic improvement in transportation and in over-all productivity.

III. *Agriculture and Forestry*

There has been little direct government technical help to agriculture, and agricultural techniques are usually primitive. Production is notably diversified and that of many cash crops on medium- to large-sized farms has been vigorously expanded in recent years.

The major crops are coffee, cotton, sesame, sugar, rice and corn. Sorghum, beans, cacao, yucca, tobacco, bananas and plantains and a variety of other fruits and vegetables are also important. Altogether more than 35 crops are grown commercially and tests have shown a number of others could probably be successfully raised for home or foreign markets. Livestock and timber production with their by-products are important associated activities. Cattle-raising, in particular, promises to become a major industry in the future.

In 1951 the total value of agricultural production was around

$91 million or nearly $90 per capita. Total exports exceeded $36 million, with seven products having export values in excess of one million dollars. As a result of increases in the world price, the value of coffee exports more than doubled from 1948 to 1951. By 1951, however, expanded production of major crops increased the value of other exports to approximately that of coffee exports. With the expansion, difficulties have appeared in the external marketing of certain crops, cotton in particular, and constitute a problem of increasing concern to the government.

IV. Industries

Nicaragua's industrial output is of considerable range, but almost all of it is produced either in homes or in small, poorly equipped factories. In 1950, according to estimates by the Central Statistical Bureau, manufacturing industries contributed around 64 million cordobas to the national income and home industries around 81 million cordobas—together less than 10% of the national income.

Leading manufactures include sugar, beer, soft drinks, textiles, cement, cigarettes, soap and matches. With some exceptions, output has been generally static for the past few years. Only a few firms are expanding operations or installing new equipment.

The wide variety of agricultural products offers the opportunity for a balanced growth of small industries using local raw materials, particularly cotton, meat, hides, dairy products, and fats and oils.

V. Transportation and Communications

Before World War II, there were almost no motorable roads in the country. Today the beginning of a comprehensive highway network has emerged on the west coast. It includes the Inter-American Highway from the northern to the southern frontier, the initial stretches of the projected road to Rama on the east coast, the roads under construction or projected from Managua to Granada, Leon, Chinandega, Jinotega and the Tuma Valley, and the roads to Masachapa and Poneloya.

The road investment program has already yielded a rich return to the economy. Wherever the mission travelled, there was impressive evidence of development stimulated directly by good roads.

The road program has, however, concentrated on main highways. The country now needs a system of access and farm-to-market roads to take the fullest advantage of the main highway program. On the west coast, the local roads most urgently needed are feeder routes into the main highways and main railway stations. On the east coast the need is for penetration roads from the navigable rivers. The local roads on the west coast are intended to improve productive efficiency in relatively mature areas. Those on the east coast and in the central area will be developmental roads to open new areas for agriculture, cattle raising, and forestry.

The proposed main highway program will parallel large sectors of the present railway system. The aged and often obsolete equipment of the rail lines has been heavily overburdened in the past few years by increased foreign and internal trade and a cotton boom on the west coast. When the road network is completed, much of the traffic that now goes by rail will move by truck, bus, or automobile, and certain sections of the line will probably have to be abandoned when a road network is available to Granada and from the Inter-American Highway to San Juan del Sur.

The communications services, operated as a unit to include the postal, telephone and telegraph systems, run at heavy deficits, subsidized by the state. Much of their equipment is also worn and obsolete.

VI. *The National Income*

Gross national product in 1951 amounted to approximately $170 million, with an average per capita income of around $155.

With a concentration of income in the hands of a relatively small sector of the population, and a system of taxation which rests very largely on consumption, average income for the overwhelming bulk of the population, after taxation, is probably less than $100 per year.

While two thirds or more of the population are directly engaged in agriculture, forestry and mining, the gross value of product of this sector accounts for slightly less than half the national income. Commerce, manufacturing, construction, finance and services make up the other half of the national income.

VII. *The Balance of Payments*

Nicaragua for many years experienced difficulties in meeting its international payments. Partly this arose from its small exports and partly from budgetary deficits and other inflationary factors which increased the volume of money in circulation and led to a demand for imports in excess of the small earnings of foreign exchange.

The limited exchange accumulated by the end of the war (U. S. $6.67 million) had, by the end of 1949, dwindled to $3.71 million. By the end of 1950, even though exports had increased by $10.67 million over those of the previous year, Nicaragua's net exchange position was negative.

Severe import controls and licensing having proved ineffective, new monetary and fiscal policies were introduced in 1950. These brought rapid improvement in both the internal monetary situation and in the balance of payments. The 1949-50 and 1950-51 national budgets were brought into balance and the government ceased borrowing from the National Bank. The National Bank in turn adopted selective credit policies to stimulate production of export crops. At the end of 1950, an exchange law established new exchange rates, abolished import controls, and provided for exchange surcharges of one and three cordobas per dollar on luxury imports. The effective buying rate was set at 6.6 cordobas to the dollar and the basic selling rate at seven cordobas, giving a spread of 0.4 cordobas.

As a result of these measures, Nicaragua's balance of payments showed a surplus of $6.3 million in 1951. There has been further improvement this year. In May 1952 gold and foreign exchange reserves reached $16.3 million. In spite of increasing development expenditures, the budget has continued in balance, and it is expected to be in balance the next fiscal year.

Exports, because of the rise in coffee prices and expansion of agricultural production, increased from $26.6 million in 1948 to $34.8 million in 1950 and to $45.8 million in 1951. The expansion of exports, the increased degree of internal monetary stability, and the rise in monetary reserves have provided a sound framework for the projected development program.

VIII. *The Monetary and Fiscal System*

Although there are several small private banks and a government-owned mortgage bank, their credit role is limited. The bulk of the commercial credits of the country are handled by the state-owned National Bank which combines central and commercial banking functions. Although the Bank has a number of branches and agencies in various parts of the country, many areas have no banking facilities. There is no effective source of medium-or long-term credits. Costs of short-term private credit are high, from 18% to 60% a year. Even short-term credit from the banks may, with various charges, run from 9% to 10%. There are almost no facilities for small credits, either for agriculture or industry.

In the past the fiscal system has been based almost exclusively on consumption taxes and import duties. These have averaged 83-87% of all revenue over the past few years. With the introduction of an export tax on coffee in 1950 and of special taxes on the net income of coffee and cotton producers in 1951, the first steps have been taken towards a more direct and flexible system of taxation.

IX. *Government Enterprises*

In addition to the National Bank and the Mortgage Bank, both government-owned, the government operates the railroad, the telephone, telegraph and postal services, and the power and light plants of the capital and a few other towns. The government also owns a half-interest in the national airlines, and maintains a match monopoly. In spite of these extensive operations, net receipts to the government from its enterprises are small since the profits from the railroad are offset by the losses of the communications services, while the returns from other enterprises are minor.

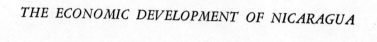

THE ECONOMIC DEVELOPMENT OF NICARAGUA

CHAPTER ONE

The Basis for Development

I. *THE ECONOMIC POTENTIAL OF NICARAGUA*

From its nearly year-long travel in the country, the mission concluded that few underdeveloped countries have so great a physical potential for growth and economic development as does Nicaragua. In area this is the largest country in Central America. In relation to its present population, it has almost unlimited land for development. The land can grow nearly every tropical crop and many nontropical crops.

By making effective use of its land resources, the country can become, in the future, an important exporter of meat and dairy products and of a diversified list of other agricultural products. It should continue as a producer of timber and minerals. It should develop a sound and well-balanced relationship between industry and agriculture.

The population of the country is a little over a million and, in contrast to its land, its manpower resources are relatively small. Compared with many underdeveloped countries the ratio of manpower to land is favorable. Though this small ratio of labor to land will impose manpower shortages, the use of modern industrial and agricultural techniques can offset this handicap.

The physical resources of the country provide a sound basis for economic development. The variety, quality and extent of these resources are assessed in the technical sections of this report.

II. *STRUCTURAL WEAKNESSES IN THE ECONOMY*

Nicaragua has many of the social, economic and governmental weaknesses typical of underdeveloped countries. Its Government is keenly aware of this.

The principal weak points in the past have been:

(a) generally low standards of health and education;

(b) an archaic fiscal system inadequate to advance the country's economic development and to encourage rising standards of living;

(c) a transportation system improved in recent years but still inadequate;

(d) an ineffective credit system, especially for the provision of medium- and long-term agricultural and industrial credits;

(e) an absence of long-range planning, and of a concrete investment program and policy coordination within the government;

(f) a system of public administration requiring a general overhaul to carry out a development program.

Many of the weaknesses in the economic structure have been accentuated by conditions peculiar to the country. Though its people are notably cheerful and high spirited, they have had an unhappy and depressing history. There have been many civil wars in the past. These have been frequently accompanied by foreign intervention in the nation's political affairs. During the civil war of the 1920's there was direct foreign military intervention. The restoration of peace was followed by a major earthquake which destroyed the capital city. The economic depression of the 1930's seriously disrupted the export trade of the country. World War II brought fewer economic benefits to Nicaragua than to many Latin American countries.

This long history, together with the general backwardness and poverty of the country, discouraged economic progress and the establishment of a sound administrative and fiscal structure in the country. Until very recent years these remained much as they had been in the nineteenth century or even in colonial times.

During the past two years the government has shown a clear awareness of the need for improvement and of the areas where

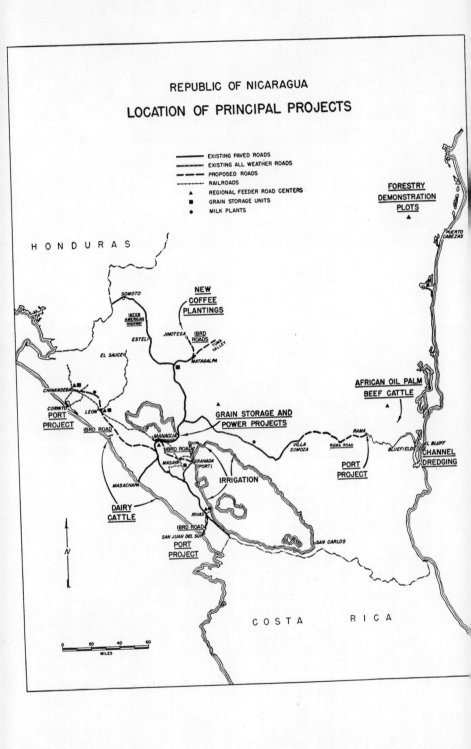

REPUBLIC OF NICARAGUA
LOCATION OF PRINCIPAL PROJECTS

improvement is necessary. It has demonstrated both the imagination and will to move forward with vigorous action.

Economic conditions have reinforced the determination of the government. During the past two years, the economic and financial position of the country has been stronger than ever before. The national income has never been higher. These conditions, together with the administrative changes being undertaken by the government, can provide the stimulus for very rapid economic development and a promising future.

III. *PROGRESSIVE MEASURES UNDERTAKEN*

During the past 12 months the Government of Nicaragua has undertaken a number of progressive measures. It has:

(a) brought into operation a National Economic Council, formed at the Cabinet level, to coordinate over-all monetary and fiscal policies with the long-range planning for development;

(b) undertaken the formulation of a five-year development program in transportation, communications, agriculture, industry, education, health and power, with major construction activities already under way;

(c) completed plans for a National Development Institute to plan and finance the long-range agricultural and industrial program;

(d) undertaken a sharp increase in national budget development expenditures, to go into effect in 1952-53;

(e) taken the first steps to institute a major fiscal reform (including the proposed introduction of an income tax, more effective enforcement of existing direct taxes, the removal of inequitable consumption taxes, and a revision of the tariff system);

(f) taken the first steps toward the improvement of the system of public administration;

(g) taken measures to improve its statistics through the first national agricultural census and the first study of national income.

These steps, taken in cooperation with the mission of the Bank, represent the achievement of a government alive to the needs of the country and with the will and desire to progress.

Within the last 18 months the Government has also taken measures to check inflation by (a) balancing the budget, (b) providing increased control of internal credit, and (c) revising the foreign exchange system. These moves have contributed to increased internal financial stability and are an essential basis for a long-range development program.

The various steps taken have been an important preliminary to the program of general economic development. They should be a solid foundation for further progress.

CHAPTER TWO

The Five Year Development Program

I. *THE AIM*

The aim of Nicaragua's development program is to raise the standard of living of its people.

In the formulation of its recommendations the mission has made this aim its main objective. To construct a practical development plan for Nicaragua has been a complex undertaking. The country lacks adequate roads, schools, hospitals, housing, sanitation, ports and power. Its basic agricultural and industrial economy has long been weak and unstable. Its system of public administration is far from adequate. The mission has had to balance short-run against long-run needs. It has weighed the need for capital investment against the need for larger consumption and improved standards of living, the needs of the cash export crops against those of crops for internal consumption and the need for communications facilities against the needs for power. It has measured the needs for private credits against the urgent fiscal requirements of the government. The program had to take account of the financial capacity of the country, including its credit standing abroad, and the institutions and personnel available or needed for carrying out such a program.

II. *THE PROGRAM*

The program formulated by the mission is designed to enable the country to go forward simultaneously in health, education, transportation, agriculture, industry and power. It is designed to raise the standards of living by strengthening the over-all economy.

In drawing up a five-year program for Nicaragua the mission has tried to develop a balanced plan, taking into account both the needs and potentials in all sectors of the economy. For this reason, the agricultural and transportation experts attached to the mission worked in cooperation to formulate a program to improve the transport sector, vital to agricultural growth. The agricultural program was drawn up to promote agricultural production and land settlement in areas to be opened up or made more accessible by improved road transport.

Proposals for the formation of new industries have been geared to expected increases in agricultural production and, for investment in power, to the need for new industries and anticipated growth of the urban population. The basic educational and health programs are designed to increase productivity in all sectors.

The five-year development program, presented in summary form, in Table 1, outlines the main investment objectives during the period. The bulk of the investment will be in transportation and agriculture but, because of their urgency, the education and public health sectors have also been assigned a substantial share of the investment expenditures.

The objectives are stated in terms of minimum and optimum goals. The minimum goals, of a first priority category, are those which the mission believes must be carried out to attain a minimum rate of development for the country. The optimum goals, the second priority group, are highly desirable but not so urgent. The mission hopes the country may be able to attain not only the minimum but also the optimum goals in the five-year period.

TABLE 1

THE OVER-ALL DEVELOPMENT PROGRAM 1952-1957
First Priority (Minimum Program)

	Foreign Exchange Costs	Local Currency Costs[1]	Total Costs
I. *Agriculture*			
A. *Instituto de Fomento*			
1. Coffee Plantings	$ 250,000	$ 2,750,000	$ 3,000,000
2. Cattle	1,500,000	2,500,000	4,000,000

	Foreign Exchange Costs	Local Currency Costs[1]	Total Costs
3. African Oil Palms	—	500,000	500,000
4. Soil Conservation	1,500,000	500,000	2,000,000
5. Irrigation	400,000	600,000	1,000,000
6. Agricultural Machinery	2,000,000	—	2,000,000
7. Land Colonization	300,000	1,700,000	2,000,000
8. Grain Storage Units			
a) Managua	550,000	150,000	700,000
b) Others	175,000	75,000	250,000
9. Miscellaneous Credits	—	1,550,000	1,550,000
B. *Ministry of Agriculture*			
1. Extension Services	50,000	600,000	650,000
2. Land-Use Studies	—	1,000,000	1,000,000
3. Forestry	250,000	750,000	1,000,000
4. Servicio Tecnico*	150,000	200,000	350,000
	7,125,000	12,875,000	20,000,000
II. *Transportation and Communications*			
1. Railway	1,290,000	460,000	1,750,000
2. Main Roads	9,000,000	4,500,000	13,500,000
3. Local Roads	3,000,000	1,000,000	4,000,000
4. Ports and Airfields	1,320,000	1,405,000	2,725,000
	14,610,000	7,365,000	21,975,000
III. *Education**			
1. Elementary Schools	525,000	1,650,000	2,175,000
2. Vocational Training	325,000	325,000	650,000
3. Literacy Campaign	—	300,000	300,000
	850,000	2,275,000	3,125,000
IV. *Public Health**			
1. Pure Water and Sanitation	1,500,000	1,500,000	3,000,000

	Foreign Exchange Costs	Local Currency Costs[1]	Total Costs
2. Health Clinics	750,000	750,000	1,500,000
3. Disease Control	250,000	250,000	500,000
4. Hospitals	1,000,000	1,000,000	2,000,000
5. Professional and Technical Training	450,000	450,000	900,000
	3,950,000	3,950,000	7,900,000
V. *Industries*	1,310,000	490,000	1,800,000
VI. *Power*	3,500,000	1,000,000	4,500,000
Total Minimum Program	$31,345,000	$27,955,000	$59,300,000

Second Priority (Additional Program)

	Foreign Exchange Costs	Local Currency Costs[1]	Total Costs
I. Agriculture	1,000,000	6,000,000	7,000,000
II. Transport and Communications			
a) Feeder Roads	750,000	250,000	1,000,000
b) Telecommunications	1,265,000	425,000	1,690,000
III. Education	250,000	500,000	750,000
IV. Public Health	2,125,000	2,125,000	4,250,000
V. Industries	1,500,000	500,000	2,000,000
Total Additional Program	$ 6,890,000	$ 9,800,000	$16,690,000
Total Optimum Program	$38,235,000	$37,755,000	$75,990,000

[1] Cordoba costs converted to dollars at seven to one.
*Represents additional funds over existing level of expenditure.

In agriculture, transportation, communications, industries and power, the proposed expenditures represent the total investment program in these sectors. They include projects already planned and under way as well as new projects reaching the planning stage. They do not include the ordinary administrative expenditures of the ministries or departments in charge of the program. They also do not include funds required for annual crop loans from the National Bank.

The projected use of funds represents desirable expenditures in education, public health and for the *Servicio Tecnico Agricola* additional to those now made by the government in these sectors.

Estimated costs have been given in dollars, since dollar values are used by the government in many of its statistical computations. The costs have been broken down into those for foreign exchange and local currency. Local currency costs have been converted to dollars at the rate of seven cordobas to the dollar. Estimates are as accurate as is possible at this time, but the relative proportions are very much subject to future change.

III.   *GENERAL AND SPECIFIC OBJECTIVES*

The general objectives of the program are to expand and diversify the basic economy in order to raise the general level of living and to improve educational and health standards. The program aims (a) to increase real per capita income by 15% in the next five years, allowing for the natural growth of population during the period, and (b) to increase the physical volume of agricultural and industrial production by 25%.

The specific objectives include:

(a) completion of a major highway network linking Managua with Granada, Leon, Chinandega, Jinotega, San Juan del Sur, the Tuma Valley and with the east coast;

(b) establishment of a complete network of farm-to-market roads;

(c) modernization of the railway;

(d) rehabilitation of the major ocean ports and improvement of lake transportation;

(e) establishment of pure water and sanitation facilities in the main towns and many of the smaller communities;

(f) expansion of the present power capacity of Managua to triple its present size, and formation of a grid to connect Managua with other important cities;

(g) increasing the number of coffee trees by 25% and expansion of cattle production to the status of a major industry;

(h) establishment of several new industries, as well as a number of grain storage plants;

(i) reduction in the rate of illiteracy and a rise in vocational and technical education and training;

(j) creation of an adequate medium- and long-term credit system and technical assistance for industry and agriculture.

In order to carry out a program of these dimensions, the mission has proposed certain structural changes in the administrative system of Nicaragua, including:

(a) establishment of an *Instituto de Fomento;*

(b) improvement in the organization and staffing of the Ministry of Finance to carry out the program of fiscal reform and better budgetary techniques and practices;

(c) reorganization of the banking system, including the establishment of a central bank; [1]

(d) reorganization of the Ministry of Public Works to embrace all construction activities of the government;

(e) improvements of staff and organization in other government departments;

(f) reorganization of the railway, power, and postal, telegraph and telephone services as autonomous public utilities.

The mission has not set out to prepare an easy program. The goals are high. They require that Nicaragua do as much in five years as she has accomplished in several decades. The program will require the most vigorous and constructive leadership in its execution.

---

[1] The International Monetary Fund is preparing a report on this subject.

The mission believes that the goals are within the capacity and ability of the country to attain on the following grounds:

(a) The program of fiscal reform, if successfully carried out, should place the minimum investment program well within, and the optimum program within, the financial capacity of the country;

(b) A substantial part of the total investment costs, particularly the foreign exchange costs, will be covered by external loans or grants already authorized. The mission believes that the financial position of the country will justify additional external loans;

(c) The balanced budget and increased monetary stability attained in the past year provide a sound framework for a development program, while the foreign exchange holdings which have increased more than fourfold in the past 18 months give the country a strong reserve position;

(d) The highway program, which involves expenditures amounting to nearly 30% of the minimum investment program, will be carried out by a highly efficient Ministry of Public Works. The mission hopes that all construction activities of the program will eventually be placed under the same ministry;

(e) The sanitation and educational programs and a substantial part of the agricultural program will have the assistance of United States Point Four personnel under programs already agreed upon between the two governments;

(f) A number of well-trained and competent Nicaraguans are available for posts in the Institute de Fomento and elsewhere. Where necessary, foreign technical personnel can fill the gaps until Nicaraguans can be trained for all important administrative positions;

(g) The production goals are set on the basis of the present relatively low level of gross national product from which percentage growth can be rapid.

The present level of gross public and private investment in Nicaragua appears to be about 6% of the national income with the private investment sector accounting for about 4%. The minimum program would raise the total investment level to approximately 11% of the national income, and the optimum program to 14%.

In addition to an increase in investment, the program contemplates a diversion of investment expenditures from nonproductive to productive uses, particularly in the private sector. This diversion will increase the effectiveness of the projected over-all rate of investment.

IV. *THE FIRST YEAR OF THE PROGRAM*

The first year will be the most difficult of the five. The development program depends for its success on the introduction of ideas new to Nicaragua. There will have to be new institutions, new budgetary techniques, new laws and generally new approaches. The mission recognizes the difficulties that are bound to arise, especially in the initial stages.

For this reason, in outlining the investment program for the first year, the mission has tried wherever possible to make it a simple expansion of the program already planned by the government. It has tried to keep new activities to the minimum compatible with the need for the rapid advancement of the development program. It expects, however, an acceleration of the new program beginning in the second year.

For the first year, therefore, the mission suggests the following additions to the road, educational, grain storage and health projects already devised by the government:

(a) expansion of the present very modest feeder road program;
(b) further and prompt attention to the power needs of Managua;
(c) expansion of the water and sanitation program being developed with technical assistance from the United States Government;

(d) intensification of the literacy campaign.

The mission also suggests the following as an additional, and essentially new, program:

(a) organization of the Instituto de Fomento and, in its first year's activities, concentration on the promotion of the cattle industry, coffee and African oil palm plantings, the establishment of a good technical staff, and the extension of credits to the proposed new industries;

(b) rehabilitation of the railroad and reorganization of the government-owned public utilities;

(c) institution of land-use studies and forestry demonstration projects;

(d) improvements in the public administration.

V. INVESTMENT BY THE GOVERNMENT AND THE INSTITUTO DE FOMENTO

In proposing the formation of an Instituto de Fomento, the mission has considered that one of the chief tasks of the Instituto would be the technical planning of future development projects of the government. The actual execution of the work on the bulk of the projects will be carried out by the government itself through its departments or agencies and enterprises.

Between 30-35% of the over-all development funds will be in the form of agricultural and industrial credits or direct investments in productive enterprises by the proposed Instituto de Fomento. Another 10% of the funds for the minimum program will be invested in state enterprises. The remaining funds will be direct government expenditures.

VI. FINANCING THE PROGRAM

A. Foreign Exchange and Domestic Costs

The program calls for the expenditure of $59-76 million over the next five years in both domestic currency and foreign exchange. The foreign exchange costs are quite manageable for the country. The first priority program will cost a little over $31 million. Authorized United States Government grants of $8 million for the completion of the Inter-American Highway and the Rama Road, $3.7 million in International Bank loans already approved but not disbursed, and another $2 million in foreign exchange set aside from the proceeds of the coffee export tax for road building, are included in these figures. These funds add up to 44% of the foreign exchange requirements of the minimum program for the next five years.

The mission, in formulating its program, has assumed that the credit standing of the country will be sufficient to enable her to obtain external loans amounting to half the remaining foreign exchange costs of the program.

The additional foreign exchange required averages only 4% per year of Nicaragua's 1951 exports. There should be no problem in finding the necessary exchange even if exports do not hold to the high 1951 level.

The domestic costs (the cordoba costs of local labor, material and credits, as well as the cordoba equivalent of the remaining foreign exchange costs of the program) will range from around 250 million cordobas for the minimum program to 350 million cordobas for the optimum or between 50 and 70 million cordobas per year. Since the 1951-52 level of public investment was around 20 million cordobas, the recommended program represents an increase of 30 to 50 million cordobas a year.

The main domestic source of funds for the development program will be the national budget, including:

(a) funds from present and future coffee export taxes and the recent special income taxes on coffee and cotton;

(b) additional revenue from the improved collection of existing direct taxes and the proposed general income tax;

(c) miscellaneous sources, such as funds now allocated to the *Banco Hipotecario,* as well as a part of the profits of the National Bank;

(d) diversion of funds in the budget from nonproductive to productive purposes;

(e) funds from the exchange surcharges where necessary for urgent projects which cannot be financed by other means.

In addition to funds from the budget, sources will include:

(a) earnings of government enterprises;

(b) revolving funds of self-liquidating projects of the Instituto de Fomento and profits from its subsidiary enterprises;

(c) domestic bond issues and sales of shares by the Instituto.

B. *Government as a Source of Development Funds*

Fiscal and Tariff Reforms. The present level of government revenue is too small to finance a development program adequate to meet the country's needs. Therefore, one of the first tasks of the mission was to recommend measures for the improvement of the existing fiscal structure.

The over-all long-range objective of the fiscal reform, now under way, is to achieve a level of government revenue from direct taxation of 35-40 million cordobas a year. This objective is both possible and feasible. It would provide, if added to the present budgetary level of investment, sufficient funds to carry out nearly the entire optimum program.

The fiscal reform will not, however, have immediate effects. The general income tax will not produce revenue until the 1953-54 budget. Because of its administrative complexities, it will not be fully effective, in any case, in its first year or two of operation. More efficient collection of other direct taxes probably will not produce any great increases in revenue until 1953. The mission believes, however, that half or more of the over-all goal for direct taxation can be reached in the 1953-54 budget, particularly if the export tax on coffee is increased.

The major purpose of the tariff revision is to reduce its present heavily regressive character, but it is quite probable that the revision (including the merger of many of the existing exchange surcharges into the new tariff) would not only introduce a fairer system of import duties but also increase their over-all yield.

Nondevelopmental Budgetary Expenditures. In the 1951-52 budget, only about 13% of total expenditures is allocated directly to development and about 40% to the budgets of the economic ministries directly responsible for development.

Some development expenditures do not appear in the budget because of rather faulty budgetary presentation which underestimates the amount of money spent for development purposes.

A substantial share of budgetary expenditures goes to non-economic purposes. Because of internal political factors connected with these expenditures the mission is not disposed to criticize them but would like to indicate the desirability of a very careful examination by the government of all budgetary expenditures for nonproductive purposes. They represent a drain on the economy and an impediment to progress. They should be weighed very carefully in the light of the country's urgent over-all needs.

The Earnings of Autonomous Agencies. The recommendations of the mission in regard to the reorganization of autonomous agencies are to be found elsewhere in this report. This section considers only the financial aspects of the recommendations which aim to introduce business standards of operating efficiency into these agencies. Greater efficiency will decrease operating costs or losses and give substantial savings to the government. It should also make available additional development funds.

a. *The Railway.* The present level of earnings of the government-owned railway is sufficient not only to cover the costs of the projected railroad investment program but also to provide an additional contribution to the government's development budget for other sectors of the economy.

Part of the investment in the railways will be self-liquidating. The proposed introduction of diesel locomotives should save enough in operating expenses over the next five years to pay for the initial capital cost.

The mission believes that an amount up to $2 million, and

possibly more, should be available from railway profits over the next five years to cover the costs of the railway investment program and of other development projects.

b. *Communications.* At present the communications services have an annual operating loss of around three million cordobas. The proposed reorganization of the services to place them on a pay-as-you-go basis should substantially diminish, if not entirely eliminate, this drain on the national budget.

c. *Power and Light.* The investment program in power contemplates, as a part of the reorganization plan of the government-owned power company, that the proposed investment costs will not only be borne by the enterprise but also that there will be an ultimate reduction of costs of electricity to the consumer.

C. *Private Sources of Funds*

The mission believes that bonds of the Instituto de Fomento can be sold, with a government guarantee, to the private banks, to the local insurance company, and to private individuals.

In addition, a part of the investment in the public sector is predicated, (the mission hopes too pessimistically), on the unwillingness or inability of local private capital to undertake risks in industry and agriculture because of psychological factors, a preference for commerce, land speculation, usury or other factors. The Instituto de Fomento is planned to take risks, to make medium- and long-term loans, and to help the country's productive growth first of all. Some of its credits will turn over rapidly, however, and some of its enterprises, if imaginatively conceived and executed, will make substantial profit. To the extent the Instituto is successful in being a risk-bearing but profit-making enterprise, and in inducing increased private investment, the fiscal burden on the country will be reduced.

D. *Other Sources of Investment Funds*

A number of other sources of funds for development purposes have been noted, including an increased coffee export tax, the funds presently going to the Banco Hipotecario, the earnings of the Port of Corinto, the customs reserve funds which are largely in foreign exchange, the exchange surcharges temporarily, and an increased share of the Government in the profits of the National Bank. In addition, the "special" reserves of the National Bank offer a source of long-term development funds for the Instituto de Fomento as the present loans are repaid to the Bank.

The development program, if skillfully managed, can be carried out with a minimum of inflationary impact on the country. To do this will require clear-cut monetary, credit and banking policies coordinated with a sound fiscal policy to promote development while maintaining monetary stability.

VII.   "FACADISM"

Because of its limited fiscal resources the Government of Nicaragua has not, to the extent so often practiced in underdeveloped countries, engaged in "facade" development—the large and handsome hospital building that has poor equipment and untrained staff, the expensive but spectacular economic project ill adapted to, or premature in, a country's economy.

Because this is a natural tendency in underdeveloped areas, it may occur in Nicaragua, particularly when the fiscal reform is completed and the government finds itself with additional revenue to finance such projects. The whole aim of the development program will miscarry if this occurs.

Funds available to the government will be limited and the mission cautions that they must be used judiciously. Each economic project should be carefully tailored to fit the country's capacity and potential growth. Much of the program planned by the mission is for agricultural credits, the training of teachers, nurses, foremen and health specialists, and the provision of pure water or modest educational facilities. None of these is spectacular but the effects will be cumulative and will show marked results in five to ten years. The program provides for few public buildings. The public works provided are, for the most part, confined to the basic transport or health needs of the economy.

In a country which lacks the most urgent basic needs, "facade" expenditures are a costly luxury which adversely affect the future health and productivity of the country.

VIII. *REVISION OF THE PROGRAM*

The presentation of the investment program that follows is long and detailed. It represents the considered judgment of the mission in July of 1952 as to the best lines of future investment, growth and progress.

The program should not be regarded as an inflexible and rigid plan. Conditions change rapidly in the world and an investment program should be flexible and responsive to them. The mission hopes and urges that the program be thoroughly reviewed each year in the light of current fiscal, trade and economic conditions. If future economic conditions are not as favorable as they are at present, it may be necessary to make this a six-year program or even longer. If they continue favorable, the mission hopes the optimum program can be attained.

While the mission was in Nicaragua, the government often modified and improved upon the mission's suggestions and recommendations to adapt them to the particular characteristics of the country. The mission hopes that the investment program will be· similarly adjusted to future conditions and circumstances in the country.

It is essential, however, that modifications in the program be motivated by sound and overriding, long-range economic reasons and not by temporary economic or political considerations.

CHAPTER THREE

Investment by Sectors of the Economy

I. *SANITATION, EDUCATION AND PUBLIC HEALTH*

Expenditures to improve sanitation, education and public health should, without question, be given first priority in any program designed to increase the long-range growth and development of the Nicaraguan economy.

Without exception, the mission found that in every sector of the economy high disease rates, low standards of nutrition, and low educational and training standards are the major factors inhibiting the growth of productivity. Farm mechanization, improved transportation, and modern industrial machinery will increase total production, but there is a limit to such increase without a basic improvement in the health, the living conditions and the productivity of the country's limited manpower.

Improvement in these sectors, moreover, involves more than raising gross physical production as measured by national income statistics. It means raising the standard of living directly through better health, greater life expectancy and general physical well-being. The program of sanitation, public health and education tackles jointly the problems of increasing the physical productivity of the country and that of improving the living standards of the people. This program is an integral part of the agricultural, industrial and transport investment program. The following deserve first priority within the sector:

(a) provision of pure water and adequate sanitary facilities;

(b) DDT campaigns and other disease control measures;

(c) literacy campaigns and the provision of elementary education;

(d) vocational training in all sectors of the economy.

The mission feels more strongly on point (a) than on any other presented in the report. The provision of pure water and sanitation facilities should take overriding priority not only over such projects as observation towers or handsome public buildings but also over such desirable projects as a modern automatic telephone system.

A. *Public Health and Sanitation*

No single factor is so basic a guide to the well-being of a country as the health standards of its inhabitants.

The primary aim of the public health and sanitation program should be to raise the general health level by stamping out malaria and intestinal parasites. These are the two chief causes of the high mortality rate and low productivity of the people. Continued expansion of the existing program to provide pure water supplies, sanitary sewage disposal and continuance of the DDT campaign for the elimination of the mosquito breeding grounds can accomplish this aim.

Other health menaces, such as alcoholism, venereal disease, tuberculosis and Hansen's disease, need substantial further control to protect the general welfare.

The health needs of the country are so great that the very large total expenditure provided in the five-year development program could be effectively spent within this one sector alone. Unfortunately, this is not possible. Careful study will be needed to obtain the greatest benefit from the available funds.

There should be a careful balance of expenditures between installation of water and sewage systems and provision of additional hospitals and health centers. Though additional hospitals are needed, the program must be realistic. There are not enough nurses to staff the existing hospitals properly. The Managua General Hospital should be finished at an early date but other hospital construction should be kept to a minimum and planned with the available supply of nurses and doctors in mind. Duplication of facilities should be avoided at all costs.

A series of clinics should be set up to care for rural health. Each of these should be manned by at least one doctor and two nurses, and equipped with X-ray facilities, an emergency operating room, a two- to four-bed ward and a dispensary. The function of these clinics would be to provide general dispensary services, to permit emergency operations, to institute and maintain a campaign to eliminate malaria and intestinal parasites, and to detect cases of tuberculosis and other infectious diseases. All cases, not of an emergency nature, requiring long or specialized treatment should be sent to an established hospital.

B. *Education*

Nicaragua needs people trained in mechanics, carpentry, agriculture, accountancy and other skills. These are educational needs above the range of ordinary elementary schooling. The country needs more than the mere teaching of reading and writing. The public education program should be developed for the benefit of adults as well as children. It should be directed not only toward the reduction of illiteracy generally but also toward the practical domestic and mechanical arts.

The public education program should be directed toward the development of the community type school, oriented to the reduction of illiteracy and the upgrading of living standards. Instruction in the elements of sanitation and personal cleanliness, in home economics, and in the practices of the workshop and the farm would fit well with the production needs of the country.

While the program should be adapted to the needs of each individual community, the basic purpose should remain the same in all cases: to educate the people so that they may be properly prepared to earn a decent living.

In some cases the education and sanitation programs may be combined effectively. For example, the carpentry class might undertake the design and construction of sanitary privies for a whole community. Elementary animal husbandry classes could stress the proper care and confinement of animals and fowls to prevent the spread of intestinal parasites.

A satisfactory educational program demands both teachers and buildings. Building schools will not solve the problem of education unless there are enough teachers. Teachers must be provided with adequate buildings and with proper books and teaching aids. Special attention should be paid to the rural areas where the lack of teachers is particularly acute.

The salary scale for both teachers and administrators needs raising to attract suitable people to this work, a measure already undertaken in part by the government in the coming fiscal year.

Training facilities must be adequate to supply the number of teachers needed for an expanded program. Teacher training may be facilitated by providing out-of-country scholarships in educational administration and supervision, by expanding the normal school system and by continuing a program of in-service training for all teachers.

Both vocational training and professional education are important. Skilled labor is needed for the development program, as are engineers and agricultural experts. Nurses and doctors are needed for the health program. Much can be done within the country to improve these aspects of its educational system, but advanced study in professional fields should be encouraged by providing additional scholarships for study abroad.

The vocational school in Managua should be placed in operation as soon as possible both to provide skilled labor for the development program and to train teachers for the rural areas.

The agricultural school should be improved and enlarged to provide the trained personnel required by the agricultural program.

The medical school should be moved to Managua to take advantage of the capital's superior hospital facilities and to attract the best doctors to the faculty. Establishment of a school of nursing in connection with the General Hospital would provide on-the-job training.

C. *Estimated Cost*

The mission does not feel that it is qualified to present detailed programs in the fields of education, sanitation or public health. This task should be undertaken by special committees consisting of representatives of government agencies, foreign technicians, qualified doctors, teachers, and other community leaders. The mission does wish to call attention to the many problems involved and to indicate the broad fields where available funds could be most profitably spent.

The national government alone cannot undertake the entire job of improving education, health and sanitation. Local communities must assume an important share of the job. Local committees working in cooperation with government agencies can accomplish a great deal. They can solicit voluntary contributions, in time, materials or money, to supplement government funds and to help in raising the educational and health levels of their own communities.

Expenditures proposed in this report are additional to the funds now allocated to these three fields in the budgets of the national and local governments and to sums which may be contributed by international agencies or by the United States Point Four Program in the form of technical assistance.

TABLE 2

FIVE-YEAR EDUCATION AND PUBLIC HEALTH PROGRAM
Proposed Increase in Expenditures 1952-57

Estimated Cost:
  (a) Health and Sanitation: $3,950,000 local currency; $3,950,000 foreign exchange.
  (b) Education: $2,275,000 local currency; $850,000 foreign exchange.

First Priority

I. Education

    A. Elementary Schools

1. Teacher training program	
Scholarships	$ 150,000
Expansion of normal schools	750,000
In-service training	100,000
2. Building program	
Classrooms	500,000
Equipment and furnishings	250,000
3. Teaching materials, books and supplies	400,000
B. Vocational Training	
1. Managua Vocational School	150,000
2. Agricultural School	500,000
C. Literacy Campaign	300,000
	$ 3,100,000

II. Public Health

A. Hospitals	
1. Construction	1,000,000
2. Equipment	1,000,000
B. Clinics	1,500,000
C. Malaria Control, Medicines, and Other	500,000
D. Professional Training	
1. Medical School	400,000
2. Nursing School	500,000
	$ 4,900,000

III. Sanitation

A. Water Supplies	2,000,000
B. Sewage Disposal	1,000,000
	$ 3,000,000
Total	**$11,000,000**

Second Priority

I. Education
   A. Elementary Schools
      1. Building program
         Classrooms 250,000
         Equipment and furnishings 100,000
      2. Teaching materials and books 100,000
   B. Professional Training
      Engineering School (additional equipment and staff) 300,000

                                                        $ 750,000

II. Public Health
   A. Clinics 500,000
   B. Hospitals
      1. Construction 400,000
      2. Equipment 350,000

                                                        $ 1,250,000

III. Sanitation
   A. Water Supplies 2,000,000
   B. Sewage Disposal 1,000,000

                                                        $ 3,000,000

                                Total $ 5,000,000

The minimum program, to average over $2 million a year, represents a very sharp increase in the present relatively modest level of health and educational expenditures. The program would approximately double the expenditures on illiteracy and disease control, greatly increase expenditures on hospitals and clinics and set up almost totally new programs in other fields, particularly sanitation. The program provides for roughly 500 urban or rural schoolrooms, either to add new facilities or to replace inadequate existing facilities, and for pure water and sanitary facilities in eight to 10 of the larger cities.

II. *AGRICULTURE*

Agriculture is the mainstay of the nation's economy, but government promotion of agricultural development has lagged far behind. The country has rich soils which can grow a large variety of tropical and semi-tropical crops but these soils have been only partially and rather haphazardly exploited. Agriculture has been too long conducted on an extensive basis, with a low return per acre. No credits have been available for soil conservation improvement or for installation of permanent facilities. Instead, credits have been restricted to current production loans which go, for the most part, to a relatively small number of large land-owners.

Urgent problems have arisen that need solution. The rapid introduction of mechanized equipment has created special problems—soil depletion at a more rapid rate than ever before and serious erosion. The lack of experience in, and facilities for, maintaining equipment also causes much trouble and wasted effort.

Nothing has yet been done to repair the damage to the economy of the East Coast caused by the passing of the banana trade.

Agricultural production must expand if the country is to progress and carry out an over-all development program. This expansion, however, must be accompanied by soil conservation and lower production costs.

A. *Aims and Methods*

Increasing agricultural production implies more than planting additional acreage.

Most present crop yields can be increased by 25% or more simply by the use of better seeds, fertilizers or green manure crops, better cultivation and harvesting practices and by proper farm storage of the crop. The yields of other longer-term crops such as coffee cannot be increased as easily because such crops present special problems. Much research remains to be done on them though partial solutions of their special problems are available.

Some of the concepts that need to be applied in increasing crop yields are new in Nicaragua. Only a very limited number of people have a knowledge or appreciation of what may be accomplished by fertilization, crop rotation, soil conservation and seed selection. This is also true of measures to improve cattle and dairy production.

The first problem then is to educate the farmers. Two agencies will work on this phase of the program, the Ministry of Agriculture and the Servicio Tecnico Agricola.

The Servicio Tecnico is primarily a reasearch agency. Its purpose is to study the fundamental problems related to crops, soils and animal production in order to develop the information that farmers must have to improve their productive practices. The Servicio is also concerned with training in agricultural research and with certain extension services, including educational services.

The Ministry of Agriculture is responsible for disseminating to the farmers the results of the reasearch and experimentation carried out by the Servicio Tecnico as well as other relevant information on farming practices.

Although the development and dissemination of information can, in time, do a great deal to help agriculture, a proper system of farm credits must be developed as an integral part of the program, so that farmers can have the financial means to apply the knowledge they gain.

To carry out this important phase of the program, a third agency, the Instituto de Fomento, will be charged with supplying adequate medium or long-term credits for permanent improvements. These credits should be extended mainly for the introduction of new crops, more extensive cultivation of existing crops, the improvement of the cattle industry and the general improvement of soil practices. Some provision, however, for short-term credits to the small farmer who lacks adequate facilities for this purpose should also be included in the Instituto's program.

B. *The Agricultural Development Program*

In presenting a detailed program, it is not always easy to indicate the interrelation of all the factors involved. It is not enough, for example, to ask for increased milk production, unless, at the same time, outlets for milk are developed.

In this respect, the agricultural and industrial programs should go hand in hand. The various phases of the programs must be worked out simultaneously and one part cannot be pushed ahead of the other or the whole program may become unbalanced. In some cases, additional credits will be needed for a considerable time after the initial five-year period covered by this report. There is no assumption that all the problems confronting the country will be solved by the end of five years. Undoubtedly the program itself will create many new problems which will demand modifications and changes in the program.

The over-all agricultural program is divided into two parts, first priority and second priority. The projects in the first priority group are those which the mission feels *must* be carried out. They represent a minimum development program. The projects in the second priority group are as important as those in the first group but are more easily deferred. Both groups together comprise the *optimum* program for agricultural development. This is the one which *should* be carried out.

The cost estimates for this program are liberal in order to assure sufficient funds to carry the projects to completion. Costs of administration and supervision of credits are not shown separately but are included in the totals.

The majority of the credits are long term, but some short- and medium-term credits are also included. As the latter turn over and produce earnings they will help in later years to reduce the amount of new funds required from the national budget.

C. *First Priority*

1. *Coffee.* In terms of value, coffee is now the country's most important crop, but the increase in income from this source

over the past few years has arisen mainly from better world market prices rather than increased production.

Little or no effort has been made to extend plantings or to increase yields from existing trees in recent years.

It is unfortunate that new plantings did not start earlier and there is a certain element of risk in recommending additional plantings at this time. Nevertheless, the risk should be taken in order to strengthen the whole economy. Nicaraguan coffee is a high-aroma specialty coffee used in blending with the harsher types from other countries. The long-range market outlook appears favorable for this quality coffee.

The total proposed cost of the coffee program is $3 million. This includes $2 million for the clearing, planting and cultivation of trees on new coffee lands. Of the total amount $430,000 is assigned for coffee processing and $570,000 is unassigned. The goal of the program should be to increase the number of coffee trees by 25%; this means the planting of 16,000,000 trees within five years.

TABLE 3

INVESTMENT PROGRAM FOR COFFEE

Estimated cost: $2,750,000 local currency; $250,000 foreign currency.

	Local Currency	Foreign Currency
1952-53		
Clearing and planting 1,000,000 trees	$ 100,000	$ —
1953-54		
Clearing and planting 2,000,000 trees	200,000	. —
Cultivating 1,000,000 trees	10,000	—
	210,000	—

	Local Currency	Foreign Currency
1954-55		
Clearing and planting 4,000,000 trees	400,000	—
Cultivating 3,000,000 trees	30,000	—
Processing facilities	20,000	40,000
	450,000	40,000
1955-56		
Clearing and planting 4,000,000 trees	400,000	—
Cultivating 7,000,000 trees	70,000	—
Processing facilities	40,000	80,000
	510,000	80,000
1956-57		
Clearing and planting 5,000,000 trees	500,000	—
Cultivating 11,000,000 trees	110,000	—
Processing facilities	120,000	130,000
	730,000	130,000
Contingencies	180,000	—
Unassigned	570,000	
Total 1952-57	**$2,750,000**	**$250,000**

No repayment of loans should be required until the sixth year after planting.

The pulping and drying of coffee is such an integral part of coffee cultivation that provision for additional processing facilities ought to be part of the agricultural rather than the industrial program. The installation of *beneficios,* either directly by the Instituto de Fomento or through credits to producers or cooperatives, should proceed approximately as scheduled.

The unassigned amount of $570,000 may be used for seed purchases, to establish nurseries to insure an adequate supply of seedlings and to obtain coffee specialists to oversee and direct the program.

Some additional credits for the cultivation of the later plantings will be needed until 1961.

2. *Cattle Industry.* The mission believes that cattle raising and the production of dairy products, meats, hides and other by-products, will be the most important future activity in Nicaragua. In 1950 the total value of its production was nearly equal to that of coffee, but eventually it should substantially exceed that of coffee. To accomplish this much remains to be done and the proposed five-year program will be only a small start toward this long-run objective.

The program is divided into two parts, dairying and beef-raising. Dairying requires a cow that gives large amounts of milk on the least feed, while beef-raising requires an animal that gains weight rapidly. There is no such thing as a dual-purpose cow. An animal can eat only a certain amount of feed per day and this goes either into milk or weight, but not into both. Draft animals are not good beef producers since their energy goes into work. There is ample room for both dairy and beef production in Nicaragua, but both products should not come from the same herd.

The country divides naturally into two cattle regions with some overlapping. The western plains, near the main population centers, are predominantly suitable for dairy cattle. The east coast with abundant rainfall to maintain year-round pastures is particularly adapted to beef cattle.

a. Dairying. The goal is to raise milk production by 50% and to market it as fluid milk rather than cheese. This goal could be attained easily by taking better care of the present stock. The long-run objectives, however, should be broader. They should include the selection of animals so as to raise the levels of individual production, the handling of milk under sanitary conditions, and the provision of more milk at lower cost. The proposed program also involves the preparation of pastures, silos, hay and concentrated feeds, in order to maintain an even milk flow throughout the dry season and dipping and spraying equipment to protect the animals against ticks and *torsalo*.

The processing of milk is such an integral part of the dairy program that, as in the case of coffee, funds have been assigned for this purpose in the agricultural rather than in the industrial sector. Transportation and storage of the milk are equally important to the program in order to provide now isolated areas with an outlet for fluid milk. Credits and technical assistance for this program should be provided by the Instituto de Fomento.

TABLE 4

INVESTMENT PROGRAM FOR DAIRYING

Estimated cost: $1,100,000 local currency; $900,000 foreign currency.

	Local Currency	Foreign Currency
1952-53		
Milk coolers, refrigerated trucks	$ 20,000	$ 40,000
Barns and milk houses	40,000	—
Herd improvement	80,000	20,000
Pasture improvement, equipment for hay and ensilage making	25,000	25,000
Total	165,000	85,000
1953-54		
Milk coolers, refrigerated trucks	20,000	40,000
Barns and milk houses	40,000	—
Herd improvement	70,000	30,000
Pasture improvement	25,000	25,000
Condensed or powdered milk plant in Rivas area	50,000	100,000
	205,000	195,000

	Local Currency	Foreign Currency
1954-55		
Milk coolers, etc.	20,000	40,000
Barns and milk houses	40,000	—
Herd improvement	100,000	50,000
Pasture improvement	50,000	50,000
Condensed, powdered milk, or pasteurizing plant in Leon—Chinandega area	50,000	100,000
	260,000	240,000
1955-56		
As in 1954-55, except processing plant should be in Juigalpa area	260,000	240,000
1956-57		
As in 1954-55, without processing plant	210,000	140,000
1952-57 Total	**$1,100,000**	**$ 900,000**

Beef-Raising. Here the goals are to increase the number of breeding stock by 50% and to make an immediate start on upgrading quality by animal selection. The methods by which this program is to be carried out are similar to those of the dairying program. Feed should be available the year round so that the animals on the western plains do not lose weight during the dry season. Pastures are green throughout the year on the east coast, but high protein feeds should be made available to supplement pastures with low nutritive value. Efforts should be made in both regions to keep the animals free of ticks and torsalo. In both cases the herds require testing for tuberculosis, mastitis, and other diseases, and all diseased animals should be culled out and destroyed if no medication is available.

TABLE 5

INVESTMENT PROGRAM FOR BEEF-RAISING

Estimated cost: $1,400,000 local currency; $600,000 foreign currency.

	Local Currency	Foreign Currency
1952-53		
Herd improvement	$ 75,000	$ 25,000
Pasture improvement, equipment for hay and ensilage making	100,000	50,000
	175,000	75,000
1953-54		
As in 1952-53	175,000	75,000
1954-55		
Herd improvement	175,000	75,000
Pastures, equipment, etc.	100,000	50,000
Miscellaneous	75,000	25,000
	350,000	150,000
1955-56		
As in 1954-55	350,000	150,000
1956-57		
As in 1954-55	350,000	150,000
1952-57 Total	$1,400,000	$ 600,000

3. *African Oil Palm.* Although the east coast, with its associated regions, comprises nearly two thirds of the total land
area, it contributes little to the economy of the country. While
much still remains to be learned about the potentialities of the
region, there is evidence to show that the soils and climate are
well adapted to the cultivation of African oil palm, and the
labor surplus in the area can be used for this labor-intensive
crop. Its development should begin at once.

It is recommended that sufficient credits be made available to plant 6,000 acres to this crop, following approximately the schedule outlined in Table VI.

TABLE 6

INVESTMENT PROGRAM FOR AFRICAN OIL PALM
Estimated cost: $500,000—all local currency.

1952-53	
Clearing and planting 600 acres	$ 36,000
1953-54	
Clearing and planting 1,200 acres	72,000
Cultivating 600 acres	6,000
1954-55	
Clearing and planting 1,200 acres	72,000
Cultivating 1,800 acres	18,000
1955-56	
Clearing and planting 1,500 acres	90,000
Cultivating 3,000 acres	30,000
1956-57	
Clearing and planting 1,500 acres	90,000
Cultivating 4,500 acres	45,000
Contingencies	41,000
1952-57 Total	**$500,000**

No credit repayments should be required until the eighth year after planting.

The minimum planting in any one area should be about 200 acres, and the optimum 300 acres. No single individual will have to plant the whole acreage but several persons could plant jointly within a small area in the vicinity of the processing plants.

Some additional credits, for the cultivation of later plantings, will be needed until 1962.

4. *Soil Conservation.* The soils of the west are composed of deep, fertile, volcanic ash. Although there are some steep slopes, they are for the most part gentle. However, the deeper and cleaner cultivation resulting from the introduction of mechanized agricultural equipment has brought about serious soil erosion. Erosion occurs mainly during the rainy season, but some comes from strong winds during the dry season. Erosion from heavy rains can be stopped by proper terracing and by contour cultivation. Damage from wind erosion can be checked by maintaining a protective cover on the soil during the dry season.

The first type of erosion is the more serious. The land must be protected if the soils are to continue fertile.

The goal should be to protect 50,000 *manzanas* (87,000 acres) of land against erosion. Land owners should be able to obtain medium-term credits to cover the actual cost of terracing. The equipment needed for this work—bulldozers, plows and graders —may be provided by the Instituto de Fomento either by directly buying the equipment and hiring operators or through credits to private individuals for purchases of the equipment.

TABLE 7

INVESTMENT PROGRAM FOR SOIL CONSERVATION

Estimated cost: $1,500,000 local currency; $500,000 foreign currency.

	Local Currency	Foreign Currency
1952-53		
Equipment	—	$100,000
5,000 manzanas protected	$ 100,000	—
	100,000	100,000

	Local Currency	Foreign Currency
1953-54		
Equipment	—	200,000
10,000 manzanas protected	200,000	—
	200,000	200,000
1954-55		
Equipment	—	200,000
10,000 manzanas protected	200,000	—
	200,000	200,000
1955-56		
10,000 manzanas protected	400,000	—
1956-57		
15,000 manzanas protected	600,000	—
1952-57 Total	**$1,500,000**	**$500,000**

5. *Irrigation.* At present, only limited use is made of existing irrigation possibilities.

Three regions particularly lend themselves to the development of low lift pumping, the area between Managua and Tipitapa, and the areas near Rivas and on the northeast shore of Lake Nicaragua. The latter two areas can use water from Lake Nicaragua. All these areas need water for pastures and rice production. The first area also requires it for raising vegetables. Individual farmers, in addition, need small dams and pumping equipment and require credits to finance them.

No definite goal can be set for this phase of the program. The most important need is to start planning for the use of the irrigation waters which are available.

TABLE 8

INVESTMENT PROGRAM FOR IRRIGATION

Estimated cost: $600,000 local currency; $400,000 foreign currency.

	Local Currency	Foreign Currency
1952-53	$ 60,000	$ 40,000
1953-54	120,000	80,000
1954-55	120,000	80,000
1955-56	150,000	100,000
1956-57	150,000	100,000
1952-57 Total	$600,000	$400,000

6. *Agricultural Machinery.* Some machinery has been included in the preceding estimates for the agricultural program. It is largely specialized equipment not suitable for general use. The total proposed program also includes provision for credits for crop production equipment such as tractors, plows, cultivators, and especially harvesters.

Harvesting equipment has not yet come into general use. Hand labor is still used to pick corn and to cut and thresh rice and sesame, although mechanical equipment can do this work faster and at lower cost. The prospective labor shortage will certainly force early adoption of this type of equipment.

Provision is also needed for adequate repair facilities and spare parts, since there are no good tractor repair shops in the country. Most repairs are made, in the field, by traveling mechanics, too often with unsatisfactory results. It is imperative that several well-equipped shops be set up in the principal agricultural regions to make major engine repairs.

The lack of spare parts is causing some trouble at the present time. Spare parts are unobtainable because of the critical materials situation in the United States for some brands of equipment. Local machinery dealers, however, are chiefly responsible for this scarcity. They generally do not carry large enough stocks because of lack of credit and, sometimes, poor planning. The proposed program will help to remedy the lack of credit, but it will be up to the individual dealers themselves to carry the proper supplies in stock. If necessary, the Instituto de Fomento should undertake to do this work.

TABLE 9

INVESTMENT PROGRAM FOR AGRICULTURAL MACHINERY
Estimated cost: $2,000,000 foreign currency.

1952-53	
Repair facilities	$ 50,000
Spare parts	80,000
Machinery	270,000
	400,000
1953-54	
As in 1952-53	400,000
1954-55	
Repair facilities	40,000
Spare parts	60,000
Machinery	300,000
	400,000
1955-56	
As in 1954-55	400,000
1956-57	
As in 1954-55	400,000
1952-57 Total	$2,000,000

7. *Land Colonization.* The aim of this part of the program is to make land available to small farmers of ability and ambition who would not otherwise be able to buy land, and to provide them with credits and sound advice so that they can work the land properly.

The mission does not suggest an ambitious colonization program. There is no idea of relocating thousands of families, nor is there any thought of attracting large numbers of immigrants. The goal is to allow Nicaraguans from the lower income group (about 95% of the population) to improve themselves, although selected immigration, particularly of Dutch dairy cattle farmers, should also be considered.

Government lands should be opened for "homesteading", with a provision for clear title to the land passing to the occupant after he lives on and works it for some specified period, say five or seven years. Homesteading should be restricted to those who do not now own land and have not the means to do so. Furthermore, no one person should be allowed to claim more than a reasonable amount of land, perhaps 100 manzanas (175 acres).

Such a colonization program is complex and needs careful planning. The first steps necessary are to find out exactly what land the government owns and for what purpose it can be used. This phase of the program should be conducted by the Ministry of Agriculture. The period from 1952-53 should be used to locate suitable lands and to plan the details of the program: the types of buildings needed, the animals and tools necessary, the amount of credit needed for crop loans, and the medical, sanitation and educational facilities required. It is suggested that any payments for land be spread over a 20- to 30-year period, and for implements and buildings over a 10-year period.

TABLE 10

INVESTMENT PROGRAM FOR LAND COLONIZATION

Estimated cost: $1,700,000 local currency; $300,000 foreign currency.

	Local Currency	Foreign Currency
1952-54		
Planning phase	—	—

	Local Currency	*Foreign Currency*
1954-55		
Land clearing	$ 50,000	$ 50,000
Buildings	50,000	—
Animals and equipment	75,000	25,000
Medical facilities and sanitation	50,000	—
Crop loans	100,000	—
Contingencies	75,000	25,000
	400,000	100,000
1955-56		
Land clearing	150,000	50,000
Buildings	75,000	—
Animals and equipment	100,000	50,000
Medical facilities and sanitation	75,000	—
Crop loans	250,000	—
	650,000	100,000
1956-57		
As in 1955-56	650,000	100,000
1952-57 Total	**$1,700,000**	**$300,000**

8. *Grain Storage.* The central grain storage plant, now under construction in Managua, will cost an estimated $700,000; $550,000 of this is foreign currency.

This large storage plant will be able to handle the needs of the capital city. Several small collecting stations also will be needed to process grain in other communities, and to channel the dry grain to the main silo or to the export market.

Each station, under the management of the main plant of the Instituto de Fomento, should be equipped with a cleaner, a drier, and some storage capacity. They should be planned so that additional storage capacity may be added as required.

The first unit might properly be placed in Chinandega to serve both the domestic and export markets. Other units will be needed in the areas served by Leon, Nandaime and Sebaco. The final choice of locations should take into account the requirements of both the existing plants and local needs.

It is suggested that five small units be built, one during each year of the program. It is estimated that each unit will cost $50,000, of which $35,000 will be in foreign currency.

9. *Other Products.* The agricultural program provides for funds to extend cacao plantings on the east coast, as well as to expand citrus orchards, vegetable growing, hog and poultry raising and other production, including the principal domestic food crops. All these are important to the future of Nicaragua, but it is difficult to set goals or assign costs to them now. This is a matter that can best be decided by the planning body of the Instituto de Fomento.

A total of $1,550,000 is assigned for this phase of the work, with around $300,000 to be made available each year of the program. These funds probably will be almost entirely in local currency.

D. *Second Priority*

1. *Coffee.* In the first priority group, funds for coffee were assigned entirely for new plantings. Production can be increased, however, in existing plantings by better cultivation practices and by replanting with higher yielding trees. The present nation-wide yield per tree averages only 0.5 pounds, but some individual growers obtain as high as 1.5 pounds. While present coffee prices are exceptionally good and there is a wide margin between costs and external prices, production costs are rising. Increasing the yield per acre on existing coffee lands will place Nicaragua in a stronger competitive position in the future.

The purpose of the proposed additional program is to make credit available to aid growers in replanting with high yield trees. It is somewhat difficult to fix any definite goal, but it is believed that at least 10,000,000 trees can be replaced with the proposed funds.

In carrying out the program it might be advisable for the Ministry of Agriculture to prepare the seed beds and then distribute seedlings to the growers at cost. The larger and wealthier growers should be required to pay cash for the seedlings, while smaller growers should be given credits repayable after the trees come into production.

Funds in the amount of $1,000,000 local currency are proposed for this program, to be allocated as they become available.

2. *Land Colonization.* A further sum of $3,000,000 is assigned to land colonization projects for approximately the same uses as the funds for the minimum projects.

One fact must be continually kept in mind. Nicaraguans normally should be given the first opportunity to receive aid under this program. If, in the later stages of the program, there are unexpended funds and no further qualified Nicaraguans are available, then well-qualified, carefully selected immigrants should be considered for settlement credits.

3. *Crop Storage.* Losses on crops harvested in the rainy season run as high as 40% because of spoilage during storage. The large grain storage unit being constructed in Managua will help cut these losses. It will not, however, be able to store all the crops grown in the country. Better storage facilities are needed on the farms to allow farmers to store feed for livestock through the dry season, to provide feed for dairy cattle and, most important, to store crops to sell at advantageous prices. Storage facilities are also needed at the ports to expedite exports.

The sum of $1,000,000 is proposed for credits for private storage units. Approximately half of the amount will be needed in foreign currency. It is suggested that the amount be expended more or less evenly throughout the five-year period.

4. *Unassigned.* An unassigned sum of $2,000,000 will go into a contingency fund, for credits not previously considered and for programs given above which may need additional funds to achieve their objectives.

E. *The Role of the Ministry of Agriculture*

For a country whose economy is so dependent upon agriculture, the Government has paid surprisingly little attention to this sector. The Ministry of Agriculture could and should be an energetic driving force in agricultural development, but its small budget restricts its activities to the most routine duties. Most of its money is assigned to the Servicio Tecnico for research purposes.

To carry out its share of the total agricultural program the Ministry should be enlarged through the organization of a section for extension service.

In close cooperation with the Instituto de Fomento, the Ministry should also undertake land-use studies. Their purpose should be to determine what lands are suitable for irrigation, the planting of new crops, or the extension of old crops. These studies should form the basis of the agricultural credit program of the Instituto de Fomento.

Finally, the Ministry should organize a forestry section to help protect existing forests, to inaugurate reforestation projects in the east coast pine area, and to prepare the legislation to make lumber exploitation less damaging to the forests in the future.

These improvements in the Ministry of Agriculture are of the first importance to the successful completion of the general agricultural program.

1. *The Extension Service.* Through an extension program, new information and techniques can go promptly to farmers. To obtain good coverage, 24 extension agents will be required: 16 in general and specialized agricultural crops, four in animal husbandry, and four veterinarians. All should have ample transportation and travelling expenses. Most of these agents should be Nicaraguans with advanced training abroad or in the Servicio Tecnico. They can be added gradually to the staff at the rate of five or six per year as the program expands.

A small agricultural laboratory, with services available to the public at cost, is needed for soil and plant analysis as well as for the analysis of irrigation water, feeds and fertilizers. It should also analyze agricultural products before they are exported. This would be a very useful service. For example, cottonseed cake sold abroad is priced according to its protein and oil content, but shippers, with no local laboratory, do not know the value of the cargo until it has arrived at the port of entry, where it is sampled and analyzed.

The laboratory should also be used to check the purity of local food products, such as milk, butter, cheese and meat.

TABLE 11

THE COST OF THE PROGRAM FOR MINISTRY OF AGRICULTURE

Estimated cost: $600,000 local currency; $50,000 foreign currency.

	Local Currency	Foreign Currency
1952-53		
Establishment of Extension Service	$ 50,000	—
1953-54		
Extension services	100,000	—
Laboratory	25,000	$25,000
	125,000	25,000
1954-55		
Extension services	100,000	—
Laboratory	35,000	15,000
	135,000	15,000
1955-56		
Extension services	125,000	—
Laboratory	20,000	5,000
	145,000	5,000
1956-57		
As in 1955-56	145,000	5,000
1952-57 Total	$600,000	$50,000

2. *Land-use Studies.* A land-use survey group should be organized to conduct land-use studies. It should work closely with the Instituto de Fomento on the potentialities of the various regions and subregions. Studies should be made of the types of vegetation and the characteristics of the soil and water supplies, as well as of the sociological and economic conditions in the different regions. The Instituto de Fomento should use these studies as a basis for evaluating the desirability of certain projects, such as the development of a particular crop or a particular type of farming. It could then decide which projects were best adapted to the various regions and most deserving of support.

The land-use survey group should:

(a) collect information regarding the past, present and potential future uses of land;

(b) coordinate all relevant information regarding physical, biotic and human resources being utilized or capable of being developed and utilized;

(c) prepare suitable reports and maps setting forth this information;

(d) work closely with the Instituto de Fomento regarding the potentialities of the various regions and subregions.

The colonization program cannot be worked out without a land survey. This is needed to help in the selection of the most promising undeveloped areas. It can be used to indicate what may be grown in those areas, to advise on the condition and care of the soils and on the health and transportation problems which will be encountered. Such surveys will also be of great value in locating additional lands for coffee planting, paddy rice cultivation, and oil palm and cacao planting.

A minimum of five people will be required to carry on this program: an ecologist, a general agriculturist, a livestock and range manager, an engineer and a forester. A team of this size can cover up to 1,000 square miles a year. It will require supporting staff and facilities.

Key personnel needed for this task is not available within Nicaragua. The mission suggests that the Government ask assistance of FAO, which has been increasingly concerned with this type of program and is developing the facilities to carry it out.

TABLE 12

COST OF THE PROGRAM FOR LAND-USE STUDIES
Estimated cost: $1,000,000 local currency.

1952-53	
Organization	$ 50,000
Coffee studies	50,000
Land colonization studies	50,000
	150,000
1953-54	
Land colonization studies	50,000
Coffee studies	50,000
Irrigation studies	50,000
Cacao and miscellaneous studies	50,000
	200,000
1954-55	
Irrigation studies	50,000
Forestry studies	50,000
Cotton and miscellaneous studies	50,000
Land colonization	100,000
	250,000
1955-56	
Land colonization studies	100,000
Forestry studies	50,000
Miscellaneous crop studies	25,000
Water conservation studies	50,000
Agricultural and forestry legislation studies	50,000
	275,000

1956-57

Forestry studies	50,000
Miscellaneous studies	75,000
	125,000
1952-57 Total	**$1,000,000**

3. *Forestry.* Although lumbering has long been an important part of the economy, little attention has been given to the protection or renewal of the forests. The lack of adequate fire protection in the pine region near Puerto Cabezas is especially critical. The custom of burning the pastures destroys the young seedlings and there is no natural regeneration to replace trees now being cut for lumber. Only a few years of cutting remain in this region and, unless measures are taken to control fire, the area may never again produce lumber.

The same problem applies, in general, to the pine regions of Ocotal and Somoto.

Much remains to be learned about the resources of other forest regions. Mahogany and other valuable woods are becoming less plentiful and more expensive to cut, while lesser known woods remain unutilized. A thorough study of all the forest areas would be too large a program to plan for now, although eventually this should be done. Such a study demands a large staff of competent foresters who are not presently available. However, by starting a program of fire control, a small staff can be trained now and later enlarged as qualified personnel become available.

The principal purpose of the forestry program is to demonstrate the immediate benefits of fire control in the Puerto Cabezas pine region. Later, the program should be extended to the Ocotal area.

The effects of uncontrolled burning, controlled burning, and no burning can be demonstrated on three plots af about 10,000 acres each. Although these plots would have to be on private lands, it is hoped that landholders will make the properties available without charge for the demonstration. Later, the land-holders may be persuaded to undertake their own fire-control program, when the experiments have demonstrated the need and benefits of control.

The tests should be supervised by an experienced forester, who should receive sufficient funds for additional men and equipment to build fire breaks, fight fires and patrol the areas.

TABLE 13

COST OF THE PROGRAM FOR FORESTRY SERVICE
Estimated cost: $750,000 local currency; $250,000 foreign currency.

	Local Currency	Foreign Currency
1952-53		
Establishment of service	$ 50,000	—
1953-54		
Selection of plots	—	—
Fire control equipment	—	$100,000
Personnel and supplies	100,000	—
	100,000	100,000
1954-55		
Fire control demonstration	—	—
Personnel and supplies	100,000	25,000
Mapping of pine region	100,000	25,000
	200,000	50,000
1955-56		
As in 1954-55	200,000	50,000
1956-57		
As in 1954-55	200,000	50,000
1952-57 Total	**$750,000**	**$250,000**

4. *Servicio Tecnico Agricola.* Funds for the Servicio Tecnico are fairly adequate, but there is need for additional facilities, such as extra transportation equipment and machinery, and for additional technical and field help. The organization also needs a central headquarters building. In order to continue and expand this valuable program, additional funds will be needed for the Nicaraguan share of the cost as shown in Table 14.

TABLE 14

ADDITIONAL COST OF THE PROGRAM FOR SERVICIO TECNICO AGRICOLA
Estimated cost: $200,000 local currency; $150,000 foreign currency.

	Local Currency	Foreign Currency
1952-53		
Main building	$100,000	$ 50,000
Additional equipment and personnel	20,000	20,000
	120,000	70,000
1953-54		
Additional equipment and personnel	20,000	20,000
1954-57		
As in 1953-54	60,000	60,000
1952-57 Total	$200,000	$150,000

5. *Mapping.* At present there are no good, reliable maps of the country. Surveys and maps of all types, topography, soils, cadastral, and power sources are essential for the development program. The government, in cooperation with the current United States geodetic mission, is now working on a first-order survey of Nicaragua, but this will not be finished for many years.

The development program provides for funds to survey the forest area, to make land-use studies, and to undertake any other surveys needed in the land-colonization program.

Some of the surveys will be of a local nature, and not part of a general program. Any mapping done in the west coast area can make use of the data already obtained by the United States geodetic survey. First-order triangulation has been completed in the area and the data obtained can be of direct use after aerial maps of the region have been made. It is possible that they can be prepared by the Nicaraguan Air Force. A single plane can be fitted for the work, and the flying crew and ground personnel can get technical training from either the United States Air Force or from a commercial concern. This would permit the completion of the survey of the west coast in a short time. At the same time, equipment and experienced Nicaraguan personnel would become available for other special surveys as may be required for the development program.

The cost of such a program is not easy to estimate, but it is likely that a considerable portion can be borne by the military budget, since it would give specialized training to pilots and ground personnel.

III. *INDUSTRY*

A number of small- to medium-sized industries should be developed that could contribute to a reduction of imports and to a better utilization of native raw materials and skills.

Nicaragua now imports cotton and leather goods, vegetable and animal fats and oils, bagging, milk products and other products which can be manufactured domestically.

The industries proposed in the development program are intended to be, and should be, attractive outlets for private capital, either for direct investment or through the purchase of securities of the proposed Instituto de Fomento. Most of the industries suggested are so important for the development of the economy that the Instituto should use its own funds for their construction when the requisite private capital is not forthcoming.

In some cases, such as dairy products, the processing facilities have been considered so integral a part of the agricultural program that they are included in the cost estimates for that program. The industrial section of the Instituto de Fomento should direct the investment of the necessary funds.

Development of the following industries is suggested as a part of, and complementary to, the agricultural development program.

A. *First Priority*

1. *Slaughterhouse and Refrigeration Facilities.* As already indicated the most promising field for future agricultural development is in the production of dairy and meat products, both for export and domestic consumption. Meat should be processed locally for the export trade. Live animal exports should cease as soon as sufficient sanitary slaughtering facilities are available in the country.

A slaughterhouse, with by-product recovery, normally needs a kill of around 200 head per day to be successful. However, Honduras has successfully established small slaughterhouses with a kill of only 25 head a day, which provide chilled meat shipped by air to the United States market.

Nicaragua's chief future markets for meat and dairy products should be El Salvador, Panama, Peru, Venezuela and Puerto Rico. Air transport to these countries will not always be practicable, so that plans should be made for refrigerated land and sea transport.

Several years will be required to develop these markets properly, since it will necessitate a large refrigerated storage capacity, the purchase of refrigerated trucks or rail cars and arrangements for refrigerated ships to call at Nicaraguan ports. However, some of these steps may be eliminated by using air transport for the nearby markets. An early start could be made on the export of chilled meat with a low initial investment by following the Honduras plan.

2. *African Palm Oil Extraction.* With the assistance of the Servicio Tecnico, some 500 acres of African oil palms have been planted by private landowners and are now coming into production, but the fruit cannot be utilized because of the lack of a processing plant. A plant is urgently needed to provide an outlet for the crop now coming from private lands, and to assure future planters that processing facilities will be available as needed.

The proposed agricultural program of 6,000 acres of new plantings will require not less than 20 processing plants. While most of these will only be needed after 1957, a definite plan should be formulated now. Until then, three plants, properly located, will be able to handle all production from present plantings.

It is suggested that the first pilot plant be placed under the supervision of the Servicio Tecnico at El Recreo. Credits for the remaining plants can be given to individual planters.

3. *Oil Hydrogenation.* The establishment of a vegetable shortening plant would eliminate lard imports and provide an additional outlet for local cottonseed oil. The same equipment can also be used to hydrogenate local nonedible oils for soap manufacture. No additional oil mill will be needed since the mills now in operation are expanding and will soon be able to handle all cottonseed production. It is recommended that credits be made available to these industries to enable them to complete their processing plants.

4. *Feed Mixing Plant.* The availability of balanced feeds will be a major factor in determining the goals of the dairy and beef program. High protein concentrates, molasses and other feeds are readily available in the country but they need blending into a balanced ration for best results. A small mixing plant should be established, perhaps in connection with the grain

storage silos, to make good feeds for cattle, hog and chicken raisers.

5. *Cement.* At the present time, the cement production of 400,000 bags per year does not quite fill the needs of the country. During the next few years demand for cement will increase because of the expanded road program, private construction and the general development program. An increase of cement production will be needed to meet such demands.

6. *Other Industries.* Other industries which should be expanded include textiles, leather and food processing, but it is not possible to formulate a definite program for them at this time.

In the textile industry, credits will be needed to expand the processing of artificial fabrics, both woven and knitted, as well as for modern equipment for the production of knitted cottons. The very urgent need for a new cotton spinning and weaving plant is now being filled through private investment. This relatively large investment need not be considered as a part of the Instituto de Fomento.

The leather industry will need both technical advice and credits for machinery. It would be advantageous for the Instituto to place a leather technologist on its staff to aid local tanners.

The food processing industry is still primitive. Such industry as exists is crude and unsanitary. There are a number of opportunities for making candy, preserves and jams, and biscuits.

Any program for the three industries mentioned will need further study by the Instituto. About $460,000 will be needed for their development over the five-year period.

The industrial program includes the estimated over-all cost in foreign exchange and local currency of the proposed plants. In certain cases where private capital is not forthcoming, the Instituto may have to construct the plant and bear the whole of the original cost. More often, however, the Instituto will probably need to bear only a part of the costs either in the form of an

extension of credits or joint participation with private capital
in the establishment of the industries. The estimated costs are
outlined in Table 15.

TABLE 15

FIRST PRIORITY INDUSTRIAL PROJECTS

Estimated cost: $490,000 local currency; $1,310,000 foreign currency.

	Local Currency	Foreign Currency
1952-53		
African palm oil extraction plant	$ 10,000	$ 20,000
Slaughterhouse and refrigeration plant	50,000	50,000
1953-54		
Cement plant	—	600,000
Slaughterhouse and refrigeration plant	100,000	100,000
Oil hydrogenation plant	25,000	75,000
Feed mixing plant	25,000	25,000
Miscellaneous industrial credits	40,000	75,000
1954-55		
Slaughterhouse and refrigeration	100,000	100,000
Miscellaneous industrial credits	40,000	75,000
1955-56		
African palm oil extraction plant	10,000	20,000
Miscellaneous industrial credits	40,000	75,000
1956-57		
African palm oil extraction plant	10,000	20,000
Miscellaneous industrial credits	40,000	75,000
1952-57 Total	**$490,000**	**$1,310,000**

B. *Second Priority*

1. *Hardboard Mill.* The establishment of a hardboard mill
would strengthen the east coast economy and allow the exploita-

tion of presently unused woods. Considerable study will be needed to determine the best location of the mill with regard to raw materials, shipping and markets. Most of the product will have to be sold on the export market, but with the completion of the Rama Road an increasing share of the production can probably be used on the west coast.

It is estimated that a small hardboard mill can be installed at a cost of about $1,000,000.

2. *Warehouses.* There is insufficient warehouse space at the principal ports to handle today's exports. If exports increase to the extent contemplated by the agricultural program, the situation can become critical. With the present transportation situation, the goods need to be on the dock when a ship enters the port. More warehouses are needed to handle the growing traffic. These should be built by private individuals but some medium- and long-term credits will be needed to help finance them. For this purpose $500,000 should be adequate.

3. *Wire Products Manufacture.* A large quantity of barbed wire, staples and nails is imported each year. It would be desirable to import only the wire and do the manufacturing in the country. The machinery is quite cheap and simple. An investment of around $50,000 should install a small plant capable of turning out all the local needs for barbed wire, staples and nails. Later, as the market expands, it may be possible to add a wire drawing mill and only wire billets will then need to be imported.

4. *Other Industries.* Two or more large cotton gins will be needed and the local saw mills need general improvement in equipment. The Instituto may also find it desirable to establish a cooperative coffee beneficio to process the crops of the small growers in order that they may get a fairer price than is now possible. The amount needed for these possible projects is around $450,000.

IV. POWER

A. Needs for Power

It is axiomatic that in any development program power is basic. Nicaragua needs power, however, not solely for the future development program but to meet present industrial and domestic requirements. No city, town or village, except the self-sufficient mining towns, has adequate power to meet normal demand. Only five cities have continuous 24-hour service. The remainder have service for periods varying from six to 18 hours daily. All generating facilities are overtaxed.

In Matagalpa the line voltage seldom rises above 60 volts. The lights are so dim that the electric company itself must use lanterns to light the generator house. In Managua, if one generator goes out a whole section of the city must be blacked out to prevent dangerous overloading of the remaining units.

Industries and commercial enterprises have been able to avoid the power shortage by installing their own power plants. This adds considerably to their investment costs. None of these private plants would have been necessary had sufficient public power been available.

Managua, with a population of over 100,000, has an effective public generating capacity of only 3,500 kilowatts. The installation of a new 3,500 kilowatt generator now under way will not substantially alleviate the situation, since the new generator will give only the necessary stand-by protection that the city has previously lacked. It will not provide additional power for new customers. In addition to the more than 5,000 kilowatts of generating capacity now installed by private interests, there is still a large unfilled demand for power for electric stoves, appliances and air conditioning, as well as for the proposed industrial plants.

It is essential that power be given first priority in the development program. It will demand the most careful attention of the government for many years to come.

B. *Hydroelectric Potentials*

Since the country has no known deposits of coal or oil, hydroelectric power is the most logical development. In early 1951, a preliminary survey of possible water power sources was made by the United States Bureau of Reclamation. The report indicated three areas which would have possibilities for development: the Tuma River, the San Juan River, and the Tamarindo River.

Maps and stream flow records of these areas were completely lacking so that, of necessity, additional study was recommended. This study is now under way. Preliminary reports indicate that the Tuma River provides the greatest possibilities. Detailed studies are now being made of the topography and flow of the river.

It now seems certain that power can be generated on the Tuma river, but the best location for a hydroelectric power development has not been determined. How much power can be generated and what it would cost remains uncertain.

It will be necessary to keep stream flow records for a number of years to learn what water storage capacity will be needed and how much firm power can be obtained. The longer these records are kept and the better the data, the more likely will be the success of the project. A minimum of two years will be needed before any idea can be gained of stream flow, but even this is not long enough to learn what minimum flow may be expected during dry cycles. Five years altogether will be required to gather sufficient data for a plan for hydroelectric development. Consequently, there can be no additional public power from hydroelectric installations within the next eight to 12 years. Nor is there any certainty that the cost of such a development will be within the means of the country at a later date.

Power is needed now. The country cannot wait for the Tuma River development. To take care of immediate needs, the only alternatives are diesel or steam generating facilities. The mission considers that steam power is preferable to diesel power.

C. *Immediate Objectives*

Managua as the center of commerce and industry has the most urgent need for additional power. There appears to be an immediate demand in the area for at least 10,000 kilowatts.

The objectives of a five-year power program should be to:

(a) install in Managua 10,000 kilowatts of steam generating capacity, made up of two 5,000 kilowatt units, using the present diesel units for stand-by;

(b) extend transmission lines in three directions: (i) to Tipitapa; (ii) to Casa Colorado, Diriamba, Jinotepe, San Marcos, Masaya and Granada; and (iii) eventually toward Leon;

(c) tie into a network the existing facilities in these towns;

(d) renovate the Managua transmission network and provide for the metering of all services as well as the revision of the rate structure.

The mission believes that the power company of Managua can finance the proposed expansion program, including amortization of new equipment, out of earnings. It can do this by reducing generating costs and line losses, by metering all sales, and by stopping the use of free current by the various government offices.

D. *Timing*

In order to meet the objectives of the program, a rigid schedule should be drawn up. The mission suggests the following:

1952-53

1. reorganizing the utility companies and rate structures to place them on a sound business basis;

2. finishing the installation of the 3,500 kilowatt diesel unit;

3. making a thorough study of the distribution network and planning a new network;
4. planning for the additional generators, including the necessary financial arrangements;
5. placing orders for line equipment and the steam turbine generators.

1953-54

1. starting work on distribution lines;
2. starting installation of the first 5,000 kilowatt steam unit.

1954-55

1. finishing work on the distribution lines;
2. finishing installation of the first steam unit.

1955-56

1. starting installation of the second 5,000 kilowatt steam unit.

1956-57

1. finishing installation of the second unit.

E. *Estimated Cost*

It is believed that the program can be carried out with a total expenditure of $4.5 million, with $2.7 million for the generating equipment and $1.8 million for the improvement and extension of the transmission lines. The funds will be needed approximately as follows:

1953-54	$1,575,000
1954-55	1,575,000
1955-56	675,000
1956-57	675,000
Total	**$4,500,000**

Not less than $3.5 million of the total will be in foreign currency.

V. *TRANSPORTATION AND COMMUNICATIONS*

Over the past 12 years there has been rapid progress towards the construction of a network of main roads. Many sections of the country, however, still remain isolated from markets during much of the year. The growing volume of exports is imposing a strain on the railroads and the port system. A further increase of production and exports resulting from the agricultural program could cause a severe crisis in the existing transportation system.

For this reason the mission recommends a program, second only in size to agriculture, having as its goals:

(a) improvement of the operating efficiency of the railroad system;

(b) completion of all major highways, as well as a country-wide network of farm-to-market roads. This would mean expansion of the west coast highway network, completion of the Rama road as an east-west route, and construction of a local mesh of farm-to-market roads in each region;

(c) modernization of the major ocean ports and improvement of lake transportation;

(d) construction of additional airfields for inland transportation.

TABLE 16

SUMMARY OF TRANSPORTATION AND COMMUNICATIONS
INVESTMENT PROGRAM 1952-1957
(First Priority)

	Foreign Currency	Local Currency
Railways	$ 1,290,000	$ 460,000
Main Roads		
Inter-American Highway	4,000,000	2,000,000
International Bank roads	2,500,000	1,000,000

	Foreign Currency	Local Currency
Rama road	2,500,000	1,500,000
	9,000,000	4,500,000
Feeder Roads		
Equipment, fuels, and supplies	3,000,000	—
Labor	—	1,000,000
	3,000,000	1,000,000
Ports		
Corinto	625,000	625,000
San Juan del Sur	125,000	125,000
Rama	125,000	125,000
El Bluff (dredging)	250,000	250,000
Lake ports	185,000	190,000
	1,310,000	1,315,000
Airfields	10,000	90,000
	$14,610,000	$7,365,000

A. *Ferrocarril del Pacifico de Nicaragua*
(the state-owned railroad)

Gross tonnage carried by the railroad will tend to decrease with the completion of the roads from Managua to Leon and Chinandega, Masaya to Granada, and Rivas to San Juan del Sur because of truck competition for intercity hauling. Nevertheless, the railroad is, and for a number of years should continue to be, an important and necessary link in the transportation system of country. There can be no thought of abandoning the system at the present time. To do so would impose an impossible burden on the country, which would have to undertake more road construction and a heavy importation of trucks and buses. It would also have to reconvert the Port of Corinto. In the opinion of the mission, the railroad has a useful life of at least 10 to 15 years, provided that it can be rehabilitated to provide fast and efficient shuttle service at lower cost. It also will need to reorganize its administration. This is discussed more fully in Part III of this report.

Specifically, the mission recommends:

(a) scrapping the pre-1925 steam locomotives now in service and replacing them with a few new diesel-electric engines;

(b) introducing diesel rail cars for passenger traffic and a number of additional freight cars;

(c) re-equipping the repair shops to handle the maintenance of the new diesel-electric locomotives and rail cars;

(d) improving the right-of-way from Managua to Corinto by replacement of track and ties;

(e) abandoning, as planned, the isolated spur from Rivas to San Juan del Sur;

(f) abandoning the line from Managua to Granada when the parallel highway is finished.

The mission believes that four 600 h.p. diesel locomotives will be enough to perform efficient shuttle service between Managua and Corinto and to replace the bulk of the pre-1925 steam engines now in use. They should, in addition, be able to repay their entire cost within five years through savings in fuel and maintenance costs. To this may be added further savings in operating time and freight car turn around.

The main line requires rehabilitation by ballasting, the replacement of some ties and rails, and some realignment of the track. This must be done for the efficient operation of the proposed new locomotives and heavy-duty freight cars and to raise the present low maximum safe running speeds.

Freight haulage should be separated from passenger traffic as far as possible by the introduction of three self-propelled rail cars each seating 90 passengers. Each car would be able to make several round trips per day from Managua to Corinto, providing the rapid and comfortable service so urgently needed.

A few of the better steam locomotives can be used for switching and service from Leon to El Sauce and from Chinandega, to Puerto Morazan.

Upon completion of the road to Chinandega, many of the intermediate railway stops can be eliminated. The railroad should concentrate on fast, nonstop service moving import and export freight between the main towns of Managua, Leon, Chinandega and Corinto.

It is estimated that the rehabilitation of the railroad can be carried out at a gross cost of $2 million as follows:

TABLE 17

RAILROAD REHABILITATION COSTS

	Foreign Currency	Local Currency
1952-53		
Ballast crushing plant	$ 25,000	—
Reballasting 69 km.	—	$137,500
Replacement of ties	—	100,000
Relaying 1500 tons of rail	157,500	5,000
1953-54		
Reballasting 69 km.	—	137,500
Replacement of ties	—	200,000
Relaying 1,500 tons of rail	157,500	5,000
4—600 h.p. diesel-electric locomotives	425,000	—
30 freight cars	175,000	—
3 self-propelled passenger cars	325,000	—
Relaying 1,500 tons of rail	125,000	25,000
Total	**$1,390,000**	**$610,000**

The net capital cost would be only about $1.75 million since 50% of the total cost of tie replacement would be chargeable to normal maintenance and the remainder of about $150,000 to capital funds. Other funds, totalling perhaps $100,000, can be recovered from sales of scrapped rolling stock and rail from abandoned lines. The mission believes that the investment program can be financed from the railroad's earnings. In order to relieve the recurrent seasonal strain while the recommended rehabilitation is being carried out, the following operation reforms should be instituted:

1. operate freight trains separately from passenger trains as much as present motive power permits;

2. arrange for maximum freight service at night, and passenger and express service during the day;

3. run nonstop freight trains at night between Corinto and the main stations of Chinandega, Leon and Managua;

4. increase demurrage charges during the peak season on cars held longer than 12 hours;

5. reassign the best and most powerful locomotives to freight service exclusively;

6. collect forecasts from shippers as to their car requirements several weeks in advance;

7. institute, if necessary, a system of priorities for the movement of essential freight during the peak season from December to March.

B. *Roads*

Nicaragua needs good roads and a land link between the east and west coasts. Good roads would reduce inland transport charges and open up areas now undeveloped because of their inaccessibility. A land link would make an east coast port available for west coast import-export trade and open a new, though limited, domestic market to west coast products.

The program prepared by the mission has two main goals: the linking of the main cities and ports with good, all-weather roads and the construction, improvement and maintenance of a system of feeder and access roads to cover the entire country. This should be carried out as promptly as possible.

1. *Main Roads*. (a) Inter-American Highway. Nicaragua is already committed to improving the northern stretches of this highway from Sebaco to the Honduras border. The present road is to be realigned and hard surfaced, its grades and curves reduced and bridges installed. This will give a high-grade road of the same quality as the Managua-Rivas section of the road. The completion of this work will provide a stimulus to inter-regional trade and to international trade with Honduras and El Salvador.

The total cost of this work is estimated at $6 million, with $2 million scheduled to be paid by Nicaragua and $4 million by the United States Government.

(b) International Bank Roads. In 1951, Nicaragua secured a loan from the International Bank to finance the foreign exchange costs of five new roads:

1. Matagalpa—Jinotega;
2. Matagalpa—Tuma Valley;
3. Managua—Leon—Chinandega;
4. Managua—Masaya—Granada;
5. Rivas—San Juan del Sur.

These roads will all be hard surfaced, although the specifications are not quite as high as those for the Inter-American Highway.

Since work has already started on these roads, it is estimated that, from mid-1952 on, a sum of $3.5 million out of a total cost of $5 million will still be needed for their completion. Of this amount $2.5 million is in foreign currency to be financed by existing loans, and $1 million is in local currency.

(c) Rama Road. This project, which will connect Managua with the east coast port of Rama on the Escondido river, cannot be assessed on purely economic grounds. Although its future value to the economy cannot be measured entirely in financial terms, the mission believes that the road should be completed in order to provide the first land link with the east coast. This road will not only connect the west coast with the port of Rama, but will also open up new agricultural lands along its route. By providing the first physical link between the east and west coasts it will help to speed the social, political and economic unification of the country.

If built to the specifications of the Inter-American Highway, such a road might require an expenditure of $8 million. In view of all other competing demands on its resources, this would be too heavy a financial burden for the country. Fortunately, the United States has now authorized, but not yet appropriated, $4 million as a grant-in-aid for this project, to be spent over the next two years. The mission believes that $4 million is enough to build a simple, two-lane, all-weather route of gravel or crushed stone, suitable for bus and truck traffic.

In 1950, Nicaragua imposed a coffee export tax to accumulate funds for the completion of the Rama road and certain feeder roads in the coffee regions. This was to provide an alternative source of revenue if the United States Congress did not appropriate money for the Rama project. By mid-1952 accumulated funds amounted to about $2 million.

The mission suggests the following, as a proper disposition of these funds: First, to pay all expenses of the Rama project, except those for actual road construction, e.g. the costs of the port at Rama and of dredging at El Bluff. Second, to transfer whatever remains unspent to the development budget for essential projects either in transportation or other sectors.

Preparation of dock and shore facilities at Rama, plus the dredging of the bar at El Bluff and the bank in the Bluefields Lagoon to a depth of 15 feet probably can be completed at a cost of about $750,000. Foreign exchange costs will amount to about half this total.

2. *Feeder Roads.* The need for feeder and access roads is general throughout the whole country. On the west coast the most

urgent need is for feeder roads into the main highways and main railroad stations. On the east coast the primary need is for penetration roads from the navigable rivers into the lands beyond the present narrow strip of cultivation.

The mission is not in a position to recommend a definite work schedule, indicating which roads should be built first and how much mileage should be built each year. This should be decided by interested government agencies, working with the National Economic Council, which would take full account of the over-all development needs of the country. The goal should be to build, as rapidly as possible, an extensive network of feeder and access roads. At a minimum, motor trucks should find these passable during the dry season. It would also be desirable to build a number of miles of all-weather roads each year. This will mean savings on road construction in the long run.

In order to carry out this program, it is suggested that the country be divided into nine regions:

1. Managua and surroundings;
2. Leon;
3. Chinandega;
4. Rivas;
5. Masaya—Granada;
6. Matagalpa—Jinotega;
7. Chontales—Boaco area;
8. South Atlantic Coast;
9. North Atlantic Coast.

In each region there should be a road crew whose sole duty and full-time job would be to build, improve and maintain the local feeder and access roads. Equipment for each crew should consist of six trucks, a tractor bulldozer, a motor grader, a pick-up and a DW-10 rubber-tired tractor. Every three crews might share a power shovel and a crusher. Rollers, adequate shop equipment, hand tools, and spare parts would also be required.

The minimum cost of such a program is estimated at $4 million. There would be $3 million in foreign currency for equipment, fuels, lubricants and supplies, and $1 million in local currency for labor costs. Some of the foreign currency costs, about $400,000 can be covered from accumulated proceeds of the coffee export tax.

If the optimum development program is undertaken, then an additional $1 million should be allocated to the building of feeder and access roads.

C. *Ports and Airfields*

In order to cope with the growing exports and to reduce handling charges, it is essential that the leading west coast ports be improved and their facilities expanded. On the west coast, the mission recommends that improvements be confined to the ports of San Juan del Sur and Corinto and that all efforts to convert the open roadstead of Masachapa into a sheltered port be stopped.

In Corinto, increased safety as well as expansion of capacity could be gained if a separate tanker berth were constructed away from the freight pier. This would allow the present pier to handle two ocean-going freighters at the same time. The over-all cost is estimated to be $1.25 million.

In San Juan del Sur engineering studies should be made to determine the feasibility and approximate cost of building a pier that would eliminate the need for lighterage. Actual construction, however, should be deferred until after the termination of this program. For the present, the existing lighter pier and services could be improved and additional warehouse space constructed. The cost is estimated to be about $250,000.

The need for a port at Rama and for the dredging of the mouth of the Escondido river was covered in the discussion of the Rama Road.

In addition to improving ocean and river ports, better landing stages will be needed on Lake Nicaragua to serve communities having no other means of access to the main towns. At Granada the pier location should be changed to a more sheltered position and a new pier installed for truck rather than railroad operation since the latter should be abandoned shortly. Piers should be lengthened at the principal centers around the lake so that the ships can be loaded directly instead of using lighterage service. The cost will be around $375,000.

In a few completely isolated communities landing strips capable of handling DC-3's should be constructed. In particular, fields should be laid out at San Carlos and Jalapa to provide regular air service to these areas.

D. *Communications*

First Priority. In its first priority investment program, the mission has no scheduled or recommended capital investment for communications. It believes, however, that administrative reorganization of the telephone, telegraph and postal services should be given high priority. All service should be put on a commercial basis to reduce the present heavy operating deficit. Detailed recommendations for improving the operating efficiency of these services will be found in Part III of this report.

Second Priority. Although there is a great need for a modern telephone system in Managua, the mission believes that it is not as important to the over-all development of the country as the construction of roads and ports. However, it does deserve to be included in the optimum program.

It is estimated that the cost would be $1.7 million, of which around $1.3 million would be in foreign exchange.

CHAPTER FOUR

Problems And Policies In Development

The previous chapter has outlined a five-year public investment program in the principal sectors of the economy. This chapter considers the fiscal and administrative problems that Nicaragua will have to face in carrying out so extensive an investment program.

I. *THE NATIONAL INCOME*

A. *Income for 1950 and 1951*

The first preliminary calculations of national income, without the adjustments and refinements to be made later, was completed by the Central Statistical Bureau in June 1952. These showed gross national product in 1950 at about 1,027 million cordobas.

TABLE 18

GROSS NATIONAL PRODUCT

1950

(million cordobas)

Agriculture	416
Mining	60
Construction	54
Manufacturing	145
Transportation and Communications	37
Power	11
Commerce and Finance	108
Government	63
Professional and domestic services	27
Other services, including hotels, residential imputed and paid rents, interest payments, etc.	106
Total	**1,027**

Similar calculations have not yet been made for 1951, but the mission believes that the gross national product in 1951 exceeded 1,200 million cordobas, as a result of increased export values in that year, the devaluation of the cordoba and internal price rises. This would be $170 million, or a per capita income close to $155. At this level of income it is possible to carry out the kind of full-scale development program recommended by the mission.

B. *The Distribution of Income*

In the absence of representative family budgets and samples of income distribution, it has not been possible to estimate the distribution of the national income between different income groups. The mission's data on costs and earnings in industry, agriculture, construction, commerce and other activities indicate, however, that more than 25% of the national income accrues to about 1% of the population. Within the top 1% there is a further concentration of income at the upper level.

Under the present fiscal system little of the tax burden falls upon the upper 1%. Most of it is borne by the remaining 99%, whose average income, after taxation, is probably less than $100 per year.

While a concentration of income of this kind is not unusual in Latin America it has probably been accentuated in Nicaragua by several years of inflation, which has tended to shift upward the shares of the national income. An additional factor has been the rise, in the past two years, in export values. The value of coffee and cotton exports rose from 23 million cordobas in 1949 to 71 million cordobas in 1950 and to 158 million cordobas in 1951. Between 70-75% of the coffee and cotton crops are produced by some 950 growers.

C. *Investment Share of the National Income*

The mission has not been able to determine precisely the level of gross investment in 1951, but from data on truck and tractor imports, imports of machinery and equipment and the estimated volume of private and government construction, the mission estimates that total capital investment in 1951 was roughly 6% of the national income. Probably 85% of this was in the private sector. Although the government had begun to allocate substantial funds to its road projects, grain storage plants and other development purposes, actual expenditures lagged well behind during the year.

Almost half of the total investment went into private construction. The bulk of this consisted of residential construction for the well-to-do, and thus made relatively little contribution toward increasing the productivity of the economy. For the most part tractor imports were financed by external loans. This somewhat reduced the amount of productive investment financed from domestic resources. The total rate of physically productive gross capital formation from Nicaragua's own resources was probably about 3% of the national income. This is a fairly low rate for a period of high incomes, especially with a concentration of income in the higher brackets.

D. *The Need for Channeling Funds into Investment*

In 1951 Nicaragua had sufficient financial means, produced by the increase in export values, to have launched a major investment program entirely from domestic resources. Yet in spite of a national income 200 million cordobas greater than the high 1950 level, only a fraction of the increase was devoted to raising the level of productivity. The country probably made smaller productive investments from her own resources than she borrowed abroad, during the year, for the same purpose.

The financial opportunity for development coincided with, and was presumably partly responsible for, the government's decision to undertake such a program. In spite of the decision, neither the government nor the country was able to take full advantage of the unexpected improvement in the financial situation. The causes of this were many, but primarily they were fiscal and administrative. The government's revenue comes almost entirely from indirect taxation, which is slow to reflect a rapid rise in the national income, especially a rise in individual incomes and profits. There has been no institution capable of guiding and encouraging private capital into the most productive channels. It was inevitable that additional funds coming into private hands should go into the usual channels: land purchases or speculation, private house construction, consumer durable goods and cars, usury and travel. A reform of the fiscal system was essential, therefore, if the country was to carry out a development program.

II. FISCAL POLICY AND DEVELOPMENT

A. The Fiscal Reform

The aim of the fiscal reform being undertaken by the government is not solely to provide additional revenue for urgently needed public works and services. It is partly intended to channel additional funds into the projected Instituto de Fomento, which would, in turn, provide private enterprise with financial and technical assistance. This would encourage the flow of capital into productive private investments, which are as urgently needed as government public works. It is partly intended, also, to make an immediate, though small, start in raising living standards by removing or reducing the present heavy taxation on standard articles of consumption, including foodstuffs.

Fiscal and monetary reform is basic to the development of the country. The first steps by the government in the direction of reform were taken in 1950 when the exchange surcharges were introduced. While these were made primarily for purposes of monetary stabilization, they later had a fiscal character as well. At almost the same time a small coffee export tax was imposed to help finance the building of the Rama road and feeder roads in the coffee regions.

Since 1950, the government has moved further towards general fiscal reform. Late in 1951 it imposed special profits taxes on coffee and cotton. It has agreed to a general income tax, and measures to improve the collection of other direct taxes. The success of the national development budget of the next five years will be largely dependent upon these fiscal reforms.

1. *The Coffee and Cotton Taxes.* In placing a special tax on net profits from coffee and cotton production, the government took account of several factors:

(a) gross receipts from coffee and cotton exports had risen from $4.6 million in 1949 to $14.2 million in 1950 and to $24.2 million in 1951;

(b) net profits had, because of the great lag in costs, increased from $2.2 million in 1949 to around $12 million in 1951 or, from 11 million cordobas in 1949 to 80 million cordobas in 1951;

(c) around $8.5 million of the net profits accrued in 1951 to some 950 producers.

A small and equitable sliding scale tax on the net profits from coffee and cotton production was passed in late 1951.

2. *Income and Property Taxes.* The imposition of special taxes on the net profits of coffee and cotton producers was a first step towards a general income tax and a revision of the fiscal system. It was a move away from almost exclusive dependence on consumption taxes and customs revenues.

The mission, in making its recommendations to the government regarding a general income tax, stressed the importance of having a relatively high exemption and of keeping the tax moderate. Both are necessary to assure that the tax be acceptable and workable. Tax rates should be high enough to provide substantial revenue, but not so high as to encourage fraud.

The government has already begun the task of improving administration of the real property tax which is now largely evaded, either by undervaluation of property or by omission of part of it from annual returns. The tax should be one of the pillars of the revenue system in the future.

The special tax on cotton and coffee profits should be merged into the general income tax. The mission believes that an export tax on coffee should be retained as a permanent part of the fiscal system of the country, along with the general income tax.

3. *The Coffee Export Tax.* The present moderate export tax on coffee was imposed in 1950, primarily for the building of the Rama road. Since the United States has authorized funds for this purpose, the coffee export tax should be revised to provide funds for the general development budget. The present coffee taxes, including both the export tax and the net income tax on coffee producers, amounts to only 7-12% of the export value. This is considerably lower than the coffee export taxes of Guatemala and El Salvador which come to about 16-17% of the export price.

The mission recommends the following scale for a permanent coffee export tax:

Export Price F.O.B. Corinto	Export Tax per Quintal
$55 or over	$7
$50-$54.95	$6
$45-$49.95	$5
$40-$44.95	$4
$35-$39.95	$3
$30-$34.95	$2
Under $30	none

This tax is much lower than the $8 per quintal tax recommended by the International Bank Mission to Guatemala, subsequently accepted by that government, and the $8.25-$9.75 per quintal tax in El Salvador. The smaller tax has been suggested, however, because of the slightly lower price of Nicaraguan coffee in New York, and the lower yields per tree.

To tie the coffee export tax into the framework of the general income tax law, it is suggested that the government allow half of the export tax to be applied towards the individual income tax payable on net income from coffee production. The other half would be a straight export tax.

The export tax on coffee will provide the government with additional revenue prior to the fiscal year in which the income tax comes into effect. It will therefore be one of the few forms of pay-as-you-go income tax suitable to Nicaragua.

If the government proceeds at any time to unify the exchange rate at seven cordobas to the dollar, an additional tax should be imposed to capture the difference between receipts at 6.6 cordobas and at the unitary rate.

4. *Consumption Taxes.* The mission has made recommendations that the government act, as rapidly as possible, to reduce or remove the most oppressive consumption taxes. The government has given full agreement to the general proposal.

The removal of the taxes on sugar and matches is particularly stressed. Both items are prime necessities for the entire population, but the price of sugar is held artificially high by a sugar cartel, and the match factory, a monopoly, is an inefficient producer of an inferior product. The taxes are an added burden on the purchaser of these products. The tax on meat slaughtering affects the price of an article which is in many family budgets, though not as widely consumed as sugar and matches. The mission believes that the fiscal resources available to the government during the coming fiscal year will be large enough to justify the removal of these taxes early in the fiscal year.

B. *A Development Budget*

The mission has recommended to the government the introduction of a general development budget which is intended to form an integral part of the government's over-all budget. Development expenditures should be clearly defined and separated out both in the general budget and the budgets of the individual government departments and enterprises. The aim of such a budget is to:

(a) assure that all, or most, increases in revenues, except for minimum operating and administrative expenses, including the service of the public debt, will go to specific development projects within the framework of the five-year program;

(b) assure that all projects in the development budget will be carefully screened for their urgency and priority;

(c) enable the government to show fully the efforts it is making to increase the development of the country and the very heavy costs involved; and

(d) give the public confidence that any additional taxes imposed will be assigned to urgent development projects within the five-year program.

This particular type of budget requires great care and skill in handling. It is not the same as a capital budget. It should specifically exclude capital expenditures undertaken by the Presidency, the Army, the Legislature and for all public buildings not used for health, educational or economic purposes. In some aspects, however, it is intended to be broader than a capital budget, since it would include DDT projects or literacy campaigns which, in an underdeveloped country, can be considered as direct contributions to the development of the economy.

C. Municipal Financing

The extremely weak state of the municipal finances of the country is a heritage from colonial days and a reflection of the strong centralization of the government. It is a particularly unfortunate aspect of the fiscal system, since the provision of many of the basic services of the country such as water, sanitation, street paving and lighting, local markets and, to some extent, general health and educational services are, and properly should be, a function of local government.

The municipal budgets of the three largest cities of the country apparently come to less than three million cordobas ($450,-000) annually, or under $3 per capita, although it should be pointed out that the mission was not able to obtain fully adequate information on municipal financing.

The government, through the National Economic Council, has approved a policy of coordinating municipal development plans with the national development program. This is most important since a substantial part of the health, sanitation and educational expenditures proposed for the next five years should come from municipal budgets.

It is strongly suggested that in the future all municipal budgets require the review and approval of the Minister of Finance. The preparation of municipal budgets is an inappropriate func-tion for the Ministries of *Gobernacion* and the *Distrito Nacional* since these Ministries do not participate in the coordinating work of the National Economic Council. Municipal taxes or public works are not now referred for approval to the appropriate national fiscal authorities.

The mission suggests the desirability either of allocating to the municipalities a percentage of the proceeds of the property tax collected by them or of making a general allocation to a Municipal Development Fund, from which it would be distributed, on a pro rata basis, to all municipal units. In either case, the national government should give close financial and technical supervision to the projects carried out by the municipalities.

D. *Tariff Revision*

The long, complex study necessary for the revision of a tariff structure, which goes back to 1917, will soon be under way.

The government deserves commendation for embarking on a tariff revision designed to overhaul its most important single source of revenue and to reduce some of the burden of customs duties on consumption. The mission's only suggestion is that care should be taken to assure that protection given to local industries should not be such as to encourage monopoly or inefficient enterprises.

E. *Government Debt*

During the period from May 1951 to May 1952, Nicaragua contracted International Bank loans amounting to $5.25 million and an Export-Import Bank loan of $600,000. During the same period it paid off $2.75 million in external indebtedness, including the outstanding amount of a Bank of America loan and normal amortization of an Export-Import Bank loan and the old Ethelburga loan. The net external debt increased by only $2.6 million during the period, to a total of $7.19 million. The outstanding debt is equal to only 15% of Nicaragua's 1951 exports.

The internal debt in the form of Treasury notes, discounted at the Central Bank in May 1952, came to only 21 million cordobas, representing a considerable reduction from the 26.6 million cordobas of May 1951.

The country can afford to incur additional external debt for productive capital investment purposes. These investments will contribute to the ability of the country to repay such loans.

One important task for the Instituto de Fomento will be to organize a local capital market to handle shares and long-term government bonds, particularly long-term investments which can be financed only with difficulty from current government receipts.

III. *COORDINATION OF DEVELOPMENT POLICIES*

Even in a small state, the technical problems and difficulties of correlating fiscal and budgetary policy, foreign trade policy, and central and commercial banking policy with long-range agricultural and industrial programming are so complex that it is essential to have an adequate administrative body to perform this task.

The size of the proposed development program is such that future coordination is fundamental to its success. The Government has established for this purpose the National Economic Council, and provided it with a secretariat. The council is still new in its operations but it is becoming increasingly effective, as it has become more aware of the need for coordination.

The problem of coordination can best be shown by example rather than by general statement.

The planting of cotton, with its spectacular if somewhat speculative growth in the last two years, has become a problem of considerable concern to a number of different government departments and institutions: to the National Bank which financed a part of the growth and negotiated external loans for the importation of tractors; to the Ministry of Agriculture, responsible for the control of insects and soil erosion; to the Ministries of Economy and Foreign Affairs, which are interested in cotton sales abroad; and to the Railway Administration which is responsible for moving the crop. The problems of warehousing and financing affect a number of departments.

When there was an unexpectedly large crop and a fall in the world price of cotton, it was necessary to improvise solutions to the problems created for the economy. There was then, and still is, no common cotton policy that will promote a balanced future growth of production and marketing.

As another example, the location of feeder roads has to be determined by the Ministry of Public Works. These are at present confined to the coffee regions but, under the mission's proposal, will be extended throughout all the principal agricultural areas. This development will place a heavy burden on the Ministry of Public Works, which should have close cooperation from the Ministry of Agriculture, the Ministry of Economy, the National Bank, the Instituto de Fomento and the Ministry of Finance, in the preparation of a program of priorities for the farm-to-market road program.

Even the educational program is not solely a matter for the Ministry of Education since the program needs close coordination with the general health program and the program for agricultural and vocational training.

The technical problems of coordination should be in the hands of an expanded secretariat of the National Economic Council. The government is small so that many of the problems of co-ordination can be handled directly by the Council but, in consideration of the work load of its members, it is increasingly desirable that only major policy matters go to the Council, and that lesser problems be handled by the secretariat. It may be desirable to designate a senior official of each ministry to work with the secretariat of the Council on the problems common to several ministries.

The final executive decisions will of course continue to be made, as heretofore, by the President of the Republic, with the advice of the Council.

The Need for Priorities. The necessity for setting up investment priorities derives from the fact that only limited funds are available for development, while the needs are great. Fixing priorities is an essential part of the general problem of coordination.

It is normal for each government department or agency to consider its requirements as the most urgent. For this reason an independent staff should make a technical assessment of the programs of each department and agency of the government, relating these programs to the financial resources and over-all requirements of the country. The Instituto de Fomento ought to be best equipped to do this job. It should coordinate the various parts of the general investment program, and make a full technical review, before the program goes to the National Economic Council.

IV. *PUBLIC ADMINISTRATION*

A. *Government Professional Staff*

In preparing its program for development, the mission has been continually faced with the weakness of public administration and of the specific administrative structure of the government departments responsible for carrying out the development program.

A comparatively small number of ministers and government employees now carry most of the burden of government on their shoulders. They have to operate under the trying and exasperating handicaps of a staff inadequate in size and quality to perform even routine tasks, let alone responsible advisory and administrative functions.

The mission realizes that it would be premature to recommend anything approaching a general civil service at this stage of the development of the country. Nevertheless, training and recruiting an adequate professional and technical staff are of sufficient importance to warrant the establishment of at least the nucleus of a professional civil service. This staff should be paid salaries large enough to enable its members to work full time for the government and should have satisfactory tenure, so that the service is attractive (particularly to the rather considerable number of Nicaraguan engineers, economists, agronomists and other technicians who are studying or working outside the country). To attain this end it is suggested that:

(a) a technical civil service be established, limited in membership to those persons who have had recognized professional or technical training in engineering, public administration, economics, public accounting, agronomy, animal husbandry and related fields;

(b) this small group be given security of tenure as a technical-administrative group, salaries commensurate with their working a full day, and promotions for merit;

(c) public employees, now in service, be eligible for admission to this group, provided they receive graduate training outside Nicaragua or specialized training in a foreign government department or with an international agency;

(d) members of the group be eligible without losing civil service tenure, to attain the post of Vice Minister of a

Department or General Manager of a state enterprise or the Instituto de Fomento. Upon appointment as Minister, tenure would be lost during the period of appointment, but would be regained upon reverting to a lower rank.

It is frankly recognized that this proposal discriminates in favor of a particular group, but the mission believes this can be justified by the urgent need for a professional and technical staff.

The Instituto de Fomento will be comparable, in every way, to a banking institution, though it will also serve as a technical planning body for the government. The mission hopes that its staff will be picked for merit and technical competence, and that the Instituto will pay salaries and have working conditions similar to those of the National Bank.

Finally, the mission suggests that the United Nations or a similarly appropriate body be asked to provide an expert during the coming year to set up a series of training programs in the various ministries. Accounting, public administration, statistics and agricultural inspection and credits are fields particularly requiring training programs.

B. *The Administrative Structure*

The mission's administrative recommendations are given in much greater detail in Parts II to IV, which deal with specific sectors of the economy. A summary of the principal recommendations follows:

1. *The Ministry of Development and Public Works.* The Ministry of Development and Public Works will be a key ministry in the execution of the development program, since 45% of the program will involve expenditures for transportation and communications, as well as for sanitation, education and health projects requiring public construction.

At present the Ministry's functions technically correspond to its titular functions, which, in turn, imply a supervision of all development and public works activities of the government. In fact, the Ministry is in charge only of the highways department, plus a number of other functions which are not directly connected with its main duties. These include:

(a) exploitation of the natural resources of the country;

(b) registration of patents and trade marks;

(c) supervision of the navigation of lakes and rivers;

(d) exploitation of hydraulic resources, including water facilities.

The "exploitation of natural resources" consists of passing on concessions given for the natural resources of the country. Because of its importance to the country, the mission suggests that this particular function be divided between the Instituto de Fomento, for technical supervision, and the Ministry of Economy, for policy approval. The trade and patents functions should go to another ministry, possibly Economy or Finance.

The main purpose of removing these functions from the Ministry is to transform it completely into a Ministry or Department of Public Works. Although the Ministry is supposed to be in charge of all public works of the government, including municipal works, the degree of supervision is nominal.

At present, each ministry is responsible for its own construction work. This means that seven or more ministries do the major construction work of the government and that, in addition, government utilities and municipal governments do still other construction. The system is not only inefficient but has encouraged waste and given rise to the possibility of fraud.

The mission recommends that:

(a) all functions not directly connected with construction be removed from the Ministry of Development;

(b) the Ministry be reorganized within the coming year as a Ministry or Department of Public Works, responsible directly to the President. There should be two principal sections: (1) highways, and (2) public works;

(c) all major construction activities, including those of the municipalities and the national government except those of the military, be placed under the direct supervision and control of the Ministry;

(d) the technical construction activities of all government enterprises be made subject to the approval and general supervision of the Ministry;

(e) the Minister and Vice Minister (or, in the event the Department form of organization is chosen, the General Manager and Assistant General Manager) as well as the chief engineers in charge of the two main divisions, be competent construction or highway engineers;

(f) the Minister have on his staff at least two foreign road engineers to act as advisers. In view of the long and close association of the Highways Department with the United States Bureau of Public Roads, it is suggested that this agency assist the government in their recruitment. This will give the Minister more time for policy formulation in connection with the general development program. The advisers would assist him and the chief of the highways section in carrying (1) the main road program, and (2) the feeder road program;

(g) the salaries conform to the urgency and importance of the Ministry to the country, and that these salaries correspond to those of the highest level of the National Bank. The Minister of Public Works should continue to be, ex officio, a member of the National Economic Council.

2. *The National Economic Council.* The National Economic Council, composed of the economic ministers and the general manager of the National Bank, has come into active operation during the past year. The Council is the principal advisory body to the President of the Republic. During its first year of operation, the functions of the Council have broadened, but they re-

quire further strengthening in order to enable it to play a more effective role in promoting the development of the country.

The functions of the Council should be to:

(a) coordinate and review all investment and development expenditures by the national and municipal governments and by government enterprises;

(b) coordinate monetary, banking and credit policies with the development program;

(c) approve all requests by any government agency for external technical assistance;

(d) approve any request of any government department or agency for external loans, including private loans receiving a government guarantee;

(e) approve the development budget of the national government, as well as the budget of the Instituto de Fomento;

(f) recommend changes in the administrative structure of the government;

(g) initiate government training programs, including external scholarships.

It is especially necessary, in order for the Council to function effectively, that each member bring to the attention of the Council the major problems and policies of the department he represents.

The Council should continue to be small in size, in order to function effectively. It is suggested, however, that because of his key position, the Director General of the Instituto de Fomento be placed on the Council with the right to vote. If a Director of the Budget is appointed at a later date, he should attend the meetings, but without the right to vote, since he will have the final task of formulating a budget affecting each of the government departments represented.

The mission suggests that the Ministers of Sanitation and of Education attend such meetings of the Council as are concerned with investment programs in their fields, and that the Ministers of Gobernacion and the Distrito Nacional attend the Council meetings to present for approval municipal development and financing programs.

3. *The Ministry of Economy.* The Ministry of Economy, a relatively new department of the government, is the ministry most directly concerned with the general economic policies of the government and the over-all development of the economy. Its high responsibility in this connection has been recognized in the appointment of the Minister of Economy as Chairman of the National Economic Council. The mission believes it desirable to centralize certain functions, as far as possible, within or under the supervision of the Ministry, including:

(a) statistical services now undertaken in other government departments, usually with inadequately trained staffs;

(b) information services of the government;

(c) government training programs, including those carried out through external technical assistance;

(d) foreign trade promotion, including the work of commercial attachés overseas;

(e) policy recommendations on relations with the specialized agencies of the United Nations;

(f) recommendations on tariff and trade policy;

(g) advice on the recruitment of technical and professional staff for government agencies, other than the Ministry of Public Works.

4. *The Instituto de Fomento.* An informal report on the mission's concept of the major objectives of the Instituto de Fomento was given to the Government of Nicaragua in November 1951.

The function of this institute will be to:

(a) make long-range technical plans for the country's development;

(b) provide adequate engineering and technical advice to new and existing agricultural and industrial enterprises;

(c) make loans involving greater risk and at longer terms than those made by existing banking institutions;

(d) help establish a capital market, and promote and channel savings into new enterprises.

The Instituto will be a planning organization as well as a credit organization. The general industrial and agricultural investment program for the Instituto as recommended by the mission, has been given in the previous chapter. In its credit program, the Instituto may extend credits directly to individuals or to organizations or cooperatives which would in turn extend individual credits. The Instituto should work closely with existing banking institutions which may often be in a position to participate in loans of the Instituto.

The mission stresses the need for an imaginative approach by the Instituto. Its powers are broad. They are, in general, to formulate development plans, to make short-, medium- or long-term loans, to issue bonds, to form new industries through the purchase or sale of shares, and to do economic and technical research. The success of a large part of the development program will depend on the skill with which the Instituto uses these powers.

5. *The Ministry of Finance.* Administrative changes in the Ministry of Finance, recommended by the mission to the government, take account of the increased responsibilities it will have to bear in the financing of the development program. The recommendations, when carried out, will mean not only greater responsibility for the Ministry but a much larger technical staff. The major suggestions have been:

(a) the merger of the Customs Administration with the Ministry;

(b) the reorganization of budgetary procedures and the establishment of a budget bureau;

(c) the establishment of a division to handle the assessment and collection of the property tax;

(d) the use of modern mechanical equipment for billing and collecting;

(e) the introduction of modern accounting systems;

(f) the training of a technical staff in accounting and tax and budget administration;

(g) the establishment of an impartial tax court of appeals.

The preparation of the annual budget, now a function of the Ministry of Finance, is a time-consuming responsibility which will grow as the development of the country increases. The Minister of Finance has approved the institution of a budget office in the Ministry. This is an important step forward.

In the longer run, however, the government should consider setting up a separate budget office, headed by an official of cabinet rank whose responsibility would be to make of the national budget a comprehensive financial plan for the year. This recommendation should not, however, be considered as of immediate urgency, since the formation of an efficient budget bureau is the first task.

6. *The Ministry of Agriculture.* The Ministry of Agriculture will have a major role in the execution of the agricultural sector of the development program.

At present, the Ministry's duties are largely routine. Its principal functions are to handle the program of the Servicio Tecnico Agricola and the agricultural school, to collect agricultural statistics, and to enforce such special legislation as that on agricultural pest control. The Department of Labor is now in the Ministry of Agriculture, but a separate Ministry of Labor is to be created shortly.

Under the mission's program, the Ministry of Agriculture will be a prime force in the promotion of increased yields through better farming practices. The Ministry will concentrate on such important aids to agriculture and forestry as research and education, the extension services, marketing and the general problem of better rural credit facilities.

The mission recommends that the Ministry be organized in four sections to cover extension services, land utilization, agricultural research and education, and forestry.

The mission believes that the operations of the Servicio Tecnico should be reviewed. Instead of seeking further to diversify crop production, major emphasis should be placed on improvement of the numerous crops which are already known to grow well. The mission recommends that the Servicio Tecnico should:

(a) undertake an intensive program designed to show how coffee yields may be improved through seed selection, better pruning methods and proper cultivation;

(b) introduce or develop new rice and sesame varieties which can be harvested by mechanical methods;

(c) demonstrate to farmers proper techniques of mechanical farming so that optimum use may be had from equipment already in the country;

(d) demonstrate proper erosion control;

(e) demonstrate the way to improve soil fertility by the use of green manures.

A part of this program will not require original research, but only modification or adaptation to local conditions of research already carried out elsewhere.

C. *Public Utility Administration*

1. *The Railroad.* The rehabilitation of the physical properties of the railroad will need, at the same time, reorganization of the management.

Although the mission believes that the railroad should remain under government ownership, its administration should be that of an autonomous public enterprise. It should have its own Board of Directors, charged with the responsibility of operating the carrier efficiently. The Board of Directors should be free to select its operating staff on the basis of competence and technical knowledge.

The company should be operated as a public utility designed to earn a reasonable return on the investment of the government. However, the government, in turn, should make prompt payment out of the budget for all services rendered to it by the railroad.

As a part of the reorganization, an outside firm of auditors should be employed to make a general audit of the company, its assets and liabilities and its inventories, and to set up an adequate system of accounting records and controls. The rate structure also requires review by a competent authority.

The power and light company should be divorced from the railroad and set up as an autonomous unit. For the time being, the port of Corinto should remain under the management of the railway, but diversion of funds for the creation of a harbor at Masachapa should be discontinued.

It is questionable whether the railroad should continue to operate the boats on Lake Nicaragua. If it is necessary to continue subsidizing this service, it may be desirable to consider transferring the operation to some other branch of the government.

2. *Power and Light.* A reorganization of the power and light companies is desirable not only for the improvement of the present service but to build an organization capable of managing and operating the hydroelectric plants projected for the future. Since the *Empresa de Luz y Fuerza Electrica de Managua* is the largest of the present companies and has the best technical staff, the reorganization should center around this company.

The mission recommends that:

(a) the power company be separated from the *Ferrocarril del Pacifico de Nicaragua* and set up as an autonomous public corporation under its own Board of Directors, composed of competent government officials and representatives from commerce, industry and agriculture;

(b) the small companies operating in the areas where expansion of grid lines has been recommended be merged into the new organization by outright purchase. This move is designed to reduce over-all administrative costs and to consolidate power planning and engineering activities;

(c) an impartial audit be made of the assets and the past performance of the companies. A proper system of accounting records and controls should be set up for the accurate assessment of profits, depreciation charges and operating costs, and a proper billing system should also be instituted;

(d) the rate structure should be reviewed in order to encourage greater use of power as additional capacity is added. The company should operate as a public utility designed to earn a reasonable return on the government's investment. The earnings should be sufficient to cover the costs of expansion and still allow for a reduction of rates when more efficient generating equipment is installed.

3. *Municipal Water Supplies*. The problem of organization for companies supplying water is somewhat different from that of the railroad or power system. Usually water supply systems are confined to a single community, and there cannot be one system to supply the whole country.

Managua, with its large population and demand for water, should have a water company organized along the lines of the power company. With this kind of organization the company may become fully self-sustaining and able to finance future expansion and improvement in service from its own resources. Here too, the general policies and the rate structure need revision to place the organization on a public utility basis.

A pure water supply should be the first concern of the smaller towns. While the government will have to take the initiative, it should be carried out as far as possible with local cooperation and local financing. The government, for the protection of the communities, should supervise and approve both the plans and the construction of water facilities to insure that the water supplies are pure and that construction meets acceptable engineering standards. The Ministry of Health should approve all sources of water before construction starts. The Ministry of Public Works should oversee the preparation of plans and actual construction. The Ministry of Finance should see that an adequate accounting system and rate structure is set up to enable the enterprise to operate on a self-sustaining basis.

D. *The Need for Public Information*

Few countries, even those very underdeveloped, have so little published information as Nicaragua. There are no adequate recent histories, no reference libraries, not even a government manual or directory. A number of ministries have not published an annual report in years. Statistical bulletins of the government appear irregularly, and those that do appear frequently contain detailed tables of little or no value. The annual budget is the only published source of information on the administrative structure of the government. It is enormously detailed but gives little information about government operations.

Under these circumstances, there is considerable feeling in the country that the government is deliberately concealing information from the public and therefore must have a great deal to conceal. Without adequate information the public necessarily has little understanding of what the government is doing, what the economic problems of the country are, and what a development program means. The public, therefore, cannot understand the extraordinary complexity of carrying out such a program.

In the opinion of the mission, while the government has never taken sufficient account of public opinion, the lack of information given to the public is much less a matter of deliberate concealment than of very inadequate staffing in the public administration.

The government has recently become aware of this problem and the mission feels confident it will act increasingly to inform the country of its program and its significance to the country.

The mission believes this to be of the utmost importance. The development program planned by the mission offers the country the most rapid rate of growth and progress in her history. Because of this, it is essential that the country fully understand its significance, so that a national and not a partisan approach can be taken to the problems outlined in this report.

The mission suggests that:

(a) the President and the National Economic Council inform the country periodically of the progress made in carrying out the objectives of the five-year investment program, in a manner similar to that undertaken by the President in his annual message to the Congress in April 1952;

(b) the Instituto de Fomento, as one of its first objectives, publish studies on national income and on agricultural and industrial projects and prospects, so that they are available to the public;

(c) the Ministry of Finance publish each three months the budgetary and fiscal position of the Ministry in relation to the development program;

(d) each ministry publish an annual report of its activities within a reasonable period after the close of the fiscal year; and

(e) an over-all summary annual report of the activities and accomplishments of the government and of the country be published annually by the Ministry of Economy.

The press and radio should be used increasingly to diffuse information about the development program. The press could play a much more effective role in stimulating progress in the country if it gave full space, regardless of party, to the economic reports of the government, to fuller economic information on internal and external markets, crops and prospects, and to much more of the technical and scientific data needed by agriculturalists and industrialists than now appears.

The Nicaraguan public is obviously extremely interested in the economic problems of the country, but is not always well informed except on immediate problems of interest to the individual. Both the government and the press can do much to correct this.

V. SPECIAL ECONOMIC PROBLEMS AND POLICIES

A. The Role of Private Investment

In view of the extraordinary opportunities for private investment, which should increase further with the rising rate of public investment and the moderate tax rates, private capital has a favorable economic environment. It should play a major role in promoting the country's rapid development. It is particularly desirable that it do so.

The government's task of increasing the country's social overhead investment—on roads, ports, power and so forth—is so large that private enterprise should not only be called upon, but given every opportunity, to bear as much of the remaining burden as possible.

A main purpose in establishing an Instituto de Fomento is to encourage the flow of private capital into productive investment through adequate technical assistance and credits. Over one third of the funds allocated in the five-year program are for this purpose. The more effective the Instituto is in stimulating private investment, the more rapid will be the country's progress. If 10% of the incomes of the upper 1% of income recipients were to be invested productively, the current productive investment rate would increase by 50%.

Up to the present time, domestic private enterprise has, with few exceptions, done relatively little to develop the country's productive capacity. This has remained the case even in the last three and a half years when there has been a sharp rise in national income. During that time not a single new industry has started and few new productive enterprises, except for some cotton gins and warehouses erected by some enterprising Nicaraguans. Investments in agriculture have been largely confined to increased production of annual crops financed quite largely by bank credit.

Private enterprise often ascribes its caution to lack of confidence in the government and in government policies. This feeling is to some degree understandable. Political factors have often played a role in determining credit allocations, in approving new industries and in various indirect, psychological ways. Private enterprise, on the other hand, has often been unimaginative and unduly cautious. It has been too prone to seek either the safe investment or a quick return. It has engaged in land or real estate speculation or has sought profits from importing and exporting or from usury rather than from increased production.

Much can be done by the government to encourage the flow of private capital into more productive channels. Government policy towards business should be based on economic rather than political considerations. The government should discourage monopolies and encourage competitive enterprises. With increased freedom, adequate credits and technical engineering assistance, private enterprise should be able to assume a vital role in the future growth of the country.

According to the standards of developed countries, profits in underdeveloped countries are normally high. This was true of the early economic history of the United States and is true today of most developing economies. In Nicaragua the "curb" rate of private lending runs between 18% and 60%. Legitimate enterprise can hardly be expected to accept much lower yields and usually it anticipates even higher returns.

The mission believes that a high rate of return is normal for the country at its present state of development, that is, normal for legitimate enterprise. High profits should be the reward for true enterprise and initiative, not for inefficiency or monopoly guaranteed by the government.

B. *Export Marketing*

The problem of export marketing must be tackled simultaneously with the plan to increase production. The financial resources necessary for carrying out the program will depend on a sustained level of exports; the increased production contemplated by the plan will require wider markets abroad.

The development program aims, in addition to raising the standard of living, to strengthen and diversify an economy which in the past has often been weak and unstable. Such instability cannot be easily and immediately corrected. There are still major sources of potential weakness in the export economy:

(a) possibility of a decline in coffee prices;

(b) possibility of a subnormal coffee crop;

(c) continued difficulties in finding cotton markets abroad;

(d) possibility of a decline in gold or timber exports.

On the other hand, there are several favorable factors which should make fluctuations less severe than in the past:

(a) Recent monetary action has given Nicaragua larger foreign exchange reserves than the country has ever had previously. With intelligent central bank and treasury action, these reserves should stay stable or increase. In any case, they will act to cushion an unexpected export decline;

(b) Costs of production of coffee—at an average of $21 per bag—are still so low that any conceivable fall in coffee prices should hardly threaten the industry;

(c) Nicaragua now has nine major export products, each with an average export value in 1951 of over $1 million. This

gives the export economy a greater degree of protective
diversity than ever before;

(d) The industrial program—the textile and oil hydrogenation
plants and others—should reduce essential imports by as
much as $2 million a year.

A major purpose of the development program will be to
strengthen Nicaragua's competitive position in export markets by
reducing production and marketing costs. In many cases, more
scientific methods can increase production of agricultural crops
by as much as 25%, at little additional cost. The regional road
program, under which trucks will replace oxcarts, should very
substantially lower transportation costs.

Although a part of the development program is long range,
the main program should have direct and fairly immediate effects
on the costs of production and marketing and on the volume and
value of Nicaragua's exports.

External marketing problems will therefore be of increasing
importance to the country. Already exports have increased so
rapidly in the past two years that the country's elementary or-
ganizational structure for promoting exports has been inadequate
to take care of the expansion. There is, at present, no foreign
trade office in the government and only a single commercial
attaché in its foreign service.

The mission believes that Nicaragua should consider organiz-
ing a small trade and commercial staff in the Ministry of Economy.
It should also consider the appointment of at least one commercial attaché in Europe and another in Panama, who would
take care of her interests in the Caribbean and northern Latin
American markets. Since perhaps no more than a hundred bona
fide tourists from outside Central America enter Nicaragua each
year, funds now devoted to the Tourist Bureau could more profitably be spent in vigorous commercial information and representation abroad.

The commercial section of the Ministry of Economy should work closely with the Instituto de Fomento, the *Compania Mercantil del Ultramar* and other government agencies, as well as with private agricultural associations and importers and exporters. The work should not be confined solely to promoting exports but should also be concerned with finding the most advantageous and cheapest sources of supply abroad.

C. *The Manpower Problem*

The small manpower supply, while a problem, is a long-run asset since it will be generations before Nicaragua feels the population pressure typical of so many underdeveloped countries. The population is, however, expanding at the rate of nearly 2.5% a year and this high rate of growth makes the need for developing the country's resources the more urgent.

The development program can be expected to put a severe strain on the relatively small labor supply, particularly of the technical, foreman, and semiskilled type of labor. During the harvest of the coffee and cotton crops of 1951-52, there were local shortages of unskilled labor, giving a forecast of the serious labor shortage that may develop within the next few years as development proceeds. The 1951-52 shortages were aggravated by the combination of a good coffee crop and cotton plantings more than double those of the previous year.

The labor shortage, together with the present absence of effective trade unions, indicates that the country can proceed into full-scale mechanization of industry and agriculture without objections from organized labor and without fears that mechanization will cause widespread unemployment. Instead, the growing labor shortage will force rapid mechanization and more efficient use of labor to increase productivity per man-hour.

Nicaraguan labor, on the whole, is willing and, when properly trained, capable of highly skilled work. Many Nicaraguans find ready employment in the neighboring countries of Central America.

In general, there is little unemployment, but in some areas, notably the east coast, there is a surplus labor supply arising from structural changes in the east coast economy (e.g., the loss of banana exports). Migration to the west coast is difficult not only because of the lack of transportation but also because of the difficulties of language.

The present working population is estimated at around 324,-000, of whom 274,000 are men. The large untapped female labor force offers a source of supply for health and educational work, small industries and agricultural labor.

Another source of supply lies in neighboring countries. In the past there has been considerable emigration to the rest of Central America, Mexico, Venezuela and the United States, ranging from the professional class to the laborer. Much of this emigration has resulted from the low wage scales, the lack of opportunity for skills, or political conditions in the country.

The development program is not only likely to stop such emigration but to reverse the process by attracting Nicaraguans back to their country, and perhaps also to attract some immigration.

The mission believes it desirable that, as the development program proceeds, the government plan a practical program, through the offer of concrete jobs, to attract back Nicaraguans who have found opportunities elsewhere.

The Instituto de Fomento should have, as one of its first tasks, the compilation of the technical, professional and scientific roster of Nicaraguans, in the country and elsewhere, which has been planned for some time by the government. This roster would serve as a basis for placing skilled Nicaraguans in positions that would help in the development of the country.

D. *The Need for a General Development Law*

The Government of Nicaragua has recently begun to revise its long-standing policy on concessions given to stimulate the development of the country.

A law of 1925 which permitted free import of machinery and equipment to those holding government contracts, formed the basis for many sweeping concessions given thereafter. Contracts were awarded which virtually gave away large tracts of public lands for the free exploitation of timber and minerals. Industries, in general, were protected from any increase in taxes or from any future taxes; freedom from export taxes and many import duties was assured; the right to use the railroad at reduced freight rates was often conceded; and in many cases industries were allowed to dispose of foreign exchange independently of any exchange controls. Although individual contracts varied considerably as to terms, most of the important concessions received such benefits.

In 1940, a law made it possible for the government to grant loans directly to new industries. As far as can be ascertained, the only loan granted under this law was to the local cement company.

In general, neither this law nor the concessions law has aided to any great extent the industrial growth of the country, although the latter undoubtedly stimulated mining in the depression days of the thirties.

Although foreign concerns have received the majority of the concessions, many were given to Nicaraguans, particularly for local industries such as sugar, cement and beer, which received long concessions in regard to taxes. The concessions for sugar and cement also permitted free disposal of foreign exchange except for a specified percentage to be turned over to the National Bank.

The future of the country depends, in considerable degree, on legislation to encourage the free flow of capital, both domestic and foreign, but concessions of the type previously given are no longer needed.

Nicaragua needs a general development law which will give full incentive and protection to foreign and domestic capital and which will, at the same time, protect the legitimate rights and interests of the country.

In drafting such a law the mission suggests the following points as appropriate for legislation on new industries:

(a) Foreign capital should be assured equal rights with domestic;

(b) Original imports of machinery and equipment should be given duty-free import privileges, and raw materials not found in Nicaragua should also be admitted duty-free;

(c) Foreign capital should be assured the right to transfer profits;

(d) Only in exceptional circumstances should general concessions be given for industry, while those for mining exploration should be limited to a period of 10 years;

(e) Tax-free privileges should be limited to a period of not more than five years after construction has been completed;

(f) With the exception of (e), all industries, foreign and domestic, should be made subject to existing or future tax legislation;

(g) All persons should be given full and free opportunity, without regard to political conditions, to engage freely in any industry.

The mission suggests that the government review, with due regard to the validity of the contracts, existing concessions to determine whether the industries to which they have been granted can be brought within the tax system of the country.

E. *Gold Mining*

The rise of coffee prices since 1949 has brought coffee exports into the first place position in the list of Nicaraguan exports, which had been held uninterruptedly by gold from 1939 to 1949.

The gold mining industry, operating under long-term concessions of the type which the mission has described, has been relatively profitable in the past. Rising production costs and depletion of high-grade ore reserves, however, have brought the industry much closer to the point where its operations may no longer be profitable. The companies, on the whole, are making a serious effort to lower production costs by making substantial investments in new machinery and techniques.

Higher costs, the use of lower-grade ores, and the relatively fixed price of gold give to the industry, the chief support of an estimated 25,000 people, a future which is by no means clear or certain. The mission believes the government and mining companies should give increasing attention to the problems facing this major industry. The government and the industry have been, for too long, mutually exclusive. The mission suggests that the mining companies might consider voluntarily offering to pay to the country future income taxes in those cases where they can be offset against income taxes in their home country.

F. *The East Coast*

While the government has considered the east coast (acquired as late as 1897) as an integral part of the country in spite of the marked differences in the racial, linguistic and religious composition of the area, it has, thus far, done relatively little to aid its development. Certain measures taken by the government to protect local industry have frequently been detrimental to the east coast economy.

In many ways, the area is even more underdeveloped than the "Interior", as the west coast is called in the region. The area has almost the only completely indigenous Indians of the country, a substantial English-speaking Negro population and a relatively large foreign population. The development of the area has been very largely in the hands of foreign corporations engaged in lumbering, fruit or mining operations.

The government has been increasingly aware that the area has special problems, dissimilar to those of the rest of the country. This is one reason for the urgency with which the government has sought the completion of the Rama Road, the first land link between the east and west. While such overland communications will be of some assistance in providing cheaper transport to the area, particularly of products such as staple food items which, although produced in Nicaragua, now have to be imported by the east coast, the road will not even begin to solve the problems of the area without concerted action and planning by the government.

Part of the mission's investment program has given specific attention to the east coast. This is true of its plans for African oil palm, cattle, cacao, forestry and feeder roads. The program also provides for completion of the Rama road, the construction of the port at Rama and the improvement of the Port of El Bluff. The very high disease rates of the area also merit special attention under the public health program.

The area will need a longer period to improve and develop than the west coast. Its problems should be considered by the government as those of 10 years rather than five. For this reason, early action is needed to implement the program devised by the mission for the coming five years.

CHAPTER FIVE

Industries

The Basis for Industry

Nicaragua will continue to be a predominantly agricultural country for the foreseeable future. Industrial development must necessarily be subordinate to, and dependent on, agricultural development since the products of the farms are the raw materials of industry. It is unlikely that any large-scale industrialization can take place but, if a well-balanced economy is to be achieved, the country will need sufficient industry to process a number of domestic products, particularly those which are now exported as raw materials and imported as finished products.

A coordinated and carefully planned growth of small industries will bring greater stability and independence to the economy. To achieve this objective industry should be primarily, though not exclusively, concerned with processing domestic agricultural materials. Most important among these are: *cattle,* which supply milk, butter, cheese, meat, tallow and leather; *cotton,* for textiles and oil; *sugar,* which may be used in canned and frozen foods, preserved fruits, jams, jellies and candies; *hogs,* for meat and lard; *coarse fibers,* for textiles and bags; as well as *timber, oil-producing crops* and others.

The mineral resources of the country are still very largely to be explored and developed. Only the deposits of precious metals have been explored or worked to any extent. Little use is made of the waters of Nicaragua for transportation, power, irrigation or fishing.

Nicaragua has a limited supply of labor and must take full advantage of mechanization and modernization of agriculture and industry to make the fullest use of her labor force.

Production

Nicaragua's industrial output is diversified, but much of the production is turned out by small, poorly equipped factories. A considerable portion of total output is manufactured by home industries, which produce most of the leather goods, shoes, cheese, and clothing of the country.

It is estimated that the value of industrial production for reporting industries in 1949 was around 100 million cordobas. These industries used raw materials worth approximately 37 million cordobas of which 11 million cordobas came from foreign sources. In addition 2.5 million cordobas were spent for fuel and 1.6 million cordobas for packing materials. In 1950 manufacturing industries contributed around 64 million cordobas to the national income and home industries 81 million cordobas, according to estimates by the Central Statistical Bureau.

Leading manufactures include, sugar, beer, soft drinks, textiles, ice, cement, cigarettes, soap, matches and a number of others. The estimated output of reporting industries is shown in the following table.

An idea of the size of plants can be gained from Table 2. The number of industries reporting increased from 194 in 1947 to 300 in 1949, but production increased noticeably only in the lumber, soft drink and liquor industries. Most industries followed the pattern of sole leather production. In 1947, 23 plants produced 190,031 kilos; in 1949, 56 plants produced 278,437 kilos. Thus 33 plants added only 88,406 kilos or an annual average production of 2,679 kilos each.

Industrial output has been nearly static for several years. No major production facilities have been built within the last seven years and, for the most part, existing plants have not received proper maintenance. Processing costs are rising because of the use of worn and obsolete equipment. Today only a few firms are expanding operations and installing new equipment.

TABLE 1

ESTIMATED OUTPUT OF SELECTED NICARAGUAN INDUSTRIES
1946-49

Products	Units	1946	1947	1948	1949
Sugar	quintales	na*	na	na	304,331
Milk**	gallons	390,148	441,561	427,018	419,219
Soft drinks	liters	na	1,524,700	6,907,686	5,481,579
Beer	liters	1,835,000	1,597,700	1,815,275	1,672,000
Liquors	liters	na	165,616	239,776	631,332
Cotton goods	yards	1,334,733	4,225,501	4,672,372	4,774,656
Rayon goods	yards	na	na	na	176,992
Clothing	pieces	34,580	302,343	400,313	451,102
Carbon dioxide (gas)	kilograms	54,571	65,851	101,804	101,560
Ice	pounds	29,952,200	36,936,550	29,867,150	30,489,250
Lumber	board feet	399,640	7,203,975	24,751,764	28,657,522
Cement	bags (94 lbs)	250,690	272,045	381,971	385,835
Matches	1,000 boxes	11,666	11,528	13,762	16,779
Cigarettes	millions	453	486	501	544
Soap	pounds	9,159,323	8,975,869	9,251,583	9,274,404
Bricks (cement)	number	982,783	2,188,652	3,140,664	3,549,088
Leather (sole)	kilograms	na	190,031	226,282	278,437

* Not available
** Managua only

TABLE 2

NUMBER OF MANUFACTURERS REPORTING

Product	1946	1947	1948	1949
Sugar	na	na	na	6
Milk	1	1	1	1
Soft drinks	na	27	31	33
Beer (also carbon dioxide)	1	1	1	1
Liquors	na	6	5	10
Cotton goods	1	2	2	2
Rayon goods	na	na	1	1
Clothing	1	5	12	13
Ice	10	18	19	22
Lumber	7	14	30	31
Cement	1	1	1	1
Matches	1	1	1	1
Cigarettes	1	1	1	1
Soap and oils	36	27	30	30
Bricks	5	15	16	16
Leather (sole)	na	23	44	56
Leather goods (manufactures)	na	na	10	14
Miscellaneous	na	52	35	61
Total	65	194	240	300

Because of the good crops and high world prices of the past few years, Nicaragua's exports and national income have risen sharply. Imports of manufactured goods have risen almost equally, while domestic production has remained very largely static. In other words, industry not only is failing to take advantage of its increased opportunity but it is falling behind the rest of the economy.

Industrial Technology

Most of Nicaragua's industrial operations suffer from poor technology. This term is not intended to refer to complex modern processes or elaborate machinery, but to the organization and system employed, including the proper choice of raw materials, their movement through the factory, the location of machinery for the most efficient operation and processing, and control and inspection methods which are needed to insure that the quality of the finished product meets desired specifications. It applies to such minor things as the installation of a pipe line to move oil from one kettle to another instead of using hand labor and buckets, or adapting the best technological methods to local conditions.

Differences in the scale of operations, the adaptability and cost of labor, transport and storage facilities, and the climate and temperament of the people—and especially variations of consumer preference—often call for important modifications of a standard process, modifications which have never been considered for Nicaraguan industry.

Good industrial technology takes into consideration plant location with respect to the source of raw materials and market outlets, yet a flour mill was located in Masaya although wheat comes either from the Jinotega region or from imports via Corinto. As a result the raw material must be transported to Masaya through Managua, processed, and returned to Managua, the major market for flour.

Almost none of the industries inspected by the mission practices any form of quality control. In well-organized industries each unit of production is the same as the preceding unit, and food plants are kept clean so that food products are not contaminated. In Nicaragua cheese and butter are processed under extremely unsanitary conditions, and vegetable oils are refined without laboratory control to insure that the process is completed. Salt is processed without a full understanding of the principles involved and sugar is made for the most part in small, submarginal mills whose output is of varying quality.

As a result of inadequate technology or quality control, production costs are higher than they need be and the poor quality of local manufacture compels the consumer to turn to imported goods. An example is the textile industry which has ignored the market needs for good quality fabrics with the result that millions of yards of cloth are imported each year. Upper leather for the better grades of shoes must also be imported, because of the generally poor quality of local hides and leather.

Technical and Specialized Industrial Training

Only one engineering course, civil engineering, is offered in Nicaragua. Anyone wishing training in other technical fields must go abroad. This of itself is not serious because the number of students desiring technical training is too small to warrant establishing a comprehensive engineering school, and fellowships and other aids for study abroad are, and will be, increasingly available. What is more important from the industrial standpoint is the complete lack of vocational training facilities for developing skilled mechanics, carpenters, plumbers, bricklayers, repair men, engine operators, and other skilled laborers. It is as important to have a qualified mechanic looking after the maintenance of a pump or power plant as it is to have an engineer plan and oversee its initial installation.

Power, Fuel and Water

Power is generated for the most part by government plants. Because of old equipment and inefficient transmission and distribution systems, the price of purchased industrial power is excessive in relation to that found in many countries. In Managua the average industrial rate is about 0.35 cordobas ($0.05) per kilowatt-hour. Moreover, public service installations, already at capacity, cannot absorb additional industrial loads. This impediment to industrial development has been partially overcome by the installation of private power plants. Although the generation cost with these plants is lower than for purchased power a larger initial capital investment is required on the part of the industrialist.

INDUSTRIES 115

While there appear to be good potentialities for hydroelectric power development, several years of study will be needed before the potential is fully known.

There are no known coal or oil deposits in Nicaragua, although a future survey may change this picture. At present wood is the only local fuel widely used in factories and sugar mills. Other fuels (gasoline, diesel oil, etc.) are imported, and as Nicaragua develops, these imports will necessarily increase. Every effort should be made to hold fuel imports to a minimum through the use of the most efficient equipment attainable in order to obtain the maximum value per unit of fuel imported.

To date, the water supply available has not seriously affected industry; however, most large consumers of water in cities have had to drill their own wells because the municipal installations are deficient. In the lower elevations, there seems to be no shortage of ground water but in the higher elevations the water supply has to be carefully considered in establishing a plant, since some areas are short of water during the dry season. For example, lack of water hampers coffee processing in the Carazo region.

CHAPTER SIX

Factors Influencing Industrial Development

Capital and Credit

The concentration of incomes in the hands of a relatively small part of the population should be a favorable basis for increased industrial production through private capital formation.

High crop returns have cut down the incentive to invest in industry, since agricultural or commercial profits are attainable with less work and worry. There is no mechanism available for medium- or long-term industrial credit or for the mobilization of capital for industrial enterprise. Bank credit is restricted to short-term crop and agricultural loans, while industry is limited to short-term financing of raw material purchases—usually for not more than six months.

Industry follows the prevailing tendency of Nicaraguan farmers or businessmen to over-extend their limited resources. All available cash is invested in land or plant facilities, and insufficient amounts are set aside for working capital. In consequence, credit is needed continually for ordinary expenses.

Political Factors

The mission heard complaints from many groups throughout the country that certain business activities are reserved for high government officials; that concessions are granted to a favored few; that bank credit is unavailable or restricted because of political beliefs; and that the principal bank is sometimes used as a personal lending agency for government officials. Whatever the truth may be in these charges, the mission believes that the widespread belief in them has hampered the development of the country, particularly in the industrial sector.

Nicaragua is potentially one of the richer countries in Latin America but its full potential cannot be realized if business is subject to, or believes itself subject to, outside influences over which it has no control. Local capital may be justifiably hesitant about investing in a new enterprise unless it knows whether such investment conforms to official wishes. The right type of foreign capital, which can play an important role in the future development of the country, will shy away from investments unless it has the assurance that it will be allowed to operate free of political influence.

Because of the importance of private investment it should be a main task of the government and the Instituto de Fomento to overcome the factors retarding industrial development.

Marketing Practices

Marketing is carried on in the ancient tradition of low volume at high prices, in contrast to the reverse pattern which has made possible the rapid growth of production in the more highly industrialized countries of the world.

In many cases, local manufacturers complain that because of a small market it is not possible to achieve optimum factory size and therefore costs of production are high. With a low sales volume the manufacturer requires a large profit on each unit to obtain a high return on his investment.

Little effort has been made to expand markets through price reduction or improvement of product quality. In many cases, the increased national demands are being satisfied by imported merchandise, which often leads to a mistaken conclusion that the tariff protection is insufficient, and demands for increased protection are made.

Unfortunately, if the tariff is high enough to allow the manufacturers to undersell imported goods, too many merchants prefer to raise the prices of domestic goods in order to make a higher profit. This has a tendency to diminish the total market available, and there is constant pressure from foreign competition.

Resistance to legitimate price competition has resulted in cartel-type arrangements or the formation of single-industry associations to fix production quotas and prices in order that small, submarginal producers can stay in business.

Low Productivity

Low productivity in industry arises from poor management, the country's low health and educational standards, the independence and indifference of labor, and poor working conditions and general climatic factors.

Management's responsibility for low productivity can be traced to a generally held belief that in all manufacturing, agricultural and commercial operations it is best to make a high profit on a low volume, with the least expenditure of money and effort. Because of this philosophy, management provides neither on-the-job training nor proper or sufficient tools for labor's use. As an example, one textile mill reports that workmen in the country cannot operate more than two looms. The fact that in Mexico, El Salvador, Cuba, and the United States one person handles many looms is not taken as a challenge by the Nicaraguans; their rationalization is that the workers of these countries, through generations of experience, have acquired skills beyond the capacity of the local labor. Actually, the higher productivity of other countries is the result of on-the-job training, the use of the best tools and machines available, and the payment of wages based upon the real value of the workers' efforts.

There is no doubt that certain natural factors affect labor productivity. How a worker feels influences his output and his skill. In most cases the worker's diet consists of rice, beans, tortillas or platanos (plantain) and only occasionally does he have meat, eggs or milk. His body is often full of intestinal parasites or he may have malaria; he is poorly clothed. Under these conditions, he cannot be expected to work intensively. This fundamental problem can be corrected only through the broad general sanitation and health program recommended by the mission.

Many of the basic problems of the labor force can be improved only by a wider and more adequate system of primary and vocational education. The few literate workers seldom have more than an elementary knowledge of reading or writing. There are no schools for mechanical or crafts training, although such a training program is being planned for the near future, nor is there any evidence of an apprentice system in the labor organizations. An exception to this general lack of personnel training has been the recent establishment of a foreman training program by a number of construction companies.

Industrial plants and large employers of agricultural labor should set up on-the-job training programs to raise the worker's level of skill as well as to instill in him a sense of pride in his work. The Nicaraguan worker, and especially the agricultural worker, has a feeling of personal independence that is not found elsewhere in Central America. He is not subservient nor is he awed by his so-called betters. With the exception of the workers of the Managua region, he cultivates a small patch of land for his own needs and works to obtain cash for clothing and what food he must buy.

This independence sometimes makes it difficult for employers to obtain labor. If the worker does not need money at the time jobs are available, he is reluctant to leave his farm. At present, the Government is finding it difficult to recruit labor for its road program and must transfer workers from the other parts of the country to the job. Many leave to go back to their own towns because of their refusal or inability to become accustomed to the new region.

The climate of Nicaragua makes hard physical and mental labor exhausting. Most agricultural work has to be done early in the day before the sun's heat becomes too great. The high humidity during the rainy season also causes discomfort. These conditions undoubtedly cause some lowering of productivity, though climate is less important than other factors.

Protective Tariff

The protective tariff, instead of encouraging industry, has frequently been a handicap to industrial development because it has destroyed the incentive to produce high quality goods at a lower price than imports. The problem is particularly serious in Nicaragua because here the marketing has traditionally depended much more upon the principles of monopoly, cartels, and scarcity than upon the alternative method of getting customers by offering them more for their money.

The consumer bears the brunt of the tariff system. Imported cement, for example, is so heavily taxed that its cost is increased by 100%, yet locally manufactured cement could meet all competition without tariff protection because its production cost compares so favorably with costs elsewhere.

In order to attract new industries it would be preferable to offer tax concessions for a limited period. In this way industry would understand that the protective period is limited, and that within this time it must become self-sustaining and able to meet all competition.

Raw Materials

The country is fortunate in having a large variety of raw materials for industrial use. In some cases industry has failed to take advantage of these materials, but in other cases it has been handicapped by the failure to produce materials acceptable to domestic manufacturers both in cost and quality.

Lack of transportation facilities increases the prices of raw materials; for example, better roads would bring down timber costs and would make some east coast lumber available to the west coast. On the other hand, the textile industry has failed to take advantage of the supply of cotton or of the market needs.

Consequently textile imports amount to a large percentage of the total imports of Nicaragua, and textile prices are high.

In the case of the tanning industry, progress has been retarded because of the poor quality of hides available. The cattle raisers for the most part do not care for the animals properly and have neglected to control the damage to the hides from insects. Every torsalo hole in the hide renders a large portion unusable; excessive branding damages the best part of the hide, and butcher cuts add to the low quality of domestic hides.

Markets

The domestic market for Nicaraguan products is limited by the small population. Nevertheless it is large enough to absorb greater domestic output if the manufacturers will use the normal incentives of price, quality and service to persuade Nicaraguan consumers to buy domestic products in preference to imports.

TABLE 1

SELECTED IMPORTS OF EL SALVADOR
value in colones
(U.S. $1 = C$2.5)

	1947	1948	1949
Live animals—beef and pork	1,488,124	2,143,465	1,626,667
Lard and other animal fats	30,003	221,387	176,288
Milk, butter and cheese	229,767	224,804	351,863
Corn	292,245	1,510,510	10,293
Beans, all classes	53,910	307,925	653,662
Vegetable oils and fats	84,388	129,721	123,694
Wood, including ties	382,186	257,419	573,328
Stearin	38,749	283,038	85,376
Hides and skins prepared	561,160	923,951	1,080,309
Soaps, perfumes, cosmetics	1,247,743	1,224,766	1,426,259

Source: *Revista de Economia de El Salvador,* Tomo I, 1950

TABLE 2

SELECTED IMPORTS OF COSTA RICA

(values in dollars)

	1947	1948	1949	1950	1951*
Cattle	188,145	93,600	109,620	na	na
Canned meats	43,090	66,628	33,176	na	na
Evaporated milk	262,808	227,622	293,704	68,955	29,809
Powdered milk	481,020	574,003	394,181	654,115	264,986
Cheese	67,670	37,127	11,791	22,735	19,365
Rice	1,549	100,147	333,978	na	na
Lard	690,882	666,411	841,309	790,313	558,289
Tallow	20,343	19,489	166,069	na	na
Tanned hides	595,964	540,581	689,481	733,629	192,658
Cotton	99,529	166,811	149,606	126,942	51,995
Cloth—artificial fiber	1,309,990	351,248	1,850,707	na	na
Cotton—unbleached cloth	560,441	319,737	531,252	na	na
Cotton—bleached cloth	1,002,685	1,304,108	1,124,558	na	na

*First six months

Source: Direccion General de Estadistica, Republica de Costa Rica

In the past, neighboring Central American countries have been largely overlooked in the search for export markets. Trade has been increasing with El Salvador but there remain many opportunities for further increases. In order to illustrate the extent of the Central American market, the tables show selected imports by El Salvador, Costa Rica and Panama. The items listed are those which, for the most part, can be produced in Nicaragua. In 1949 these three countries purchased a total of $2.8 million in dairy products alone. These are but a few of the possibilities of the export markets for Nicaraguan products.

Stimulating Industrial Development

In spite of the various factors which have contributed to the slow growth of industry, there are many opportunities to expand existing industries and establish new ones. If this industrial development is to be carried out by private industry, the old restrictive influence must be superseded by conditions stimulating to private enterprise. The Instituto de Fomento should, in its credit policies, give first preference to Nicaraguan private capital, but foreign capital should be given every opportunity to invest in the country.

To facilitate investment in new industries, the Government and the Instituto de Fomento should adopt a selective but consistent policy which should provide for:

(a) A minimum of restrictive control and political interference;

(b) Greater use of good technology and modern methods;

(c) Tariff and tax policies encouraging new industry but discouraging monopolies; tax-free privileges should be discontinued once an industry is established;

(d) A general development law granting equal rights to domestic and foreign capital;

(e) Abolition of long-term concessions to individuals and organizations;

TABLE 3
SELECTED IMPORTS OF PANAMA
(value in balboas)
U.S. $1 = B$1

	1947	1948	1949	1950	1951*
Beef—fresh, frozen or refrigerated	51,482	74,539	68,885	51,914	50,334
Pork—fresh, frozen or refrigerated	81,334	36,173	30,167	23,142	8,394
Canned meats	68,723	28,373	84,572	79,447	23,563
Sausage	63,018	76,396	69,201	85,749	26,742
Ham	430,671	365,718	334,975	408,116	192,687
Bacon	56,287	37,777	38,732	36,645	20,402
Lard	754,571	515,310	767,710	964,938	619,250
Evaporated milk	743,345	662,531	470,866	458,559	278,665
Powdered milk	519,135	582,051	688,061	615,594	494,703
Butter	683,545	793,007	615,702	591,448	367,176
Cheese	218,783	246,068	209,849	211,921	160,055
Beans	179,378	175,808	136,526	135,226	72,940
Cottonseed oil	43,772	45,284	40,667	50,128	5,005
Cotton	65,433	55,476	31,481	53,109	34,214
Tanned hides	228,913	174,858	167,386	202,303	82,084
Cotton cloth	137,771	121,359	87,046	148,882	49,891

*First six months

Source: Direccion de Estadistica y Censo, Republica de Panama

(f) Provision of adequate working, medium- and long-term capital through the Instituto de Fomento.

The enactment of a general development law will automatically do away with the individually negotiated concessions which have plagued the country for so long, and have brought little benefit, and which have been inequitable because of the wide variation in individual contracts. The law should establish standards for the granting of all future rights for timber and minerals exploitation. A share of the profits for the Government should be included. There should be no need for any industrial concessions, other than moderate tax free privileges for new industries for periods up to five years.

The general development law should provide for:

(a) Free imports of original production machinery and equipment for new industries for a period up to five years;

(b) Free imports by all industries of raw materials which do not exist in Nicaragua;

(c) Tax free privileges for new industries for a period up to five years after original construction has been completed;

(d) Equal rights for foreign and domestic capital, and a guarantee that profits may be freely transferred into foreign exchange.

CHAPTER SEVEN

The Major Industries

I. *TEXTILES*

A. *Cotton Goods*

Status

The textile industry is of recent origin; the first mill was established in 1939 and the second in the early war years. The two mills use local cotton and import only dyes and finishing materials. The first mill was established with old machinery, some of it built in the 1890's and first used in Spain, then Mexico, and finally Nicaragua. The slow, nonautomatic looms are poorly maintained and the plant appears to be beyond rehabilitation.

The second mill, while superior, also has second-hand equipment except for a new cotton gin which processes cotton for its own use as well as for export. Although automatic looms have been installed, they are operated manually with one operator handling only two looms.

The textile industry has not, on the whole, contributed very effectively to the economy of the country. It has invested its profits in other enterprises instead of increasing its own output with modern equipment, labor-saving machines and the training of workers. Even where automatic looms have been installed, insufficient advantage has been taken of this opportunity to increase productivity. The industry has failed to study the local textile market in the light of imports and consumers' preference. Neither mill makes cloth finer than 40 x 40 count, which is a coarse and heavy grade entirely unsuited to the climate.

Production

Maximum yearly capacity of the present industry is about 5 million yards; it consumes 2 million pounds of cotton. The mills have some 10,000 spindles and 300 looms. Locally produced cloth supplies less than 50% of total consumption in yardage, and under 25% in value.

Local mills currently produce some 40 different patterns or weaves. They are also experimenting with combined cotton and rayon yarns.

Market

In recent years imports have ranged from six to 10 million yards, as against annual production of five million yards. Unbleached and plain colored goods account for four to seven million yards of imports and stamped or printed goods from two to three million yards.

More "manta," or unbleached muslin, is sold locally than any other type of cloth. A finer quality cloth which has become very popular is known as "Tipo Inez." This cloth is 36 inches wide, four yards to the pound, with 56 x 60 construction. Next in popularity is a 50 x 56 construction; 31 inch, five yards to the pound, 48 x 48; and 26-27 inch, 6.75 yards to the pound. Neither local mill is equipped to make any of these cloths; their output is restricted to a 40 x 40 or coarser manta.

Other imports are: 60 x 100 cloth widely used for clothing; denim for work trousers; toweling and sugar bags. All these materials could be produced locally.

TABLE 1

IMPORTS OF COTTON YARD GOODS 1950-51

	1950		1951	
	Yards	Dollar Value	Yards	Dollar Value
Greige sheetings	2,551,240	499,239	1,484,909	344,357
Bleached sheetings	1,104,867	278,562	856,674	264,308
Dyed sheetings	1,588,591	397,410	2,047,344	642,778
Stamped goods	3,159,839	622,045	3,093,080	623,122
Woven with colored yarn	807,214	165,256	657,234	174,228
Broadcloth	1,934,023	561,422	1,565,765	494,343

Source: Memorias del Recaudador General de Aduanas.

TABLE 2

VALUE OF TEXTILE IMPORTS—COTTON
(Dollars)

Year	Yarn	Clothing			Cloth		Others
		Knitted	Other	Rem-nants	Simple weave	Fancy weave	
1946	151,801	131,681	77,525	62,774	1,523,705	763,731	554,548
1947	263,255	103,225	109,499	98,520	1,983,283	1,055,814	498,424
1948	359,782	68,604	92,575	82,900	2,464,611	989,995	617,206
1949	194,800	50,981	75,619	31,665	960,275	507,227	486,470
1950	128,821	na	na	na	na	na	na
1951	129,475	na	na	na	na	na	na

Source: Memorias del Recaudador General de Aduanas.

TABLE 3

TEXTILE IMPORTS—COTTON
(kilograms)

Year	Yarn	Clothing			Cloth		Others
		Knitted	Other	Rem-nants	Simple weave	Fancy weave	
1946	59,092	26,605	11,056	41,622	558,196	318,353	326,746
1947	92,994	18,257	20,148	47,965	659,977	401,616	180,249
1948	114,606	11,962	14,843	35,354	846,015	414,154	229,839
1949	72,281	10,002	14,491	18,522	451,722	267,752	220,359
1950	57,096	na	na	na	na	na	na
1951	48,640	na	na	na	na	na	na

Source: Memorias del Recaudador General de Aduanas.

TABLE 4

ARTIFICIAL FIBER TEXTILE IMPORTS

Year	Clothing		Cloth		Others	
	Kgs.	Value Dollars	Kgs.	Value Dollars	Kgs.	Value Dollars
1946	4,982	51,852	31,948	134,578	6,982	46,361
1947	4,530	49,138	51,426	294,205	12,399	52,082
1948	6,744	62,232	62,656	322,968	27,679	93,170
1949	4,269	39,653	54,803	237,095	29,964	92,425
1950	na	na	366,106	1,045,088	na	na
1951	11,504	41,313	82,228	310,315	na	na

Source: Memorias del Recaudador General de Aduanas.

Tariff Protection

Textile duties and their application form a complex portion of the Customs Guide; it is outside the scope of this report to consider them in detail. The protection on unbleached and bleached sheetings ranges from 29% to 33% which, in the opinion of the mission, is ample to protect the local industry.

Need for a Textile Mill

Additional cotton textile processing facilities are urgently needed. The country has a present effective annual demand for four to five million square yards of cotton goods of simple construction and plain colors, which is currently satisfied by imports. It is doubtful whether the market will be able at present to support an economical domestic production of stamped or printed goods, because of the cost of the printing rolls.

It is suggested that the new mill should make the following materials: 3 million to 4 million yards of sheeting, ranging in construction from 56 x 60 up to 60 x 100; up to 500,000 yards of denims; and the remainder towelings and fancy goods woven in special patterns. A considerable portion of the sheeting production could be made into bags for the sugar industry.

B. *Artificial Fibers*

Imports of textiles made from artificial fibers amounted in 1950 to 2,643,777 yards with a value of U.S. $1,045,088. Most of these imports were rayon goods.

It is more likely that the use of rayon goods will increase since they are more suitable for hot, humid climates than other synthetic fibers.

Although local mills produce cloth of rayon and cotton mixtures, only one organization weaves all-rayon fabrics, using imported yarns. The machinery is old and not well maintained, so that only about 20,000 yards of fair quality rayon are produced monthly in a variety of patterns. With some imagination in pattern design, new automatic equipment, and increased operating efficiency, considerably more rayon goods could be manufactured locally.

C. *Clothing Manufacturing*

There is some manufacturing of knitted materials and cotton and rayon clothing, for which imported yarns are used. The quality is good and the items sell for less than equivalent imported articles. One plant is installing modern machinery and will shortly produce a wide variety of patterns.

In general there is little wholesale manufacture of clothing. Most of it is done by tailors and dressmakers on order. One firm manufactures a good shirt with a permanent collar and another maintains a small stock of locally made suits, all made with imported cloth. Comparatively little ready-made clothing is imported. Most of the clothing imports are limited to formal and semi-formal dresses, although nonluxury imports are increasing steadily.

II. *FATS AND OILS*

There are almost no statistics on production or consumption of fats and oils in Nicaragua. According to the available data, 700 tons of oil were produced locally and about 300 tons were imported in 1951, which would make present annual consumption around 2.5 kilograms per capita. This figure may be too low, since many families in rural areas raise oil-bearing seeds for their own use. In any case Nicaraguan consumption of fats and oils appears to be well below minimum dietary requirements.

Many fats and oils are produced in Nicaragua, including lard and tallow, as well as cottonseed, sesame, castor, coconut and African palm oils. Production of lard and tallow is insufficient to meet the local demand.

A. *Animal Fats*

Lard is the main cooking fat for Nicaraguans. Since there are no modern slaughtering facilities, much slaughtering is done by individuals, who frequently kill a single animal and render the lard at the same time. The product is unrefined, liquid, and frequently rancid, with an off-flavor taste and odor. The retail price of crude lard is usually very much higher per pound than that of meat from the same animal. In spite of this apparent stimulus to increased production, considerable lard is imported.

Tallow is used mainly for soap; it is produced in the same manner as lard. Its price is also frequently higher than meat, and periodic shortages necessitate importation for soap stocks. The whole situation is an anomaly in a cattle-producing country. Once the cattle herds are increased and Nicaragua gets modern slaughtering facilities, animal fats should become an export item.

B. *Vegetable Oils*

Nicaragua produces a variety of oil seeds and a small vegetable oil industry is now developing, but exports are small and irregular. There is considerable local consumption of cottonseed oil as a substitute for the more expensive lard.

Cottonseed Oil

Cotton production has risen sharply in the last three years; the 1951-52 crop is expected to double the 4,300 tons of cotton ginned in 1950-51. The 1950-51 crop produced 8,600 tons of seed for processing. Half was exported as unprocessed seed, and the remainder was processed for local consumption.

There are two cottonseed crushing plants in Managua, one with an annual capacity of 10 million pounds, the other of approximately four million pounds. The first, which is now being expanded, expects to increase its capacity to more than 21 million pounds and plans to crush cottonseed only seven months of the year and to process sesame the remaining months. This plant now removes only first-cut linters from the seed but, with expected additional equipment, it will be able to produce second-cut linters. The oil is refined and sold for cooking purposes; foots are used for soap, while the cake is sold locally or exported. Local sales of cake are expanding slowly but the price at which it is sold discourages domestic consumption.

The cottonseed yields an average of 14.5% oil and 7% linters. In 1951, the price the local mills paid for seed averaged 17.7 cordobas per quintal (1 quintal = 100 pounds) although the price went as high as 23 cordobas per quintal.

Cottonseed oil sales are increasing because its price remains constant, in contrast to lard prices which fluctuate by as much as 100 to 150% during a year. In addition the quality of the oil is more or less constant (although subject to improvement) while lard quality varies even more than price. The company, in expanding, plans to install up-to-date refining facilities to improve the oil generally and to produce a good quality salad oil.

Coconut Oil

Production of coconut oil, on which data are lacking, is confined to the east coast and Corn Island. There are an estimated 250,000 trees on Corn Island with perhaps another 200,000 trees on the coast south of Bluefields. It is believed that the yield of coconut oil may be about 225 tons per year, based on an average of 50 nuts per tree per year and 100 nuts yielding one kilogram of oil.

TABLE 5

IMPORTS OF FATS AND OILS
(dollars)

Year	Lard		Butter and Substitute		Fish and Animal Oils and Fats		Vegetable Oils Edible		Vegetable Oils Miscellaneous	
	Kgs.	Value	Kgs.	Value	Kgs.	Value	Kgs.	Value	Kgs.	Value
1946	17,163	7,679	1,290	849	18,654	10,842	10,333	7,331	31,162	8,977
1947	162,921	100,426	1,068	752	28,569	21,218	37,971	38,326	21,587	9,612
1948	49,847	31,210	1,495	1,552	21,497	15,778	18,876	20,322	43,969	26,503
1949	146,160	52,502	3,537	4,587	14,344	10,798	18,198	14,224	52,658	25,825
1950	223,438	74,029	31,220	14,967	331,674	67,518	57,708	31,436	24,688	12,059
1951	211,003	92,094	22,089	13,606	223,557	69,035	39,357	24,102	54,775	24,066

TABLE 6

EXPORTS OF FATS AND OILS
(dollars)

Year	Lard		Butter		Sesame Oil		Cottonseed Oil		Castor Oil	
	Kgs.	Value	Kgs.	Value	Kgs.	Value	Kgs.	Value	Kgs.	Value
1946	131	102	70	56	44,216	16,506	12,130	5,953	1,655	928
1947	—	—	—	—	—	—	20,283	7,840	7,972	4,048
1948	24,574	18,773	—	—	146,947	54,306	—	—	—	—
1949	42,639	34,068	10,088	12,137	29,566	12,995	—	—	9,660	5,145
1950	—	—	16,379	16,005	—	—	—	—	—	—
1951	8,153	3,894	45,686	45,630	—	—	44,812	16,557	11,997	6,719

TABLE 7

EXPORTS OF OIL SEEDS
(dollars)

Year	Sesame		Castor Beans		Cotton Seed		Linseed	
	Kgs.	Value	Kgs.	Value	Kgs.	Value	Kgs.	Value
1946	4,047,855	852,654	—	—	786,998	31,005	—	—
1947	7,467,864	2,185,040	—	—	—	—	—	—
1948	12,050,092	3,614,121	—	—	—	—	230	50
1949	17,388,844	4,125,263	—	—	686,565	31,044	7,699	1,008
1950	7,466,065	1,514,611	7,809	1,061	4,312,216	203,972	1,610	175
1951	8,177,257	2,479,498	125,186	27,244	1,429,032	113,038	2,760	630

Source: Memorias del Recaudador General de Aduanas.

On Corn Island, the nuts are processed for copra before pressing. Artificial heat is used for drying the copra and expellers are used for oil extraction.

The oil is consumed domestically; as far as can be determined none is exported. Most of it goes to the capital for soap making, after being transported by boat and barge up the San Juan River and across Lake Nicaragua, at a freight cost of 48 cordobas per drum. There is a seasonal price variation in normal times. Oil was selling at three cordobas per pound in 1951 in Managua, or more than double the world market price. In early 1952, the world price had dropped enough that coconut oil was being imported into Managua. It sold considerably below the local price and was of a much better quality.

There is ample land available to increase the planting of coconut palms, and every effort should be made to do so. At the same time the quality of the oil must be improved so that it will be equal to that of the imported oil.

The market could be expanded within Nicaragua and it should be possible to develop an export market in El Salvador and Honduras.

African Palm Oil

Oil from the African palm is widely used in soap making and in the metallurgical industry. The agricultural experimental station at El Recreo has been testing this tree for several years on soils near the Escondido River. Good results have been shown, and the station is providing seedlings and technical advice to local growers. Several hundred acres have been planted by small farmers; in addition, the Cukra Development Company, a United Fruit subsidiary, has 1,400 acres coming into production.

Unfortunately, the only processing facilities are owned by the Cukra Company. They have not been made available to the small growers, even though the company cannot yet utilize their full capacity.

The lack of a processing plant is holding up additional plantings by private individuals. It would be possible to solve this problem by installing an extraction plant at the El Recreo Station, charging a fee sufficient to amortize the plant. Such a plant can be built at a cost not exceeding $25,000 to $30,000, including the machinery, building and installation costs. With the increase of plantings, the larger individual farmers will be able to afford their own processing plants which can also process crops of smaller planters.

Miscellaneous Oils

The export of sesame seed is important to the economy; in 1951 the crop was valued at nearly $2.5 million. Only a small amount is processed locally into oil because in recent years the oil mills have concentrated on cottonseed.

Sesame oil is as good cooking oil as cottonseed oil, if not better, and should be an important domestic oil source. It is estimated that over 3,000 tons of oil can be produced locally.

Castor production has been variable. There is only a small local market for the oil—principally for use in low grade soaps. However, castor production should be expanded since there is usually an export market for the oil, especially when there is a threat of war. Although it would be possible to introduce new varieties which may be harvested mechanically, this is not recommended. Instead, small farmers should make castor plantings around their houses and care for them during spare time. This would provide the farmers with an additional cash crop and would not detract from other crops.

Need for a Hydrogenation Plant

With a shortage of good lard, and serious seasonal fluctuations in lard prices, there is a clear need for producing additional cooking fats. Oils can replace fats in some cases, but the latter are essential for a number of purposes, including baking. Hydrogenated vegetable lard can be made from cottonseed oil. This would eliminate the need for lard imports, and provide a higher degree of processing of a local raw material for local consumption. At current prices it should be possible to produce a hydrogenated shortening from cottonseed to retail at not more than three cordobas per pound, or the lowest seasonal price of lard.

Two alternatives are available: (a) the installation of a completely new plant including crushing, refining and hydrogenation equipment (plus a soap kettle) which would cost around $300,000. Such a plant would require 7,000 to 10,500 tons of cottonseed to produce two to three million pounds of lard a year (with a capacity of 10,000 pounds per day); or (b) the installation of additional hydrogenation equipment in one of the existing cotton oil processing plants. This latter procedure would cost around $100,000.

The second alternative is recommended. While the record 1952 production of cottonseed may reach 20,000 tons, or enough to supply both the 10,000-ton capacity of a new hydrogenation plant for seed and the expected 10,000-ton capacity of the cottonseed crushing plants, future cotton and cottonseed production is likely to be a variable quantity. Additional equipment in an existing plant would provide hydrogenated shortening to the country at minimum cost.

III. *SOAPS*

There are about 27 small soap factories and nearly every little town or village has some soap making facilities. The 27 plants have an average production of nine million pounds per year, valued at 13 million cordobas. The three largest factories can produce 12 million pounds annually but they operate at 50% or less of capacity. The soap is made by the "half-boiled process," in which the fats and oils are heated with the required amount of alkali and with saponification allowed to go to completion. Any glycerine formed remains in the soap. The soap is inferior to that of the full-boiled process, but more economical to manufacture.

Some typical formulations are:

1. Tallow ....1,000 pounds
   Coconut oil .... 300 pounds
   Caustic soda .... 234 pounds
   Soda ash .... 55 pounds
   Ultramarine blue .... 7 pounds

2. Tallow ....1,000 pounds
   Coconut oil .... 500 pounds
   Caustic soda .... 180 pounds
   Coloring .... 2 pounds

3. Tallow ....1,000 pounds
   Coconut oil .... 145 pounds
   Caustic soda .... 150 pounds
   Rosin .... 280 pounds

The ingredients are boiled for four hours and then are sent to cooling frames. No attempt is made to determine if saponification has gone to completion or if there is excess caustic soda. Most soap is incompletely saponified, and, in laundering, unsaponified grease remains in the clothing while the unreacted alkali weakens the cloth. Neither has there been any effort made to make soap with better detergent action by incorporating trisodium phosphate or other builders. One formulation shows the addition of rosin, but very little is made because of its darker color.

All soap is poor in quality but it can be improved by better control of saponification. The industry is hampered by too many small submarginal producers who have no knowledge of good soap processing. Full-boiled soap should be made, in order to have good quality soap, although the capital investment is much larger than that required for the half-boiled process. Unfortunately, there is hardly a market sufficient to support a single modern factory.

Soap imports, while increasing, are still too small to affect domestic production. Furthermore, imports are made up of many different soap products, some of which cannot be made locally.

TABLE 8

SOAP IMPORTS

Year	Kilograms	Value (dollars)
1948	280,077	168,207
1949	349,949	142,015
1950		
Toilet and shaving soaps	151,969	97,856
Soaps, soap powders and synthetics	225,014	64,995
Household cleaning articles	67,175	40,267
1951		
Toilet and shaving soaps	126,918	93,438
Soaps, soap powders and synthetics	224,492	69,040
Household cleaning articles	71,160	52,788

The industry suffers from too many producers competing for a small market. The only possible remedy is for one producer to undertake to get the largest share of the market by producing a better soap (using the same process) at a lower price. As his market builds up, he should be able to change over to the full-boiled process, and be in a position not only to have a large share of the domestic market but to export to neighboring countries.

IV. DAIRY PRODUCTS

It is very roughly estimated that average milk production per cow is around one liter per day. However, a few farmers with good stock and good feeding practices have yields up to 14 liters per day. The over-all average milk production can be doubled merely by the application of a few rules of herd management such as taking the calf away from the cow soon after birth, having regular milking hours, supplying all the water the cattle will drink, and providing feed during the dry season.

TABLE 9

DAIRY PRODUCTS—EXPORTS
(dollars)

	Butter		Cheese	
	Kgs.	*Value*	*Kgs.*	*Value*
1946	70	56	2,763	1,192
1947	—	—	4,533	1,827
1948	—	—	5,567	1,956
1949	10,088	12,137	34,813	13,526
1950	16,379	16,005	56,813	20,975
1951	45,686	45,630	68,339	27,346

Source: Memorias del Recaudador General de Aduanas.

The majority of the milk is produced and handled under unsanitary conditions. It was surprising for the mission to see some farms with good barns and to find that these were used only for feeding, with milking taking place in open corrals in the midst of a cloud of dust raised by the animals milling around.

The majority of the milk does not get to market in the fluid state; it is processed into butter and cheese at the farm, again under questionable sanitary conditions. There is a fluid milk market in Managua and some of the other towns but these markets are far from being adequately supplied and at times it is difficult to buy milk in Managua. The price of fluid milk rises rapidly during the dry season, decreasing as soon as the rains come.

The only pasteurizing plant in the country is located at Managua. At present it has a capacity of around 3,000 gallons per day. This organization will soon have in operation a new plant with a maximum capacity of 10,000 gallons per day. In addition a small powdered milk plant is to be added within the next year which will be able to process 3,000 gallons a day.

Milk is currently purchased by weight only. As soon as the

new pasteurizing plant is in operation, this will be changed to the normal system based on the butter fat content of the milk. At the same time, greater attention will be given to the bacteria count and the cleanliness of the milk. It can be expected that the milk producers will change their procedures to conform to the stricter sanitary code.

The lack of adequate roads and transportation prevents farmers in the isolated regions from disposing of their production as fluid milk, hence the large production of butter and cheese. With the growing network of roads more farmers will be able to sell on the higher priced fluid milk market. However, it will be necessary for them to cool their milk and to transport it to market in insulated or refrigerated trucks. A considerable investment will be needed in this type of equipment during the next few years.

A minimum of three processing plants is needed to handle milk from Leon-Chinandega, Rivas, and Boaco or Juigalpa. The one serving the Leon-Chinandega area should be a pasteurizing plant; later a condensed or powdered milk unit could be added. The other two units probably should work only on condensed or

TABLE 10
(dollars)

DAIRY PRODUCTS—IMPORTS

	Milk of All Types		Cheese		Butter and Butter Substitutes	
	Kgs.	Value	Kgs.	Value	Kgs.	Value
1946	212,819	104,649	1,174	1,316	1,290	849
1947	253,107	135,317	3,499	3,947	1,068	752
1948	247,019	149,328	4,273	5,353	1,495	1,552
1949	223,600	102,128	5,718	5,976	3,537	4,587
1950	579,899	163,306	8,640	7,956	31,220	14,967
1951	306,673	150,945	4,731	4,840	20,595	11,810

Source: Memorias del Recaudador General de Aduanas.

powdered milk for the domestic and export markets.

The export of dairy products offers an extremely large market for Nicaragua. Possible exports to Central American countries alone are estimated at over $2 million annually. Exports of butter and cheese are increasing and could reach many times their present value. Imports of milk, which are tending to increase, could be stopped entirely with expanded local production.

V. MEAT AND MEAT BY-PRODUCTS

It is estimated that the cattle population is about one million head, but the number will be known more accurately when the agricultural census is completed.

A permit is required before an animal is slaughtered. The official kill is around 70,000 cattle and 75,000 hogs per year but it is believed that the actual kill is much greater because of the many clandestine operations. In the Managua area, around 25,000 cattle and 30,000 hogs are slaughtered annually.

Animals are slaughtered under extremely unsanitary conditions. The meat is sold the same day as slaughtered since there is no refrigerated storage available. Only two or three people have small refrigerators that can hold one or two carcasses at a time. These people, on a limited scale, are attempting to cut and sell meat as it is done in the United States.

There is a limited amount of meat processing, especially of hams, bacon and sausage (*chorisos*), usually poorly cured.

Live cattle exports since 1947 (with the exception of 1950) have averaged around 19,000 a year. It is expected that this will increase unless their export is prohibited. It would be even more advantageous if all animals now exported alive were slaughtered locally, in order to have use of the by-products.

Only the meat, hides, and some fat are currently recovered from the animals. There is no production of tankage or fat rendering in the usual sense. Managua alone, with a daily kill of 200 animals, could support a modern slaughterhouse with full by-product recovery and refrigerated storage.

TABLE 11

SLAUGHTER OF CATTLE AND HOGS

	Cattle (number)	Hogs (number)
1945	57,819	67,985
1946	72,868	71,106
1947	66,329	67,838
1948	67,727	70,185
1949	70,746	76,178
1950	71,743	80,279

Source: Direccion de Estadisticas, Ministerio de Economia.

TABLE 12

LIVE ANIMAL EXPORTS
(dollars)

	Cattle		Hogs	
	Number	Value	Number	Value
1946	4,921	265,775	—	—
1947	17,815	1,016,369	—	—
1948	21,074	1,198,926	605	10,890
1949	19,518	1,202,079	495	9,454
1950	4,491	291,314	162	3,240
1951	18,298	1,141,461	977	19,019

Source: Memorias del Recaudador General de Aduanas.

The export of chilled or frozen meat in large quantities involves a number of transportation problems. However, with a modern plant, slightly larger than required for the needs of Managua, some meat could be exported by air to the better markets. Such a plan is in successful operation in Honduras, where the meat is being sold on the United States market. There the meat is chilled to a bone temperature of 36°F. It is then carefully packed in a plane and arrives in Miami at a temperature of 39°F. Since the time in transit is short, elaborate refrigeration facilities are not needed in the plane.

Nicaraguan meat can be sent to the United States only if the slaughterhouse meets certain rigid specifications and if the meat is inspected by a properly qualified veterinarian. Nicaragua might also be able to reach the markets of El Salvador and Panama by air. This method offers an opportunity to initiate meat exports with a relatively low investment.

VI. *HIDES AND LEATHERS*

Nicaragua produces more than 75,000 cattle hides per year. Virtually all were consumed locally in the past, although 1951 exports amounted to 150,000 kilos. Exports are confined mainly to skins of alligators, wild pigs, sharks, tigers and deer. Many skins also are used locally but no records are available to show the total slaughter of wild animals.

Imports are confined to high quality leathers, shoes, and some specialty items such as industrial leather, beltings and packings. Leather imports amounted to $342,000 in 1951 and have averaged $250,000 for the past five years. These are made up primarily of upper and sole leathers of better quality than can be produced within the country.

Nicaraguan cattle hides are of poor quality. The quality of leather is determined by the quality of the hide, which in turn is determined by the health of the animal. Poor feeding practices and poor care of livestock are a primary cause of poor quality hides. In addition, many of the hides are from animals slaughtered in the country, which have been dried instead of salted.

The thickness of the hide and, consequently, the thickness of the leather, increases with the age of the animal. Few of the animals in Nicaragua are slaughtered before they are three or four years old and many of them are aged oxen, too old to do any more work. Thick hides cannot be used to make high quality upper leather.

The most serious defect in Nicaraguan hides is caused by the torsalo fly. This fly deposits its eggs under the skin of the animals where a large grub develops and causes a good sized hole. Some hides with over 100 holes have been observed by members of the mission. These hides had the appearance of a sieve and were worthless for leather. Frequent spraying with Toxophen will control torsalo and all farmers in the affected areas should be taught these control measures.

A second serious defect is caused by indiscriminate and excessive branding. Every time an animal changes owners, it acquires a new brand. Nicaraguan animals bearing five or more brands are a common sight, and some animals have been seen bearing three brands of the same owner. The general practice is to brand on the hip or flank but this practice spoils the best leather. Actually, branding for the identification of the animal is unnecessary and has been outlawed in some countries in order to improve the leather quality. Nondestructive methods of identification include notching the ear, attaching a metal tag to the ear, or attaching a tag to a chain fastened around the horns or neck of the animal.

Careless flaying also contributes to the low quality of the hides. Many butcher cuts are found on every hide and each cut spoils a portion of the leather.

Hides are purchased by the tanners on a weight basis only. There are no penalties for low quality nor are there premiums for the highest quality. Under these conditions cattlemen have no incentive to improve the grade of hides.

Indirectly, the practice of exporting live cattle also contributes to the poor quality of the skins, because the animals exported are usually the best in the country—the youngest, fattest, and healthiest animals. Those that are killed locally are the second grade animals with poorer hides. If the cattle were slaughtered in Nicaragua and only the meat sold abroad, the hides and other by-products could be processed locally and would have a greater value when sold to foreign markets.

Tanning

Leather is made in numerous small tanneries scattered throughout the country. Some 44 tanneries are listed and report their production to the Direccion de Estadisticas. It is believed that there are at least an equal number of unregistered, smaller tanneries.

The tanneries range in size from those which handle only a few hides per week to one with an output of 200 hides per week. Without exception all were using crude processes and equipment. Only a few have machinery for finishing the leather and none use driers to speed up the processing. The hide is stretched on a crude frame and hung from the ceiling of the plant to dry or sometimes is placed outside in the sun.

Suggestions for Improving Leather Quality

Hide Storage—Immediately after flaying, the green hide should be cooled to room temperature and salted to prevent deterioration during storage. Although thorough drying will prevent putre-faction, it is difficult to dry large, thick hides without some decomposition taking place. When dried hides are purchased for storage they should be soaked and salted in order to maintain their quality. Salt does more than simply retard hide deterioration. There seems to be a reaction with the protein of the hide which improves the quality of the leather. Thus better leather can be made from salted hides than from green hides.

Soaking—Hides coming from the salt bin contain appreciable quantities of salt and soluble matter which must be removed by prolonged soaking in water. Pure water must be used for this step because the presence of iron or other metal impurities will cause dark stains in the finished leather.

Dry hides usually need longer soaking and sometimes limited amounts of sodium hydroxide or milder alkalies are added to speed the water take-up but careful control is needed to see that the pH of the solution does not become too high. Antiseptics (such as chlorine) should be added to the soaking water to prevent bacterial action during the long soaking period.

Tanning Operations—Many factors must be watched in making good vegetable-tanned leather; the concentration of the tannin must be adjusted to the optimum value; the pH of the solutions must be controlled in order to get good plumping and the greatest fixation without excessive swelling of the hide (plumping is also controlled by the addition of salt); tanning temperatures must be adjusted both for operating economy and to prevent hide damage; rate of penetration must be followed to insure complete tanning of the thickest parts (hides of uniform thickness should be tanned together).

Different vegetable tannins cannot be interchanged freely without making proper modifications in the process. It must be recognized also, that all vegetable tannins do not react alike with the protein of the hide, and that better leathers are generally made with a combination of tannins. For example, mangle rojo used alone gives a dark red color to the leather making it unsuitable for use where a light colored leather is desired. However, by using mangle rojo in the first stage and retanning with Divi-Divi, the leather will be much lighter colored.

Leather Products—Shoes, saddles, bags and other leather products are manufactured in many small shops scattered through the country. These shops seldom employ more than one or two workers.

It is difficult to obtain any data concerning the output or value of leather products, although the annual production of shoes is estimated at 700,000 pairs of all types.

In general, the quality of work is low and many of the products are crudely made although a few people attempt to better their products to attract the small tourist trade. It is hoped that this movement will be extended by improved vocational training in order to provide better products for local consumption.

Tanning Materials—A small amount of leather is tanned with imported synthetic materials, principally chrome tannins. The remainder is processed with materials available locally.

Mangrove (*Rhizomorpha mangle*) is the principal tannin used by the smaller tanneries followed by nacascolo (*Caesalpinia coriaria*), nancito (*Hieronyma alchornecides*), roble (oak), and espino.

Mangrove is found on both coasts in the swampy areas. It is exploited over a wide area for local use but Puerto Morazan and Corinto are the principal sources of the bark traded commercially. The bark is shipped to those larger towns which have railroad facilities. The cost per ton at the tannery averages 120 cordobas at Leon and 150 cordobas at Granada. It is estimated that the tannin content of this bark is approximately 20%.

Nothing is known of the extent of the mangrove forests nor how long they will last at the present rate of exploitation. A recent study in Guatemala showed that the mangrove forests (manglares) were only 25%; mangle rojo (*Rhizaphora mangle L*); other varieties not suitable for tanning made up the remainder. Furthermore, when the mangle rojo is cut the roots do not start a new growth, and the species is gradually crowded out by the nonexploitable varieties.

At present, there seems to be no shortage of mangrove bark. Although a serviceable leather can be produced with it, its inherent disadvantage is the red color imparted to the leather. Actually Nicaragua has available a much better tanning material that is little used—nacascolo or divi divi (*Caesalpinia coriaria (Jacq.) wild*).

Nacascolo—The pods of this tree contain 45-55% of a tannin which produces plump, light colored leather. The small amount that is being used at the present time comes from the region north of Lake Managua. Nothing is known about the tree population or concentration, consequently no estimate can be made of possible output.

The world-wide shortage of tannin materials, including nacascolo, is so great that it would be worthwhile to examine the feasibility of developing nacascolo for export. Further, a study might be made to see if additional trees could be planted to increase the amount of pods available for export. A latter possibility would be the establishment of a plant to produce a concentrated tannin extract for the export market.

Black Wattle (Acacia Mollissima)—The tannin from the bark of this tree is much in demand. Although the wattles are not native to Nicaragua, there is reason to think that it might be introduced to provide a new fast growing tree crop. It has been suggested that the region around Matagalpa would be suitable. Planting trials should be started by the Servicio Tecnico to determine if wattle will grow successfully in Nicaragua.

VII.   HARD FIBERS

A. *Sisal*

Cordage manufacture is limited to small-scale hand operations. Rope is manufactured by two small plants which use hand power and the rope walks of the last century. In spite of the crude manufacturing methods rope of good quality is made up to three inches in diameter. Many individuals throughout the country are engaged in making small-diameter twine used for wrapping twine and woven goods (harness, hammocks, nets, etc.). There is no local manufacture of bags from native hard fibers.

There is no organized cultivation of hard fibers but small, scattered plantings of *Cabuya* are found throughout the drier regions of the country. *Cabuya* is the local name applied to the agaves; *Agave sisalana* has been identified here and it is suspected that there is considerable *Agave letonae* present also.

Imports

Each year, approximately 1.25 million bags worth 5 million cordobas must be imported to handle the export of coffee, corn, and sesame as well as for the internal movement of these and other crops. In addition, imports of cordage range from 50,000 to 150,000 pounds annually with an estimated value of 700,000 cordobas to 2.1 million cordobas.

Opportunity

While sisal bags are not as satisfactory for certain crops or as easy to handle as those made of jute, they are adequate for the movement of coffee, corn and other grains. Nicaragua could save considerable foreign exchange, and would have a new agricultural crop and industry as well, if sisal cultivation were undertaken to provide for the bag requirements of the country.

It is estimated that to manufacture a million bags, nearly three million pounds of fiber would be needed annually. At least 3,000 acres of land would be required to supply this amount. Although more detailed soils surveys are needed, it appears that there are extensive areas, not now under cultivation, which would be suitable for sisal. Such areas are found near Dario, Juigalpa, Boaco, and from Esteli northward to the border.

Cultivation

The agaves are Xerophilous plants, requiring only a moderate amount of rainfall and able to withstand long periods of droughts. Henequen *(Agave fourcroydes)* requires a minimum of 30 inches of rainfall per year whereas sisal *(Agave sisalana)* does best on 50 to 70 inches of rain.

Sisal is ready for its first cutting within two to three years after planting but henequen requires five to six years to mature. Conversely, henequen may bear for 10 to 15 years while sisal has a useful life of only four to five years. Over a long period of time, both varieties will yield approximately the same amount of fiber per acre.

In general, sisal produces a finer and stronger fiber than henequen and normally brings a slightly higher price. Because of this sisal is to be recommended over henequen wherever the rainfall and soil conditions are found suitable.

Processing

Hand stripping of the leaves is satisfactory only for small scale home production. It will be necessary to adopt mechanical decortication to supply enough fiber for bag manufacture. Such units can be installed with an investment of $15,000 to $50,000, depending upon the size of the decorticator and the amount of auxiliary equipment.

To manufacture bags, the clean, dry fiber must be drawn, spun and woven. A single plant to make a million bags per year might cost up to $500,000 but it is estimated that the initial investment need not be over $100,000. Since it will take some time to expand sisal production, a small unit can be installed first and expanded later to keep pace with increased fiber production.

It is strongly recommended that circular looms be installed in place of flat looms. Circular looms have a greater capacity and produce a tubular cloth which needs to be cut and sewn at only one end to form a bag.

B. Kenaf

Whether or not the present experimental plantings of kenaf (*Hibiscus cannabinus*) are successful will largely determine the the amount of emphasis to be placed on the development of sisal.

Kenaf yields a fiber closely resembling jute which can be processed on the same machinery. Kenaf fiber makes a better sack than sisal and can be used where sisal cannot. However, in spite of much experimentation, kenaf is not yet widely grown in the Western Hemisphere because no satisfactory, economical way has yet been found to obtain a clean fiber from the stalk. To date, retting gives the best fiber—but retting requires cheap labor and an abundance of fresh flowing water. The fiber can be obtained by machine decortication but the fiber loss is high.

Some experimental work by private interests is going on in Nicaragua; other work is in progress in Cuba and the United States. However, if the solution to kenaf decortication is not found within the next two or three years, it is recommended that a sisal planting program be started.

C. Abaca

Abaca *(Musa textilis)*, commonly called Manila hemp, is grown in Nicaragua only on an experimental basis by the Servicio Tecnico Agricola and the Cukra Development Company. It has been demonstrated that it grows satisfactorily on the best soils of the east coast, and large acreages have been planted in similar soils and climates in the neighboring Central American countries.

A recent detailed soils survey of the Cukra Hill region, conducted by the U. S. Department of Agriculture, showed nearly 9,000 acres of Class II land suitable for the cultivation of abaca. Surveys of soils in other regions have failed to find good lands in tracts large enough to be feasible.

Abaca is a newcomer to the Western Hemisphere. In adopting the plant to new conditions, mechanical decortication and large plantation type operations were substituted for the hand-decortication, small-unit cultivation of the East. Due to the higher water rates and relative shortage of labor in the West, no one as yet has seen how to produce abaca without a high initial investment.

It is estimated that an investment of $4 million to $5 million would be necessary to bring the Cukra Hill area into production, which immediately takes it beyond the reach of local capital.

While it is possible to grow abaca in Nicaragua, it is recommended that its development be left to foreign capital.

VIII. *SALT*

Common salt (sodium chloride) is produced in Nicaragua by the evaporation of sea water, the average annual production being about 12,000 tons. On a few occasions some salt has been exported to neighboring countries, but generally about 300 tons are imported annually, principally by the East Coast. The industry is given some measure of protection by an import duty of $0.69 per 100 gross kilos on crude salt, and $1.03 per 100 kilos net on ground or refined salt.

There is almost a complete lack of knowledge of the principles of salt manufacture. The present process is extremely crude and wasteful of both manpower and fuel, and results in a product which is impure chemically and contaminated with beach sand. The usual practice is partial concentration of the sea water by solar energy, followed by final evaporation and crystallization in open pans heated at a wood fire. The crystallized salt is removed just before complete evaporation has occurred, and is piled on the ground for draining.

This final evaporation step requires large quantities of wood for fuel, which is wasteful because the percentage of effective heat utilization is low. By allowing almost complete evaporation, many undesirable compounds are included in the salt. Only one producer uses a true solar method to effect the final evaporation and crystallization of the salt. Although this process needs much improvement, it should serve to indicate that salt can be made without wasteful consumption of wood. The major portion of the output probably averages about 88-90% sodium chloride, and 6-8% moisture. The remainder is calcium and magnesium compounds.

The term "salt," as commonly used, applies to table salt or sodium chloride. It is used for preserving hides and meats as well as in various industrial processes. Sea water contains a mixture of compounds, one of which is sodium chloride. Some of the others are magnesium chloride, magnesium sulfate, calcium sulfate, calcium carbonate, silica, iron compounds and others. Only the sodium chloride is desirable for table and most other uses. The magnesium compounds cause the salt to be bitter and to cake. Magnesium sulfate in large amounts is a purgative, while calcium sulfate may be one cause of certain types of heart troubles. These compounds should be eliminated during the processing, and they can be removed by controlled evaporation. Furthermore, all the heat energy required can be obtained from the sun.

Sea water contains approximately 3.5% solids of which 77.8% is sodium chloride. Nearly half of the original volume of sea water must be evaporated (actually 47%) before any of the compounds will settle out. At this point calcium carbonate and the iron compounds will precipitate. Sodium chloride does not begin to crystallize until the liquid is reduced to 9.5% of its original volume. In other words, if 10 inches of fresh sea water were placed in a pan, only one inch would remain at the time sodium chloride first started to precipitate. This illustrates clearly the need for a cheap process for the recovery of sea salt, and the fuel waste involved in the present processing methods.

The pond system should be composed of several concentrating and crystallizing ponds. The ratio of concentrating ponds to crystallizing ponds will vary from 12 to one up to 25 to one, depending upon local conditions. This point can be determined only by experimentation. It is estimated that the total needs of Nicaragua can be made in a system of 500 to 700 acres.

The number of concentrating ponds should not be less than four but may be as high as 10 or 12. The fresh sea water is introduced into the first pond (called a settling pond) either at high tide or by pumping. The water should be at least 18 inches deep. Here the suspended matter of the sea water settles to the bottom and preliminary evaporation takes place. At least two settling ponds are needed. In the first, silica, aluminum and iron compounds are precipitated and in the second, calcium carbonate. If more than two ponds are used, the brine may be pumped from one to another continuously with evaporation and precipitation taking place in each.

From the settling ponds, the brine flows (either by pump or gravity) to a pickling pond where calcium sulfate precipitates. By the time the brine reaches a specific gravity of 1.198 to 1.209, most of the calcium sulfate has been deposited and the relatively pure brine may be transferred directly to the crystallizing ponds or to a "holding" pond used to supply the crystallizing ponds. (Specific gravity may be measured easily with an inexpensive hydrometer.) Since the brine is saturated by the time it reaches the holding pond, sometimes salt will be precipitated. This is desirable because if at another time the brine is not saturated upon reaching this pond, some of the precipitated salt will be redissolved to give a saturated brine.

The crystallizing ponds should be deep enough to hold 10 inches of brine and the bottom should slope so that the bittern may be drained off. At the time the specific gravity of the brine in the crystallizing ponds reaches 1.25, only a small amount of sodium chloride remains in solution. If the concentration is carried further, large amounts of magnesium compounds will be precipitated. The secret of making salt from sea water lies in knowing when to discard the bittern or mother liquor. Once the solution reaches a specific gravity of 1.25, all the remaining liquid must be drained off and discarded.

There is no need to harvest the salt from the crystallizing pond at the completion of each cycle. Fresh saturated brine can be admitted on top of the salt and several cycles can be completed before harvesting. By this means, a layer of salt up to six inches thick can be built up, reducing harvesting costs and labor needs. If the crystallizing ponds are of sufficient size, tractors fitted with scoops may be used in place of hand labor.

The salt must be washed after harvesting, first with clean, saturated brine, and finally with a small amount of clean sea water, or fresh water if available. Some salt will be dissolved during the final washing but this is not wasted as the washings should be returned to the pond system. The final washing is necessary to remove the impurities which adhere to the outside of the salt crystals. Finally, the clean salt should be piled to drain in a protected place to prevent contamination from dust.

Salt prepared in this manner will contain 99.5% sodium chloride (on dry basis) and is suitable for table use, as well as salting hides and other industrial purposes.

IX. SUGAR

Sugar production of all grades amounted in 1951 to approximately 26,000 tons. Of this amount, 18,000 tons were consumed domestically and the remainder exported. Products range in quality from semibleached "plantation white" sugar, to the crude "dulce" made by evaporating the juice to dryness.

Of more than 25 mills, only two are modern and obtain efficient yields. The largest mill, with a capacity of about 25,000 tons, has a yield of 10.25% or 204.7 pounds of sugar per ton of cane ground, with a sucrose extraction of 91.5%. This compares favorably with mills in other parts of the world, but the best of the smaller mills obtains no more than 120 pounds of sugar per ton while in the worst, the yields are as low as 80 pounds per ton.

Cane yields in the best plantations average 50 tons per manzana (72.6 tons per hectare) on irrigated land, but only 50% of this on nonirrigated land. Yields on the smaller farms are estimated to be as low as 10 tons per manzana (14.5 tons per hectare).

Fertilizer is not used yet although a few experimental trials have been made. These showed that cane yields were increasd 8.35% on irrigated land, and 12.85% on nonirrigated land.

The many small submarginal producers, with their wasteful use of land and cane, were unable to compete with the larger mills in a free market. This led to the formation of the *Associacion de Azucareros,* for the purpose of fixing prices and allocating production quotas to the members. A natural result has been high domestic sugar prices well above world market prices and further raised by the tax on sugar consumption, which the mission has recommended abolishing.

Certainly for the good of everyone, including the submarginal mills, the sugar market should be made free and competitive, both to bring domestic prices into line with those abroad and, more important, to force more efficient utilization of the land and a greater yield from the crop.

The two largest mills usually sell the bulk of their production to foreign markets, while the others compete for the small domestic market. Actually such a market can support only one medium-size, modern mill. It is suggested, therefore, that the members of the Associacion de Azucareros abandon their present, inefficient mills and pool their resources to establish a modern mill. Whether or not such a mill is built, serious efforts should be made to divert cane from the inefficient mills. Cane reasonably accessible to the most efficient mills should be diverted there to take advantage of operating economies and lower production costs.

Much of the land now planted to cane by submarginal producers is without irrigation water. Sugar cane cannot be grown satisfactorily on the western plains without irrigation. These lands are better suited to the seasonal crops of corn, sesame, cotton and sorghum. New plantings of cane probably should be made on the fertile flats near Lake Nicaragua, which can be irrigated easily.

In the future, more fertilizer should be used to increase cane yields per manzana. Nicaraguan soils are seriously deficient in nitrogen but this can be corrected by the addition of chemical fertilizers or any green manuring. Probably both methods should be used. Chemical nitrogen can be applied yearly to the cane and a crop such as cow peas turned under before replanting. Properly used, chemical fertilizers will increase cane yields, but many field trials need to be made to determine optimum applications and types of fertilizers. In addition, full use should be made of plant residues. Fields should not be burned before harvesting; the leaves stripped from the stalks should be left in the fields as a mulch to conserve moisture and suppress weed growth. One method is to mulch alternate rows each year and to carry out normal weeding and cultivation in the mulch-free rows.

For the present, the best use that can be made of the bagasse is for fuel to power the mills. However, an efficient mill will have excess bagasse, up to 15% more than is needed for fuel. Recent developments have shown that this can be mixed with molasses (another sugar-mill by-product) and oil cake to provide a good cattle feed. Disposal of excess bagasse and molasses by this means should be seriously considered.

X. LUMBERING

Saw mills are scattered throughout the country. Those of the east coast, which saw wood for the export market, tend to be larger than those of the west coast. It is estimated that there are 51 mills in Nicaragua, including a few that are inactive for lack of logs. Some lumber, especially in the smaller towns and outlying rural regions, is prepared with whip saws.

In general, the mills are poorly equipped, have old machinery and the percentage of waste is high. On the west coast especially, much of the wastage is due to splits which develop in the green logs when they are allowed to lie in the sun. This splitting may be minimized by painting the ends of the logs with a sealer to retard the rate of drying.

Little of the lumber is seasoned before use, consequently shrinkage occurs after the lumber is used in building or furniture construction. It is a common sight to see cracks in walls, doors, windows, and furniture. Thorough air drying before use will reduce this shrinkage but for best results all lumber for local use should be kiln dried.

All lumber used within Nicaragua is subject to decay and heavy insect attack. The use of fungicides and insect repellents is well known and should be introduced into Nicaragua. While kiln drying and chemical treatment may raise the initial cost to the consumer, in the long run, by extending the life and serviceability of the lumber, it will be cheaper than using green lumber.

TABLE 13

LUMBER PRODUCTION

	1948		1949	
	Board Feet	Value (cordobas)	Board Feet	Value (cordobas)
Production of mills reporting	24,763,372	7,484,382	28,657,523	18,584,241
Other estimated production	4,713,307	2,130,416	5,169,419	2,336,577
Logs exported	8,866,182	3,514,875	5,303,288	2,428,900
Lumber exported	11,949,687	3,138,865	16,894,519	4,524,115
Ties exported	127,482	11,150	359,369	23,825
Ties for local use	1,979,482	170,754	2,072,177	159,506

XI. CEMENT

Nicaragua has one cement factory with an estimated maximum annual capacity of 400,000 bags of Portland cement. Up to 1950 the excess production was sold on the export market, but since then internal consumption has equalled or slightly exceeded the plant capacity. The company is now engaged in doubling production to 800,000 bags per year.

The major imports of gray cement are confined to the east coast which cannot now be served by the local plant. Other imports include white cement, which is not made in Nicaragua.

Private use of cement has risen steadily while government use has declined. However, it is estimated that the development plan will boost government use to about 220,000 bags per year until 1955. Private building has increased sharply since 1950 and is placing a heavy demand on the factory for cement. Imported cement, although landed at a reasonable cost, is more than double the price of domestic cement due entirely to heavy duties and internal transportation costs.

Local cement is made by the conventional wet process using limestone of marine origin. At present the company is limited to mining to a depth of 10 to 15 feet because of the high ground water level. It is not known whether or not pumping would be practical to permit deeper mining. The company could make a number of operational changes to effect some savings in production costs. More mechanical equipment should be used for mining and loading instead of the present hand operations.

A lower grade fuel oil, such as Bunker C, should be used instead of diesel oil to fire the kiln. The company should either install facilities at Masachapa for unloading directly from tankers or refit their ship, now used for cement exports, to carry the lower grade fuel from Corinto to Masachapa. A considerable saving in fuel cost could be made by this move.

TABLE 14

PRODUCTION AND DISTRIBUTION OF CEMENT
(1,000 bags)

	Government and Official	Private	Export	Total Production
1942	13.8	3.5	1.0	18.3
1943	189.4	57.5	22.1	269.0
1944	139.2	103.6	—	242.8
1945	142.0	101.3	—	243.3
1946	148.0	112.8	—	261.8
1947	108.6	140.6	18.4	267.6
1948	132.5	166.1	95.3	393.9
1949	74.7	222.3	78.1	375.1
1950	86.6	293.6	7.0	387.2
1951	na	na	na	400.0*

*Estimated

Source: Compania Nacional Productora de Cemento, S.A.

TABLE 15

CEMENT IMPORTS AND EXPORTS

	Imports		Exports	
	Kgs.	Value	Kgs.	Value
1939	8,046,423	65,636	—	—
1940	7,023,572	56,014	—	—
1941	11,748,623	126,608	—	—
1942	4,825,314	58,551	—	—
1943	3,350,059	76,852	2,344,785	83,553
1944	939,490	14,893	44	2
1945	2,641,443	80,196	—	—
1946	4,817,415	93,898	19,913	1,369
1947	2,142,449	53,469	278,562	8,409
1948	1,827,330	42,413	3,861,098	104,347
1949	1,103,842	27,023	3,585,354	95,250
1950	1,529,093	37,699	901,494	24,780
1951	1,324,392	36,604	—	—

Note: Values in cordobas through 1945, in dollars thereafter.
Source: Memoria del Recaudador General de Aduanas.

XII. *THE CONSTRUCTION INDUSTRY*

Most of the building in the past has been by "maestros" rather than by architects or engineers.

The largest number of buildings are still constructed by the maestros but the construction companies are now taking over the higher priced and larger buildings. The value of construction by organized companies now greatly exceeds that by maestros.

Reinforced concrete and concrete blocks are the common materials of construction for the better buildings. Mixed construction (*taquezal*) wood framing and masonry fill—is being used less than previously and is confined entirely to low cost building. All-wood construction is little used because of the termite problem.

Prior to 1950, the volume of construction was small, probably less than 15 million cordobas per year. Due to the good crops and prices since then, the volume has increased sharply, jumping to an estimated 30 million cordobas in 1951. It was expected that it would reach 40 to 45 million cordobas in 1952.

Government construction expenditures have been low during the past two years but are expected to increase in the future. Commercial and private construction account for the largest share of the total but church and nongovernmental school and hospital construction are expected to amount to seven million cordobas during 1952.

For the better class buildings, costs are estimated at 300 cordobas per square meter for homes, 350 cordobas for first floor commercial, 400 cordobas per second and third floor commercial, increasing by 50 cordobas per square meter for each additional floor.

The construction industry is on a cash basis since there are no direct credit facilities available for this purpose. Most house buyers meet this problem by using their bank credit facilities for agricultural purposes, which releases funds for construction.

XIII. *MATCHES*

Only one company is engaged in the manufacture of matches. Although the plant is privately owned, the industry, in effect, is a government monopoly, since the entire output is sold to the government. The government in turn sells to the retailers, after imposing a tax amounting to a third of the retail price.

The matches are of an extremely poor quality. Fully 25% of the matches per box either break when struck, fail to light, or the heads fly off. Manufacturing operations, as seen by the mission, are crude and wasteful of both manpower and materials. It is estimated that less than 25% of the wood entering the plant to be used for boxes and sticks leaves as a part of the finished product. The wood itself is not the kind best suited for match sticks, since it breaks easily.

In addition to providing better matches, operating costs can be lowered considerably by more careful handling of the wood and better adjustment and maintenance of the machinery. The match sticks should be increased in size in order to give them better physical strength. The formula for the head composition should be revised to give better adhesion to the stick and better striking properties.

Until this can be done, the mission suggests not only the removal of the present tax on retail sales of matches, already proposed, but the suspension of all duties on imported matches to permit the consumer to have matches of good quality and at a reasonable price.

XIV. *THE FISHING INDUSTRY*

It has been estimated that the per capita consumption of fish and other seafoods is less than one pound per year. The greater part of this consumption is confined to the coastal regions and the immediate area around Lake Nicaragua. Probably most of the catch is utilized by the families of the fishermen and thus does not enter the market at all.

Imports of fish represent only a small part of total imports, being about $70,000 in 1951. Exports, mainly live turtles, amounted to $15,000 during the same period.

Very few people are engaged solely in fishing as a means of livelihood. At least one attempt has been made at commercial shrimp fishing off the east coast, but this was unsuccessful because of high costs and a scarcity of shrimp.

Almost nothing is known of the marine resources of the country since no detailed surveys have been made. A recent report, *"The Fisheries and Fishery Resources of the Caribbean Area,"* by the United States Department of the Interior contains a good description of the coastal waters and indicates what should be found. The Humboldt current, which is rich in tuna, reaches the southern

Pacific shore of Nicaragua and fishing boats from the United States work this stream from Nicaragua to Ecuador.

However, the recent discriminatory legislation introduced in the United States almost obviates any hopes of establishing a fishing industry based on exports to that country. A thorough study might show, however, a market for fish oil and meal to support a small nonedible fish industry. Some quantities of fish meal could be consumed locally in mixed feeds, although probably not in sufficient bulk to be sole support of such an industry.

The local market for fresh fish, though small, undoubtedly can be expanded several times over today's figure. This will be facilitated by the completion of the roads to San Juan del Sur and Leon, which will make it possible to ice the fish and move them rapidly to the Managua market.

It seems likely that the expansion of the fishing industry will have to be based on the local market. However, the Instituto de Fomento should study both the domestic and export market possibilities for fish, to determine the extent to which the industry may be developed, particularly in cooperation with other Central American countries.

XV. OPPORTUNITIES FOR NEW INDUSTRIES

The best opportunities for industrial development lie in the improvement and expansion of the major industries already described. However, certain other industries not now found in Nicaragua, and in addition to those mentioned, are suitable for an industrial development program. Many have been included in the development plan of Part I; others may be left for a later date or for development by private initiative.

Meat Processing

As indicated in Part I, the most promising field for future agricultural development is in the production of animal products for export and domestic consumption. Meats especially should be processed locally for the export trade, and live animal exports should cease as soon as sufficient sanitary slaughtering facilities are available in the country.

A plan for meat exports to be started on a small scale is outlined in Part I. However, in a long-range program, Nicaragua's future markets should be El Salvador, Panama, Peru, Cuba, Venezuela and Puerto Rico, and later, perhaps, Europe. Most of these markets cannot be served by air because of the distances and costs involved. Tonnage shipments especially will require large refrigerated storage capacity, refrigerated trucks and/or rail cars, and port facilities to handle perishable cargo, although El Salvador could be served by refrigerated trucks.

Planning for these large, future markets should be coordinated with the design and construction of slaughtering facilities to supply the local market. Certainly, one of the major preparatory steps will be the passage and enforcement of legislation governing the sanitary standards of meat handling, both for local consumption and exports. A period of time will be needed also, for the training of veterinarians to serve as inspectors of animals and meat.

Consideration must be given to the complete utilization of the slaughterhouse by-products, hides, bones, blood, and other offal. At first it may be desirable to produce only hides, inedible tallow and tankage, but plans should be made for the ultimate production of a complete line of inedible and edible tallow and lard, blood and bone meal, tankage, perhaps neatsfoot oil for the tanning industry, and recovery of certain of the glands which have pharmaceutical uses.

The development of a cattle and meat products industry should be considered as a high priority project and merits the continuous attention of the technical staff of the Instituto de Fomento.

Animal Feeds

If Nicaragua is to reach the twin goals of increased milk production and improved beef cattle, the supplemental feeding of cattle will be necessary. At present the majority of the cattle are pasture fed. During the rainy season the pastures are green—the milk flow increases and the animals gain weight. However, during the dry season the pastures are practically worthless—the milk flow is reduced sharply or stops altogether and the animals lose weight.

Supplemental feedings, with all the water the animals want, are absolutely essential to even out milk production and maintain animal weight. A good dairy cow, for example, consumes from 50 to 65 kilograms of green pasture per day and also needs proteins and minerals. These may be fed in the form of ensilage, corn, cottonseed meal or hay made from legumes. Typical formulations include corn or sorghum, bean, molasses, cottonseed cake, coconut cake, or sesame cake.

All of these materials are readily available in Nicaragua. At present, the rice bran and some molasses are thrown away. The establishment of a feed plant would provide a new market for these materials. It is suggested that the first small unit be established at the new grain storage plant in Managua since adequate supplies of corn will be available and the other materials may be obtained within the Managua area. Besides, the plant is located close to the center of the main milk producing area.

The feed plant should have the following facilities; one hammermill, one dry mixer, weighing and sacking equipment and adequate storage bins for both raw materials and finished products. Later, the facilities should be expanded to include a molasses mixer, drier and the necessary auxiliary equipment. With this simple plant, a variety of feed preparations could be made for dairy and beef cattle, hogs, and chickens.

Hardboard Mill

Nicaragua's forests are extensive but relatively unexplored. In the past, only high value woods have been exploited, and the lesser known timbers have been ignored. These timbers, which are not now useful as sawn lumber, can be processed into hard board sheets or into a softer insulation board.

Recent developments make it possible to use mixed woods in the manufacture of fiber boards, and the market demand has been growing for these products. A plant to manufacture fiber board, requiring an initial investment of from $1 million to $2 million depending upon the process chosen and the size of the plant, probably could be developed in Nicaragua. The mission cannot say anything definite about the possibilities of such a program because of the lack of adequate forestry data. The following information will be necessary if such a project is to be undertaken:

1. What types of timber are readily available near possible plant sites?
2. What quantities of timber are available near the possible plant sites?
3. What types of transportation can be used to get the timber to the mill? Can waterways be used or will it be necessary to build roads?
4. Estimated life of timber reserves. Will timber continue to be available near the plant or will the forest receed with the years? This will involve questions of reforestation.
5. What are world market possibilities for fiber boards? Almost all of the production will have to be exported.

This industry may be particularly suitable for investment by foreign private capital, either on a complete ownership basis or jointly with Nicaraguan capital, including that of the Instituto de Fomento.

Wire Products Manufacture

Up to 1951 nearly 1,000 tons of barbed wire and between 500 and 800 tons of nails, tacks and staples were imported into Nicaragua each year. In 1951, these imports reached 1,900 and 1,050 tons respectively. These items are relatively simple to manufacture; an investment of approximately $50,000 would install equipment sufficient to make barbed wire, nails, and staples using imported wire. At some time in the future it may be desirable to install wire drawing machinery so that only wire billets need be imported.

Flour Milling

In 1951, flour imports amounted to 8,500 tons. Although there are two small mills in Nicaragua these process only a small amount of wheat flour, primarily because of poor location and isolation, but also because of poor equipment.

The amount of flour imported would be sufficient to maintain a small, modern mill. It could be located either at the port or near Managua. The establishment of such a mill not only would reduce the amount of foreign exchange involved, but also would stimulate the domestic textile industry by requiring increased cotton bag production. Also, it would make available bran and grits which are valuable materials for cattle feeds.

Rubber Processing

Although Nicaragua is the second largest producer of wild rubber, all the production is exported. There is no processing of rubber within the country except for the manufacture of a few hundred raincoats. The situation should be studied carefully but there would seem to be ample opportunity to introduce the manufacture of rubber heels and soles for shoes, tennis shoes of cloth and rubber, and other rubber goods. Later on, the manufacture of bicycle tires might be undertaken. The manufacture of automobile tires and tubes will not be possible within the foreseeable future.

Yucca Starch

Yucca starch is now produced in many small factories. The product is generally dirty and variable in its characteristics. Some starch is exported and it is believed that these exports could be increased by offering a better product. Also the domestic textile industry could use larger amounts if the viscosity were better controlled.

At least one central plant, of modern design, could be built to process the yucca roots from a large area. This would result in better recoveries of starch and a more marketable product.

Candy

Nicaragua has most of the raw materials (sugar, chocolate, and milk) needed to make good quality candies and other confections, but all of the better candies are imported. The imports are comparatively small, and local consumption is limited. Other countries lacking the raw materials, have been able to build up large export markets using imported raw materials. Nicaragua, with materials available locally, should be able to compete favorably in the export market.

XVI. OTHER INDUSTRIES

Many other industries have been suggested for Nicaragua but certain of these cannot be recommended for the near future, for various reasons. It is important to state these reasons in order that,

(a) the conditions now holding back certain developments can be corrected,

or

(b) projects for some industries can be discarded to save time and effort.

It is apparent that Nicaragua cannot develop a heavy metallurical or chemical industry since the basic requirements of cheap power, fuel and raw materials are completely lacking and nearby markets are small. Long-run development of hydroelectric power may permit some small electrolytic industries (such as caustic soda, chlorine and related products based on solar salt) but the market aspect undoubtedly will be the major deterring factor.

There are several industries within the realm of possibility for Nicaragua which cannot be considered within the next five years because of the lack of data on raw materials and markets. During this period the appropriate government agencies and the Instituto de Fomento should collect these data in order to determine the feasibility of the industries discussed below.

Paper and Pulp

Forests cover a major portion of the eastern part of the country, yet they are relatively unexplored. Almost nothing is known about the distribution and density of tree varieties. Exploitation has been limited to commonly known commercial timbers, such as mahogany, cedar and pine. Extensive study of the forest resources is needed to determine if paper of marketable quality can be made from Nicaraguan woods. Other factors to be considered are the lack of transportation routes in the forest areas, lack of power and fuel, the need to import chemicals, the market prospects (since the product would be sold on the export market), and the large amount of capital required for plant construction and operation.

The capital requirements almost preclude the development of a paper industry based wholly on Nicaraguan capital. The best solution would be to allow a foreign paper company to participate in the initial studies and development.

Plywood

Although the capital needs for plywood manufacture are well within the means of the country, many of the same factors retarding the development of a paper industry apply to plywood, especially the lack of basic knowledge of the woods available. A thorough study of forestry resources is imperative before funds are invested in either paper or plywood manufacture.

Paint

In 1950, all paint imports amounted to $310,900. These included paints, enamels, and varnishes, as well as printing inks and typewriter ribbons. An economic enterprise cannot be established with this volume in view of the large number of colors and types of paints. Furthermore, all raw materials would have to be imported (pigments, drying oils, and thinners).

It is recommended that no attempt be made to establish a paint industry in Nicaragua.

Shoes

Shoes and other leather goods are now hand made in many small shops which rarely employ more than one or two persons. Probably several thousand persons derive their living from this work.

It is doubtful if a shoe factory could compete in the price market at the present time, although the quality of the shoes needs improvement. The present leather workers have little invested in tools and their prices are adjusted to the demand for shoes and their need for money to buy food.

A modern shoe factory might be established within five to 10 years, but only if the labor demand increases to such a point that the excess leather workers can find other employment.

Canning

Imports of canned fruits and vegetables are small. Consumption of these goods is limited almost exclusively to the foreign colony. There is an abundance of locally grown fruits available throughout the year, so that it is unnecessary to preserve fruits. Some vegetables are not grown in Nicaragua, while others are unavailable during the dry season. Nevertheless, enough vegetables are available throughout the year to eliminate all but a small market for canned vegetables.

A canning plant would have to be based upon the export market, if it were to attain an economic volume. There might be some possibility of an export market for canned pineapple, but unfortunately many of the other tropical fruits either are unknown abroad, or cannot be canned satisfactorily. It is probable that a canning industry would have little chance of success.

On the other hand, it should be possible to develop export markets for jams and jellies. Such items as citrus marmalade, guava jelly, pineapple jam, etc., are widely used and often are made at the points of consumption, using imported fresh fruit. Papayas and mangoes could also be exported in the form of preserves.

CHAPTER EIGHT

Power

Present Power Situation

In discussing power in Nicaragua, a distinction must be made between public and private power. Public power refers to power sold to individuals and industries, whether the generating facilities are owned by the government, private companies, or municipalities. Private power refers to captive plants designed to provide power only for the owner of the plant.

In 1949, the last year for which complete figures are available, a total of 23,112,139 kwh were generated by all the public plants throughout the Republic. Of this amount, 22,214,529 kwh left the plants but only 17,995,087 kwh were distributed to buyers, representing a line loss of 4,259,442 kwh or nearly 24%. It is estimated that not more than 26 million kwh were generated during 1951, including the 1.5 million kwh increased generation by the Managua plant.

A total of 31 companies are engaged in power generation and distribution: 20 using diesel power; three using steam; five hydroelectric; three semihydro, i.e., hydro power during the rainy season and diesel power during the dry season. The facilities of the most important plants are shown more fully in Table 1. Other data, concerning distribution, costs, etc., are shown in Table 2. The generating capacity of the 16 plants in Table 1 is 7,250 kw. The total capacity of public installations is estimated at about 10,000 kw.

Data concerning private power installations are incomplete but it is estimated that the six mines alone generate in excess of 45 million kwh per year, and there are dozens of other units, ranging in size from one or two to more than a thousand kilowatts. In Managua alone, private plants have nearly 5,000 kw capacity which is considerably in excess of the public plant.

TABLE 1

Major Public Power Facilities in Nicaragua

City	Ownership of Company	Generating Capacity kw or kva	Prime Mover	Approximate Number of Customers	Hours of Operation
Bluefields	P	160	diesel	420	6 p.m. to 6 a.m.
Chinandega	P	250	diesel	1,000	12 hours daily
Corinto	P	73	diesel	460	5 p.m. to 5:30 a.m.
Diriamba	P	121	diesel	1,720	continuous
		150	hydro		
Esteli	P	50	diesel	400	6 p.m. to 6 a.m.
Granada	P	750	diesel	2,200	continuous
Juigalpa	P	37.5	diesel	500	6 a.m. to midnight
La Libertad	G	25	hydro	200	6 p.m. to 6 a.m.
Leon	P	200	hydro	700	6 p.m. to noon
		515	diesel		
Managua	G	3,900	diesel	14,000	continuous
Masaya	G	550	diesel	1,600	6 p.m. to 6 a.m.
Matagalpa	F	22	diesel	200	6 p.m. to 12 noon
		50 (est.)	hydro		
Ocotal	P	55	hydro	230	6 p.m. to 6 a.m.
Puerto Cabezas	F	150	steam	180	continuous
		66	diesel		
Rivas	P	75	diesel	650	6 p.m. to 12 midnight

P—Local Private   G—Goverment   F—Foreign

TABLE 2

PRODUCTION, DISTRIBUTION AND CONSUMPTION OF PUBLIC POWER
1949

	Kwh Produced	Total Operating Cost (cordobas)	Average Cost per Kwh (cordobas)
Production	23,112,139	3,930,988.26	0.170
1. Diesel	19,326,654	3,406,570.63	0.176
2. Hydro	516,599	43,292.74	0.084
3. Semihydro	3,268,886	481,132.89	0.147

	Kwh Distributed	Gross Revenue	Average Price per Kwh
Distribution	17,955,087	4,832,593.37	0.269
1. Diesel	14,864,490	4,120,323.73	0.277
2. Hydro	449,246	98,991.78	0.220
3. Semihydro	2,641,351	613,277.86	0.232

	Kwh Consumed	Gross Revenue	Average Price per Kwh
Consumption			
1. Domestic	6,387,775	2,353,970.11	0.369
2. Public	2,024,558	241,266.74	0.119
3. Refrigeration	3,239,765	1,036,087.19	0.320
4. Industrial	4,682,647	976,705.25	0.209
5. Free	233,348		
6. Official	1,386,994	224,564.08	0.151

All the principal cities are troubled by power shortages in varying degrees. New commercial or industrial enterprises are forced to provide their own generating units, although few private plants would be installed if adequate public power were available.

Empresa de Luz y Fuerza Electrica, Managua

This company is the largest public company in Nicaragua. It is under the nominal control of the Ferrocarril del Pacifico de Nicaragua. Day-to-day operations are managed by an engineer with extensive public utility experience.

In 1951, the company showed a net profit of 797,864.95 cordobas based on gross income of 4,773,188.5 cordobas. Although a book profit has been shown for several years, nothing has been put back into the company on a planned basis until recently. A depreciation allowance was not set up until 1951, and then only for the cost of the new generator being installed. In the absence of adequate reserves, funds are raised by borrowing whenever additional equipment is needed.

The present installed capacity is 3,900 kw but the operating peak capacity is effectively limited to 3,500 kw because of the age of some of the equipment. The company is now adding a new 3,500 kw diesel generator which will be able to absorb the full load while older units receive much needed maintenance and repairs.

The diesel generating equipment is made up of the following units:

    2—   400 kw
    1—   700 kw installed in 1941
    2—   700 kw installed in 1945
    1—1,000 kw installed in 1948

Power distribution is limited to the city of Managua and for a distance of 14 kilometers south along the Inter-American Highway toward Casa Colorado. In the past, peak loads have reached total capacity within one to three years after the installation of additional units. Total consumption in the Managua area has tripled within the last 10 years.

Residential rates range from 0.4 to 0.5 cordobas per kwh ($.06 to $.07), and while they are not excessive, they do not encourage the use of appliances. The minimum industrial rate of 0.3 cordobas per kwh ($.04), is extremely high. This, coupled with the lack of adequate capacity, has forced the installation of many private power plants in the Managua area, some of them up to 750 kw capacity.

TABLE 3

Operation of
Empresa De Luz Y Fuerza Electrica
Managua

Year	kwh Generated	kwh Station Use	kwh Sold	Percent Line Losses	Number of Customers	Annual Peak kw	Annual Load Factor %
1941	4,544,080	—	3,783,943	14.68	—	—	—
1942	5,064,900	—	4,277,886	13.99	8,228	—	—
1943	5,681,980	—	4,834,765	13.22	8,740	—	—
1944	6,910,630	—	5,531,737	18.59	9,306	—	—
1945	7,062,360	141,334	6,143,022	11.49	9,870	1,830	—
1946	8,250,010	135,971	7,139,215	11.99	10,435	1,960	—
1947	9,913,670	186,600	8,071,025	17.02	11,296	2,430	46.5
1948	11,975,281	372,000	9,812,317	15.43	12,322	2,920	46.7
1949	13,749,610	372,000	10,576,959	20.90	12,860	3,400	46.2
1950	14,724,370	372,000	12,091,832	15.35	12,931	3,500*	48
1951	16,304,708	360,000	13,470,987	15.44	14,000[1]	4,000**	53

*Limited by generating capacity
**Estimated peak if capacity were available
[1] April 1952—14,586 customers

TABLE 4

EMPRESA DE LUZ Y FUERZA ELECTRICA
MANAGUA

Rate Schedule—January 1, 1951

(cordobas)

Tariff No.	Type of Service	Minimum Billing and Rates
1.	Residential lighting, metered	9 cordobas with right to consume up to 12 kwh
2.	Residential service without refrigeration	25 cordobas with right to 50 kwh, excess kwh at 0.5 cordobas each
	Residential service with refrigeration	40 cordobas up to 100 kwh, excess kwh at 0.4 cordobas each
3.	Commercial service with refrigeration	40 cordobas up to 100 kwh, excess kwh up to 400 at 0.4 cordobas each, additional up to 1,000 at 0.35 cordobas each; all excess at 0.30 each
4.	Industrial up to 25 HP only during hours of 4:00 a.m. to 5:00 p.m. over 25 HP subject to special arrangement	8 cordobas per HP a fraction up to 20 kwh excess up to 500 at 0.35 each; all additional at 0.3 cordobas
5.	Limited lighting	4 cordobas flat rate for 2 lights with 50 watt limit
	Limited lighting and radio	6 cordobas flat rate—limited to 90 watts
6.	Government	0.25 cordobas per kwh

Potential Power Market

While the Luz y Fuerza has recently estimated that Managua's peak load demand will reach 5,700 kw by 1955, several factors appear to have been overlooked in this estimate. In the opinion of the mission, there is already today a potential demand of at least 10,000 kw. In making this estimate, it is assumed that private plants would switch to public power. There is every indication that this would take place.

The private plants in Managua have a generating capacity of about 5,000 kw which, in general, work at maximum capacity most of the time. New home construction is placing a strain on the public facilities and there has been a recent heavy demand for electric stoves and air conditioning units. The company, however, must discourage appliance loads for lack of capacity.

The savings to be gained through large central station generation, particularly with the potential demand within a 50-kilometer radius of Managua, have never been taken into account in planning additional power for the city. Most of the communities within a 50-kilometer radius of the city have even poorer service from local plants than has Managua. In order to provide better service and tap new markets, the Managua network should be extended east to Tipitapa and south to Jinotepe and possibly even to Granada, to serve the many towns along the way. Eventually a line should also be extended to Leon and Chinandega.

Residential use of electricity is in its infancy in Nicaragua. The better class homes used about 318 kwh during 1950 as compared to the 1,600 kwh used in the United States homes during the same period, while at least half of the population of Managua is without any electric service.

Hydroelectric Power Development

In a country with no known coal or oil reserves, it is only logical to think of hydroelectric development. Early in 1951, a preliminary survey was conducted for the government by the U. S. Bureau of Reclamation. This brief study concluded that three areas offered potentials for development; Lake Managua through the Tamarindo River, the Tuma River, and Lake Nicaragua.

The lack of stream flow and runoff records in these areas prevented the drawing of any definite conclusions and additional studies were recommended. The preliminary study indicated the probability that the cost of power development on the Tuma was likely to be less per kilowatt than in the other areas.

At present, detailed studies are under way, with the installation of flow gauges, mapping by air and land, and examination of soils in the area.

It is estimated conservatively that records of stream flow over five years will be needed in order to have sufficient data upon which to base a design for a hydroelectric development, and before undertaking the final design and construction of a dam.

It is fairly definite that power can some day be developed on the Tuma River, but how much, where and what the cost will be is not yet known. The stream flow is low during the dry season and water storage will be needed to firm the normal flow; a flow gauge installed during the present dry season on the Tuma, just above the junction with the Yasica River, showed a minimum flow of around 85 cubic feet per second.

Any development of the Tuma River will require a transmission line nearly 100 miles long to bring the power to Managua, the major consumption center. It is strongly recommended that the hydroelectric program be developed slowly and with full attention to technical details. While hydroelectric power still offers the long-term solution to Nicaragua's power problem, it does not and cannot answer the pressing immediate need for power, since it may be eight to 10 years before hydroelectric power can be developed. Furthermore, there is no guarantee that the hydroelectric development will be within the country's financial means.

Expansion of Generating Facilities

In order to meet the power needs of Managua and vicinity, it is essential that the present inadequate generating facilities be increased immediately to provide a minimum of 10,000 kw of firm power through the addition of diesel or steam units. It is evident that such facilities will be used a minimum of eight to 10 years before hydroelectric power may be available, with the possibility of much longer use if the costs of the hydroelectric development should prove to be beyond the means of the country.

However, the Managua plant might well fit into the future over-all hydroelectric scheme and could also be a factor in reducing the cost of the over-all program. All the projects contemplated thus far will require the storage of water for dry season power generation. Although there are not yet enough known facts, it seems probable that a separate storage dam will be needed for the Tuma project, which could well be the most expensive part of the program.

If a storage dam should prove necessary, a steam plant might be used for stand-by and dry season power, with the hydro program based on the wet season stream flow and using small diversion dams.

In view of these conditions, the best solution for the immediate power needs is the installation of two 5,000 kw steam turbine generators, using the present diesel units for stand-by duty.

Whether steam or diesel power units are chosen, the most important factor, however, is that Managua and the surrounding communities need power now; that hydroelectric power is many years away; and the major portion of the cost of the additional generating equipment can be amortized by the time hydroelectric power is available.

It is recommended that the program should include plans for the early expansion of the transmission lines to Tipitapa and Diriamba. The line to Diriamba is intended to form a part of a loop which will eventually serve Nandaine, Granada, Masaya,

Nindiri and the other communities within this area. Wherever possible, existing generating facilities should be connected to the network for stand-by or peak load power. A third line should be planned for a later stage to go toward Leon and Chinandega.

It will be absolutely essential that the distribution systems of Managua and the other towns be overhauled to enable them to carry increased loads and to reduce the now high line losses to a reasonable figure.

Reorganization of Empresa de Luz y Fuerza Electrica

Along with the technical improvements and installations, a reorganization of the company will be necessary, not only for the increased operating efficiency of present and proposed services but to have an organization capable of taking over the management and operation of the hydroelectric project when it becomes a reality.

The Empresa de Luz y Fuerza Electrica should be divorced as promptly as possible from the national railways administration and established as an autonomous public corporation under a Board of Directors composed jointly of representatives of the government, commerce, industry and agriculture.

When the reorganization has been completed, the company should make every effort to take over, either by outright purchase or exchange of stock, all the small power companies operating in the towns and villages to which the power line will extend. This will reduce administrative costs and increase future operating efficiency by the consolidation of all planning and engineering activities. Simultaneously a firm of public accountants should make an audit of present and past performances to determine the actual assets and liabilities in order to give the new company a realistic capital value. At the same time, a proper system of accounting records and controls should be set up for an accurate assessment of profits, charges for depreciation, operating costs, etc. A proper billing system should be instituted.

The rate structure will need revision with a view to fixing a rate to encourage additional use of power, when efficient equipment has been installed and distribution losses have been reduced to a minimum. In 1951, the total cost of a kilowatt-hour delivered was 0.29 cordobas; users on the 0.3 cordobas rate were therefore receiving power virtually at cost. The new unit now being installed should reduce costs considerably since it will operate on cheaper fuel and have a higher efficiency than the present units.

The goal of the immediate program should be to reduce the cost per kwh delivered to 0.17 cordobas in order to reduce industrial rates to at least 0.21 cordobas per kwh, or to half the present rate. While residential rates are not excessive, lower rates for consumption above 100 kwh per month should act to stimulate consumption. It is expected that the rate reduction would not be so low that it would prevent the company from earning a reasonable return on its investment, including amortization and depreciation of new equipment.

Financing the Expansion Program

It is estimated that the cost of installing the additional equipment will be about $2.7 million and the overhauling and extension of the distribution system about $1.8 million, or a total cost of $4.5 million for the immediate program.

In 1951, the Empresa de Luz y Fuerza Electrica showed a profit of 578,924.92 cordobas on the sale of power and 218,940.03 cordobas on other transactions, principally on sales of supplies. A reduction in distribution losses and other savings now being effected may increase profits by as much as 150,000 cordobas, based on current rates and equipment.

With the installation of the new equipment and distribution system, and an expected tripling of sales within three years, it is believed that net profits will cover depreciation, interest and amortization charges over a 15- to 20-year period on new equipment and still allow for some reduction in industrial rates.

CHAPTER NINE

Minerals

The principal mining has centered around the production of gold and silver, although claims have been denounced for other minerals.

By 1949, some 1,441 mining claims were on file with the government as follows:

Gold and Silver	1,383
Bauxite	7
Antimony	4
Mercury	2
Copper	16
Chromium	1
Tin	1
Beryllium	1
Iron	14
Manganese	2
Molybdenum	2
Platinum	1
Lead	2
Tungsten	3
Vanadium	1
Zinc	1

Of this large number, only a few are being worked at the present time.

An adequate assessment of the mineral possibilities of the country is impossible at present because of the complete lack of basic geological data. It is important that the government undertake the task of determining the full extent of its mineral resources, both metallic and nonmetallic. A systematic geological survey will require many years, and for this reason an early start should be made. Unfortunately, there are no Nicaraguans trained in this work and it will be necessary to request assistance from abroad to organize the program and carry out the field work during the initial stages. At the same time, a training program should be instituted by scholarships and supervised field work to prepare Nicaraguans to take over the ultimate execution of the program.

I. METALLIC MINERALS

Gold and Silver

For many years gold was the principal export in terms of value; in recent years it has been supplanted by coffee. Production has been relatively stable, with some expansion in each year since 1945. In general, the larger mines are increasing production while the smaller ones are reducing output or are stopping work entirely. This is due primarily to the decrease in the free market price of gold and the sudden increase in costs of supplies caused by the Korean outbreak.

Nearly all the gold production is exported. In 1949, for example, the value of production exceeded the value of exports only by an estimated $500,000.

Six mining companies account for nearly all the production. The approximate 1950 output of each in fine ounces was:

La Luz Mines Limited	51,770
Neptune Gold Mining Co.	72,200
Compania Minera La India	26,900
Empresa Minera de Nicaragua . .	47,800
Compania Minera Matagalpa . . .	4,500
Compania Minera del Jabali	25,600

In general, the largest mines are conducting their operations in an efficient manner and have modern mining equipment and processing facilities. The better grade ores run up to $10 per ton in value although one of the companies is working low grade ore worth only $3.50 per ton. Most of the ores contain varying amounts of silver which is recovered with the gold. The product shipped from Nicaragua is the combined gold-silver bullion and actual refining is done abroad.

TABLE 1

Gold and Silver Bullion Exports
(at $35 per ounce)[1]

	Gold		Silver	
	Kgs.	Value (dollars)	Kgs.	Value (dollars)
1939	3,116	3,503,266	7,416	96,227
1940	5,112	5,757,998	7,894	100,149
1941	6,514	7,323,265	8,478	93,553
1942	7,502	8,436,485	8,248	95,500
1943	6,879	7,735,757	7,835	110,694
1944	6,768	7,611,163	7,730	110,066
1945	6,329	7,117,155	7,290	114,450
1946	6,341	7,131,254	7,692	192,453
1947	6,790	7,641,382	6,833	171,331
1948	6,916	7,779,860	6,769	163,931
1949	6,816	7,659,242	6,427	151,556
1950	7,161	8,080,286	5,771	138,751
1951	7,820	8,739,586	6,450	170,554

[1]In recent years practically all gold exports have been made at "free market" prices.

Ore reserves are difficult to estimate. Some companies have been more active than others in exploration work. One company has proved reserves sufficient for nine years and possible reserves for 14 years while another company is working almost on a day-to-day basis, with less than two years' proven reserves.

All mining activities operate under government concessions which grant, among other privileges, freedom from listed taxes and future taxes, and free import of essential supplies and equipment during the term of the contract.

In 1951 the industry paid a total of $132,940 in bullion export taxes (at the rate of $17.00 per kilo) and an estimated 142,382 cordobas ($20,340) as a capital tax. In addition most of the companies maintain schools, police forces, water supplies, and hospitals for the workers and their families as required by the concessions.

It is commonly thought that the gold mining companies are making huge profits and removing large sums from the country each year. While there may have been some element of truth in this in the past, it no longer seems to hold true. It is estimated that the 1951 combined profits did not exceed $1.2 million, amounting to about 15% on gross sales. However, since the total investment of the mining companies is estimated at about $14 million, the above profit represents a return of 8.5% on the investment.

As yet the outlook for the future is favorable, but any further reduction in the free market price or any sharp increase in costs would be a serious threat to the industry.

Copper

Recent explorations by private interests have discovered a copper deposit on the east coast near Rosita. Preliminary studies indicate that the deposit is large enough for commercial exploitation although there are certain metallugical problems associated with the smelting of the ore. If these can be worked out successfully, it is to be expected that mining will be started in the near future. Test borings seem to indicate that the deposit is small and will have only a limited life. No other copper prospects have been discovered to date.

Other Metallic Minerals

The mission has heard many reports concerning deposits of iron, tungsten, and other minerals, but in no case has it been possible to verify these reports or even obtain samples for inspection.

II. *NONMETALLIC MINERALS*

Nicaragua has an abundance of nonmetallic minerals which have been largely overlooked in the search for gold and silver. Clay and limestone are utilized to some extent but their exploitation is on the basis of small, local industries and the products, for the most part, are crudely made and of inferior quality. There are a number of opportunities for the expansion of output and the introduction of new products as the deposits become better known.

Clay

Clays seem to be widely distributed throughout the country although nothing is known about their properties. At present the use of clay is restricted to the manufacture of roofing tiles and soft bricks, which are merely baked rather than fired.

Although there is some manufacturing of clay products in almost every town, the principal production is concentrated near La Paz Central where some 30 small enterprises make from 40,000 to 80,000 bricks and roofing tiles per day, depending upon the weather. Since these are first air dried without protection from the rains, production is reduced during the rainy season.

The clays of Nicaragua need study and testing to determine their properties. Better types of kilns should be introduced so that vitreous tile products can be made. A good market is probable for face bricks, vitreous roofing tile and sanitary pipe, none of which is made in Nicaragua today.

The manufacture of vitreous sanitary and soil pipe is especially recommended, if the proper clays are available, in order to reduce the present heavy imports of cast iron soil pipe. It might also be possible to manufacture a hollow clay tile to be used in building construction.

Limestone

Limestone, like clay, is scattered throughout the country. The major deposits are located along the western coast and are of marine origin. These deposits are highly fossilized, porous and friable and probably run up to 95% calcium carbonate. The cement plant, located at San Rafael del Sur, uses this type of limestone.

There are many small lime kilns throughout the country engaged in burning lime for the construction industry and a small amount for the sugar industry. However, the largest sugar mill imports burned lime because of the variable quality of the local product.

As yet the agricultural uses of lime, which offer the largest potential market for burned or crushed lime, have been overlooked. In agriculture the value of lime is threefold: it neutralizes acid soils; improves the tillability of heavy soils; and supplies calcium, magnesium and often minute quantities of trace elements required by growing crops. The second use, that of improving tillability of heavy soils, is especially important in Nicaragua which has large areas of "sonsocuite" or gumbo soils. Heavy applications of lime plus turning under of green crops should make these soils among the most productive in the country.

Gypsum

Some high grade gypsum deposits are located near Santa Rosa, Leon. This material is used in limited quantities in making cement. No other local use is known although there may be some manufacture of plaster of Paris.

Talc

Some small beds of talc are found in the Boaco area, one of which was found during the construction of the Rama Road. At present, a small amount is being used as a diluent for the insecticides mixed locally.

Sulphur

It is known that there is some sulphur associated with the volcanos of the country but, as with other minerals, nothing is known about the extent or quality of the deposits. With the present critical shortage of sulphur it might be worthwhile to make this a first study of any geological group formed.

Fuels

Although it is claimed that there are coal deposits in Nicaragua, this could not be verified by the mission and until a geological survey is made the presence or absence of coal cannot be ascertained.

Some years ago, some exploratory drilling for petroleum was done in the Puerto Cabezas area. Although no details of this work are known, it is concluded that the results were negative since the work was abandoned after a few tests. In the near future exploratory work is to be started in Costa Rica in the area between Limon and the Nicaraguan border. If these tests are successful it would provide the impetus to make similar tests in the San Juan del Norte area.

CHAPTER TEN

Rehabilitation and Modernization
of the Railroad

If the west coast had to be provided with a completely new transport network, there would be no point in building a railroad like the *Ferrocarril del Pacifico de Nicaragua* to link Managua-Granada with Corinto-Leon-Chinandega. From Managua to Corinto is only 138 kilometers by rail—too short a distance for efficient, low-cost rail haulage. The volume of goods traffic is too small to justify the much greater capital outlay required for a rail line than for equivalent motor roads. (The FCPN has been hauling an average of only 233,000 tons per year from 1947 through 1951.) Most of the carrier's goods traffic is freight in bags, sacks, cartons, cases, etc., which is ordinarily more efficiently hauled by truck. Except for oil, there is practically no heavy freight particularly suited to rail haulage, such as bulk grain, ore, coal, steel, timber, and building materials. Finally, most of the dense passenger traffic (over three million passengers in 1950-1951) would probably be moving by autobus if there were roads over which buses could run.

Traffic Outlook

Although rail traffic has greatly expanded since the war—67% more freight and 30% more passengers, comparing post-1946 with pre-1942 performance—there are good reasons to believe that it is now close to a peak and is more likely to shrink than expand in the foreseeable future. The growing workload in the last few years has been primarily the result of swelling exports and imports, increased internal trade, and a cotton boom on the west coast. Until recently this region had no motor roads at all, and it still lacks any roads by which goods can move between the main productive areas and their main ocean port. This is a temporary situation which will be revolutionized with the completion of roads now being built or programmed. By 1957, if Nicaragua carries out the road projects now under way or in sight, together with the additional projects which the mission believes she ought to undertake, much of the present traffic of the railway will presumably move by truck, bus, or automobile. At a later stage, the possibility of eventual abandonment of FCPN may have to be faced.

The present traffic of FCPN is subject to serious traffic diversion by several road projects now in progress or soon due to start, as follows:

(a) The IBRD-financed roads, as stipulated in the 1951 loan agreement, from Managua to Leon-Chinandega, from Managua to Masaya-Granada, and from the Inter-American Highway south of Managua to San Juan del Sur;

(b) the Rama road, to link the west coast with the east coast via a river-ocean port on the Rio Escondido.

When they are completed in 1955, these roads will attract: (a) the great bulk of the railway's passenger traffic; (b) most of the carrier's goods traffic except export-import freight via Corinto; (c) some of the export-import freight which can go part way by truck. At present, about a third of the railway's operating revenues come from passenger transport and about two thirds from freight haulage. Roughly three fifths of the freight tonnage is domestic goods moving between internal stations, and roughly two fifths is export-import goods going via Corinto.

The Bank-financed road to San Juan del Sur will literally put the railway spur from Rivas out of business, since it will probably be built on the permanent way of this line. When the road is completed, the spur will have to be abandoned in any case, because it will serve no further useful purpose. The carrier will thus be freed of a source of loss rather than deprived of a productive asset.

Completion of the Rama road, including port facilities and waterway dredging as well as the road proper, is bound to cut into the volume of rail-hauled export and import goods now passing through Corinto. Some of these goods are destined for, or come from, overseas areas such as Europe, the Caribbean, the Gulf Coast and Middle Atlantic States of the United States which can be reached more cheaply and quickly via the Rama road prolonged by the Rio Escondido than by ocean freighter out of Corinto with transshipment across the Panama Canal.

Need of FCPN Investment

Despite the unfavorable traffic outlook because of the road network which will ultimately crisscross its service area, the FCPN is capable of rendering essential services to the economy for an indefinite period ahead. It should be kept in good operating condition until, if ever, it becomes certain that there is no sizeable fraction of the west coast's export, import, and internal trade which cannot be hauled more efficiently by truck or bus than by rail. True, the line may cease to be a vital adjunct of the west coast economy, if, as, and when the pending road from Managua to Chinandega is extended to reach Corinto. For the time being, however, total abandonment of the FCPN is out of the question because no Corinto road exists. Nor has any clear-cut project to construct such a road yet been formulated. Construction could not in any case start before 1957 at the earliest, in view of prior commitments of the resources of the Highway Department and of Nicaragua's development budget.

Although ultimately a Chinandega-Corinto road may be justified, the advisability of constructing one in the next few years is doubtful.

In the first place, improvement of the existing rail line would probably cost much less than its total replacement by truck and bus facilities, which would involve in addition to construction of a Corinto road proper, construction of feeder roads to replace

FCPN branch lines, transformation of Corinto from a railway port into a truck port, and expansion of the motor vehicle fleet.

Secondly, with modest improvements the railroad could provide much more efficient and reliable service at much lower charges than at present, particularly if it concentrates on shuttle haulage between Corinto and a few main upline stations such as Chinandega, Leon, and Managua.

On the other hand, as closely as we can calculate, it would cost a minimum of $5 million merely to correct the major flaws—e.g. rundown track, obsolete rolling stock, underequipped repair shops —which have grown up in the last 10 to 15 years because of neglect of renewals, upkeep, and maintenance. A thorough overhaul would cost several times as much and would be equivalent, in fact, to building and equipping a complete new line. Considering the range and urgency of Nicaragua's developmental needs, her limited financial means, and the imminence of a road network on the west coast, there are much better uses for the investment funds at Nicaragua's disposal than total renovation of a rail property which will soon have outlived much of its present usefulness.

It would nevertheless be a sound investment, in the mission's opinion, to refit the FCPN for more efficient performance of certain limited but vital functions on the hypothesis that the carrier has a useful life of at least 10 to 15 years. These functions are the carriage of export-import freight out of Corinto and interurban transit between Managua and Leon-Chinandega. The main reasons for proposing that the line be refitted sufficiently to do this work are:

(a) The tremendous immediate outlay for new roads, port works, motor vehicles, etc., which immediate abandonment of the FCPN would necessitate;

(b) the multitude of farms, plantations, cattle ranches, etc., alongside or close to the permanent way of the FCPN's main line which could be efficiently serviced by a well-equipped, well-run rail carrier;

(c) the various sugar mills, brick works, power plants, ware-houses, and grain silos on the FCPN's main line which are presently set up to operate as railroad-serviced installations;

(d) the penetration of branch lines of FCPN into areas such as El Sauce and Puerto Morazan which have no access except by rail and lie outside the main thrust of the road-building program as presently conceived.

Although the mission recommends partial rehabilitation and modernization of the FCPN, it also recommends abandonment of some of the existing facilities when certain new roads now under construction come into service. Specifically, it suggests that the isolated spur to San Juan del Sur ought to be scrapped; that the lines from Managua to Masaya-Granada-Diriamba are also dispensable; and that most of the minor stations on the main line from Managua to Leon-Chinandega can be shut down a few years from now.

Program of Action

Refitting the FCPN for its reduced but essential functions ahead calls for prompt action along the following broad lines:

(a) Rehabilitation of the permanent way by some ballasting and some relaying of ties and rails on the most badly worn stretches downline from Managua;

(b) modernization of motive power by replacing the older of the oil-burning steam locomotives now in service by a few new diesel-electric engines;

(c) modernization of rolling stock by purchasing a few new rail cars to run in interurban transit between Managua and Leon-Chinandega-Corinto, and a few new freight cars capable of fast, heavy-duty work in shuttle haulage out of Corinto;

(d) re-equipment of repair shops by procuring some specialized facilities for the maintenance of diesel-electrics, rail cars, and modern wagons.

Improving the permanent way between Managua and Corinto is the most basic job of all. Long stretches of the main line are poorly ballasted (a thin covering of loose, coarse sand) or are hardly ballasted at all. The existing crossties are not only worn and rotting in large measure but are made from crooked, twisted logs of untreated low-grade timber. There has been no significant replacement of rail (60 lb. mainly) in the last 15 years or so. As a result, trains cannot run faster than 50 kilometers an hour (top running speed on open stretches without allowance for the need to reduce speed near stations, around curves, on grades, and approaching water tanks) and cannot carry more than 400 tons of goods (assuming a train of 20 cars carrying 20 tons each). It would thus be sheer waste to buy new traction capable of moving heavier trains faster without simultaneously preparing the roadbed to take such trains.

Most of the 24 main-line road-haul locomotives of the FCPN are long overdue for scrapping because of age, wear, and technical deficiencies. All of them are oil-burning steam engines dating back to the pre-diesel age. Considering the efficiency, reliability, and serviceability of diesel-electrics and their exceptional savings of fuel cost, the existing FCPN engines are functionally obsolete. Almost three fourths of the aggregate tractive effort is more than 25 years old and three fifths is more than 40 years old, including several museum pieces from the 1880's and 1890's. Only a fourth of the total capacity is less than 20 years of age; i.e. several 1928-1929 engines plus a pair of 1936 units. Many of the engines, including some of the newest, were bought second hand after heavy prior usage. Several of these are former broad-gauge engines which had to be converted, with serious loss of operational efficiency, to the special 42" gauge of the FCPN. The inevitable result of operating such a worn, aged fleet is frequent re-shopping for major overhauls—in the case of some of the oldest engines, every 600 kilometers. Even at the peak of the seasonal upswing in freight traffic from December through March some 35-40% of the motive power is immobilized for repairs. In the best of circumstances, only 16 engines out of the fleet of 24 are actually at work on the main line.

Despite autobus competition to come, the FCPN might be able to retain much of its passenger traffic if it could offer fast, frequent, and comfortable interurban transit downline from Managua. No such service is possible with the old, decrepit, and cramped coaches which comprise the present fleet. Moreover, to economize on motive power, the coaches are run in mixed freight-passenger trains which stop at every station. Auto-rail coaches propelled by their own internal-combustion engines would seem to be the obvious solution, as European experience has shown them to be fast, comfortable, and efficient. Further, if passenger traffic is carried by auto-rail coaches, the new diesel-electrics and such of the old steam locomotives as may be worth retaining can be concentrated on the urgent task of moving export-import freight.

Operating about 240 freight cars in all, the FCPN has wagons to spare during the slack season but too few wagons to move goods promptly during the busy season. At the time of the mission's visit practically all of the freight cars were out at work on the line, leaving no reserve capacity whatever in the face of urgent pressure for more and more cars to clear bulging sheds and warehouses. Few, if any, of these aged and overworked cars are fit for high-speed, heavy-duty service, and it might be more costly to rehabilitate than to replace many, perhaps most, of them. It is thus arguable that the FCPN ought to be ordering new freight cars not only to relieve peakload pressure but also, if the mission's suggestion for a shuttle operation out of Corinto is put into force, to be better equipped for the kind of work ahead. All the freight car needs of the immediate future can be met by purchasing new wagons to the equivalent of 15-20% of the effective capacity of the present fleet.

Estimates of Costs

The total job of rehabilitating and modernizing FCPN for its limited but vital functions of the next 10-15 years, need not cost more than the equivalent of $2 million. Part of this cost, such as some of the cross-tie replacements, might be regarded as current rather than capital expenditure while another part can be recovered from the proceeds of scrapping present facilities unfit for further use such as obsolete motive power and rolling stock, and rail from abandoned stretches of line. The net capital expenditure would thus be measurably less than $2 million; say $1.75 million as a rough order of magnitude.

On the basis of discussions of each project with the FCPN management, the mission recommends a five-year program of gross capital expenditure as follows:

(a) Reballasting almost the entire 138 kilometers of roadbed between Corinto to Managua at a total cost of $300,000. This allows $275,000 for materials, labor, and haulage, and $25,000 for a small crushing plant;

(b) replacing the bulk of the present cross-ties on the Corinto-Managua main line by higher quality logs at a gross cost of $300,000. Of this only half, or $150,000, need be charged to capital expenditure since, at the normal rate at which FCPN replaces cross-ties, the rest would be charged to current maintenance;

(c) relaying some 3,000 tons of rail, about a fourth of the required effort, for complete rehabilitation. The total cost is estimated at $325,000 of which $300,000 would be for rail, $15,000 for switches, and $10,000 for labor;

(d) replacing all the pre-1925 locomotives by four new 600 HP diesel-electrics at a c.i.f. cost of roughly $425,000. Embodying 94,400 lbs. of continuous tractive effort and giving 95% serviceability in normal use, these diesel-electrics can provide the full equivalent in practical work capacity of the 320,000 lbs. of nominal tractive effort they would replace;

(e) replacing about a third of the effective capacity of the 43 passenger coaches now in service by three new rail cars seating 90 passengers each and capable of running several round trips a day each between Managua and Corinto, at a c.i.f. cost of perhaps $325,000;

(f) procuring perhaps 30 new freight cars fit for high-speed, heavy-duty work in shuttle runs out of Corinto at a c.i.f. cost of roughly $175,000;

(g) procuring some specialized tools for the maintenance of the new diesel-electrics and rail cars at an installed cost on the order of $150,000.

Since the rehabilitation and modernization as recommended by the mission will take several years, it would not relieve the immediate traffic strain on FCPN. Primarily, this is a peak load problem. During most of the year the carrier's facilities are used at a fraction of capacity, but from December through March, when cotton, coffee, sesame, and other crops are simultaneously harvested, the facilities are overloaded. Shippers during the busy season cannot get all the cars they need as fast as they need them. Merchandise piles up in warehouses and sheds with serious risks of loss from fire. There is spoilage and deterioration of perishable goods for home market use. Part of the trouble is the lack of enough freight cars in good operating condition to service the peak movement. More basic shortcomings, as already mentioned, are inadequate traction and inadequate roadbed aggravated by underutilization of the existing equipment.

The present seasonal strain could be measurably alleviated by using rolling stock more intensively during the traffic upsurge from December through March. The necessary reforms require no investment at all and they can and should be put into effect even before the FCPN gets started on the general rehabilitation program recommended by the mission. Some of the specific correctives are:

(a) operating freight trains separately from passenger trains as far as the availability of motive power permits;

(b) rescheduling freight service so as to move a maximum of freight at night, a minimum during the day;

(c) running nonstop freight trains at night between Corinto and the main upline stations;

(d) reassigning locomotives so that the most powerful work in freight service and the least powerful in passenger service;

(e) increasing the present demurrage charges of 50 cordobas per car per day payable by carload shippers who hold wagons more than 12 hours during the peak season. There is no need, however, to raise slack season demurrage of only 10 cordobas per car per day;

(f) collecting advance forecasts several weeks ahead from merchants, finca owners, and industrial plants, as to their freight car requirements from December through March;

(g) coordinating freight-train schedules in the peak season with the scheduled arrival and departure of freighters at Corinto;

(h) as a last resort, if no other corrective suffices, introducing a system of priorities for the haulage of essential freight to be applied only at the height of the seasonal upsurge.

Financing of Investment Effort

The mission believes that the net expenditure of $1.75 million to rehabilitate and modernize the FCPN would be a sound investment, but that the entire cost can and should be met out of the carrier's own revenues, without recourse to the national budget. If the FCPN is now poorly equipped and badly run down, it is not for lack of income out of which to maintain and improve the property. Instead, the railroad has earned genuine and substantial profits above sizeable depreciation charges for many years past. These are by no means as large as published reports might suggest, but sufficiently large to have kept the property in good shape. Instead of being used for improvement and renewals, however, the earnings and depreciation charges have been partly diverted to noncarrier functions and partly wasted by questionable purchases of secondhand equipment, inadvisable salvage and conversion work, and abortive efforts at line expansion.

Given its present traffic and tariffs, the FCPN is a profitable enterprise which can continue earning substantial profits for at least the next five years, pending the emergence of a comprehensive mesh of good roads on the west coast. In fiscal 1950-51, according to the carrier's accounts as adjusted by the mission, net operating income approximated 3.15 million cordobas after depreciation charges of 520,000 cordobas. It was earned on a transport property valued at 22.5 million cordobas after depreciation reserves of 6.9 million cordobas so that the rate of return was about 14%. Although data for 1951-52 are not yet available, there is every reason to expect that the earnings for the full year will be at least as good as, if not better than, those of 1950-51.

The mission does not argue that the handsome earnings of 1950-51 and 1951-52 are apt to continue indefinitely, or even that they represent normal performance at a particular level of gross national product. They have been realized from much higher freight rates than the FCPN ought to be charging unless the carrier is to be thought of as a state venture in monopolistic transport, concerned with getting maximum revenues for the state. For want of motorable roads there has been no truck and bus competition. World-wide stockpiling after Korea has helped to bring about an upswing in traffic. Assuming a reduction of freight rates on the theory that reasonable transport charges are more essential for Nicaragua's welfare than a maximum of FCPN profit, and allowing for traffic diversion after the completion of the Bank-financed roads several years from now, the carrier's earning power over the next five years is likely to fall measurably short of its present earning power.

The mission has no precise forecast of 1952-57 earnings to put forward. We suggest, however, as a prudent working hypothesis striking an average between the lush earnings of 1950-51 (about 3.15 million cordobas) and the much smaller earnings of 1949-50 (about 1.44 million cordobas), when 10% less goods traffic was carried at 20% lower freight rates. The resulting average approximates 2.3 million cordobas a year; if earnings continued at this level for five years this would yield about 11.4 million cordobas equivalent to $1.6 million or close to the net cost—$1.75 million —of all the improvements recommended by the mission. This is profit after depreciation charges, an additional source of funds out of which to pay for renewals and replacements. Judging by the 1950-51 set-aside of 520,000 cordobas on account of depreciable rail and lake transport properties, depreciation charges for five years ought to bring in a minimum of 2.6 million cordobas equivalent to $370,000.

If the carrier is re-equipped and refitted as recommended by the mission, this postulate of average earnings from mid-1952 through mid-1957, about 25-30% below recent performance, is likely to prove an understatement. Huge operating economies should result from the new locomotives and cars, and the improved permanent way. The diesel-electrics alone, for example, should be able to return their full purchase price in five years through fuel savings and reduced maintenance costs. No trucks and buses will be running over the Managua-Leon-Chinandega route before 1955, so that short of a collapse of world trade or a slump in the Nicaraguan economy, the FCPN's goods traffic is likely to hold up well for the next five years. By abandoning certain lines as the IBRD-financed roads come into service, the FCPN could free itself from certain localized operating losses and some low-yield properties. Finally, our analysis of the carrier's earning power has made no allowance for income from rentals, fees, and other nontransport sources yielding 520,000 cordobas in 1950-51, but only 93,000 cordobas in 1949-50.

In short, we believe the FCPN is easily capable of paying for its improvements out of its own revenues over the next five years.

Need of Administrative Reforms

Improvement of the FCPN's motive power, rolling stock, and permanent way will have to be accompanied, in the mission's opinion, by a thorough overhaul of the carrier's administrative organization and procedures. Unless this is done the enterprise will be unable to work with reasonable efficiency, regardless of the means of transport at its disposal. First, the FCPN needs to be sheltered against pressure tending to divert its resources to non-carrier purposes. It should have a competent management empowered to determine operational policies without political interference. Finally, it should apply the same financial, accounting, and inventory controls as would a well-run railroad under private ownership. At present, none of these conditions is satisfied. This is perhaps the basic reason why the FCPN is badly run down, why it gives poor service at high charges, and why its earnings have been largely dissipated or misapplied.

As a state-owned carrier and thus a kind of public corporation in form, if not practice, the FCPN is attached to and under the immediate control of the President of the Republic. Immediately below the Chief Executive is the General Manager, a presidential appointee, who is nominally in full charge of operational activities.

Because of its direct subjection to the executive authority of the state, the FCPN can be and has been used as a source of materials, labor, and funds to help carry out a large variety of projects which have nothing to do with the operation of a railroad, a lake fleet, or rail-linked ports. Typical examples range from port construction where no rail lines reach, or are needed, to financing the acquisition of the Managua power plant. Regardless of the intrinsic merits of this extra-curricular work, the essential point is that the FCPN has been deprived of sufficient means to renew, improve, and modernize its transport properties, and thereby prevented from performing its carrier functions with reasonable efficiency.

The operating officials of the FCPN manage the property in a loose and haphazard manner. Although the property is state-owned, its accounts are unaudited except by its own personnel. There is no budgeting, except for the preparation of a list of salaries, plus lump sum estimates for equipment, materials, and supplies. Inventories are neither policed with ordinary prudence to avert losses and waste nor managed with ordinary care to forestall excessive accumulation and serious depletion. No systematic effort is made to foresee equipment needs, to assess traffic trends, or to work out specific costs. No accounting effort is made to reconcile the total inflow of cash receipts with the total outflow of cash disbursements. In short, the railway runs more by inertia than by management.

The managerial shortcomings under the present regime may be clarified by some specific examples.

Despite its bad state of disrepair, the carrier has no capital-improvement program, not even the sketchiest plans or projects. Instead of renewing facilities according to definite rules of service life, the FCPN renews them strictly *ad hoc,* that is, after they break down, or wear out. Supplies and materials as inventoried once a year are much smaller than they should be from the accounting records of initial stock plus additions minus withdrawals. Some of the ostensible holdings of materials and supplies carried as current assents in the published balance sheet are in fact plant and equipment never capitalized as such; i.e. locomotives, freight cars, and rails bought secondhand many years ago. Substantial amounts of materials and labor, including amounts which the published accounts do not disclose, have been and continue to be utilized in a questionable effort to build a breakwater and a pier at Masachapa, a road-serviced port which is not even rail-linked with the FCPN network. Other large sums are being used to salvage and reconvert craft for service on Lake Nicaragua with no prior analysis of the eventual costs relative to the eventual benefit. Part of the expenditure for line construction and maintenance as set forth in the FCPN accounts may conceal outlay for properties which do not belong to the carrier. Instead of giving all of his time and effort to supervision in a broad sense, the FCPN's General Manager has to give most of it to supervising the overhaul of locomotives, cars, and coaches in the main repair shop at Managua.

Recommended Reforms

If the FCPN is to become an efficient tool of basic transport, it must first be set up as a public enterprise with definite terms of reference to which all of its resources have to be applied and beyond which none of them can be expended. The proper functions of the FCPN, as the mission envisages them, are common carriage by rail, perhaps some lake transport as well, and the operation of rail-linked ports. This should be expressly recognized by an organic statute in the form of a law, decree, or charter as convenient. It should be spelled out by a precise statement of the functions which the FCPN is competent to perform and a definite prohibition against the use of its material, manpower, and working funds for any other purposes.

Specifically, the mission recommends that the FCPN be reorganized to take the form of an autonomous public utility corporation free from interference by other governmental departments and officials, in the use of its equipment, materials, labor, and funds. It should be run as a commercialized public utility subject to the state's claim, as owner of the property, to a reasonable return on the investment. Like other public corporations elsewhere, the reorganized FCPN should be under the control of a Board of Directors with prescribed functions, duties, and responsibilities. Since the carrier is a state-owned public utility, it is arguable that the Directors should be various ministers ex officio (perhaps the same ministers who comprise the National Economic Council) plus representatives of the railroad's users such as farmers, industrialists, and merchants. What matters, in any case, is not the precise composition of the Board but the control of the property by executives expressly charged to concentrate its resources on its own work.

In line with ordinary railway practice, the Board of Directors should be empowered to name a General Manager who would be authorized to select his own top staff such as the Chief Mechanic, the Maintenance of Way Superintendent, the Train Dispatcher, and the Chief Accountant. It is essential that the General Manager be an experienced railway specialist who gives all his time, effort, and duties to top management in the sense of deciding basic issues of operational, financial, and administrative policy. None of his energy should be dissipated on technical routine such as the repair of rolling stock, the supervision of line construction or train formation and dispatching. It is possible the Board of Directors will have to go outside Nicaragua to find a qualified technician for this job. The mission refrains from recommending the employment of a foreign manager because it is not convinced that capable Nicaraguan personnel are unobtainable.

If the FCPN were organized like most state-owned railroads elsewhere its labor force, except the top management, would be organized along career lines; i.e. permanent status after a probationary period and in-service promotion within a clearly-defined structure of duties and salaries. The mission does not propose an FCPN civil service since this would be impractical in a country which has no governmental civil service. What we do recommend is to make FCPN employment an attractive career for qualified personnel by applying certain practices common to well-run railroads, for example, selective hiring of staff, promotion by merit, and security of tenure for workers of demonstrated competence.

For the next five years, rehabilitation and modernization of the FCPN along the lines of the mission's diagnosis ought to be regarded as a first charge on its earnings ahead of the Treasury's claim to interest or dividends. This is necessary in order to simplify the financing of the program recommended and to strengthen the likelihood of its being carried out. We do not mean to imply that the FCPN should have carte blanche to go ahead with the self-financing of its rehabilitation and modernization. Instead, we suggest that a definite schedule of projects be drafted for submission to the National Economic Council as a part of the total budget of public investment, and that the carrier be empowered to carry out as much of the NEC-approved program as the government authorizes.

We stress immediate budgeting for rehabilitation and modernization, because certain improvements are urgent. Capital expenditure budgets, however, are not an emergency tool to be applied once and then laid aside. On the contrary the mission is convinced that the FCPN cannot hope to be well equipped for its post-1957 tasks unless it develops the habit of programming the purchase of new facilities well in advance of their actual need. The mission recommends periodic preparation, say at five-year intervals, and continuous review of a complete schedule of gross capital expenditure, to include not only outlay for renewals and replacements but for expansion. This budget should be the fruit of close study by the management of all the basic factors affecting the carrier's equipment needs. Such a study must take account not only of the expected service life of existing facilities, their actual wear and functional obsolesence, but also traffic trends as affected by the growth of the west coast region, the evolution of Nicaragua's export trade, and competition from trucks and buses.

In preparing the capital budget, the FCPN will necessarily have to program expected funds by source as well as required expenditure by purpose. Part of the outlay can be financed out of depreciation charges, and perhaps another part by some retained earnings above interest and dividends payable to the Treasury. The bulk of the funds, however, will probably have to be found as

additional loan or equity capital to be subscribed by the state to
the extent that the government is willing and able to finance railroad projects as part of the public investment program. In any
case, under the reorganization proposed by the mission government approval of the budget would be required before the FCPN
could undertake any capital expenditure.

Necessary Accounting Reforms

Simultaneously with administrative reorganization of the
FCPN, a reputable firm of certified public accountants should
undertake a complete audit of the carrier's books. No other means
will suffice, the mission is convinced, to ascertain the actual assets
and liabilities of the FCPN, or to determine true earnings and
their specific utilization. Although the present accounting is based
on sound concepts, forms, and procedures inherited from a
former United States management, their actual application has
deteriorated to such a degree that the carrier's financial status and
performance has become a riddle which expert accountants alone
are competent to unlock. Some of the obscurities which need to
be cleared up are: the extent and value of the carrier's free haulage of governmental freight and passengers in lieu of cash dividends; the impact on earnings of non-transport services rendered
free of charge to public and quasi-public bodies; the exact status
of some old plant and equipment which is now carried as a current asset; the reconciliation of physical inventories with recorded
inventories, adjusted for additions and withdrawals; the adequacy
of depreciation charges now computed at 5% per year of the
original cost of depreciable rail and lake transport properties; the
meaning and scope of various internal reserves which are seeming-
ly used to absorb or augment operating income as convenient; and
the balancing of cash disbursements for all purposes with cash
receipts from all sources.

In addition to auditing the FCPN accounts so as to clarify its
financial structure, the accounting consultants should set up a

proper system of records and controls. These are indispensable tools of efficient management for any type of commercial enterprise whether state-owned or privately owned. Without them, the executives and officials of the reorganized FCPN will have no reliable way to measure revenues and costs, assess profits, evaluate inventories, provide adequate depreciation, and control the utilization of revenue. It might be convenient to apply much the same accounting rules as those prescribed by the Interstate Commerce Commission for Class 1 carriers in the United States. The mission recognizes, however, that other rules may be more suitable in the specific circumstances of the FCPN. Be this as it may, it is essential to replace the amorphous accounting now in use by a rigorous, clear-cut system.

Particularly urgent, in the mission's opinion, is the need to introduce effective methods for keeping continuous track of inventories, controlling their volume, and safeguarding their utilization.

Following the initial audit and after the introduction of adequate accounting controls, the books of the FCPN should be examined regularly by independent accountants. Their job would be to verify the balance sheet, the income and expense statement, and all accompanying exhibits. They ought to certify the formal reports as submitted to the government and the public.

Review of FCPN Tariffs

In recommending that the FCPN be transformed into a public utility seeking a reasonable return on the investment, the mission is far from taking the present structure of freight rates and passenger fares for granted. On the contrary, we believe it ought to be reviewed at once by qualified specialists in railway tariffs. Present charges for the carriage of export, import, and internal goods are extremely high by comparison with other railroads in other underdeveloped countries. They average about U.S. 7.6¢ per U.S. ton-mile (1950-51 experience) compared with an average of U.S. 3.0¢ for the Belgian Congo, U.S. 4.2¢ for Ethiopia, U.S. 5.8¢ for

Colombia, and U.S. 6.3¢ for Surinam. Passenger fares, in contrast, are definitely on the low side, averaging only U.S. 1¢ per passenger-mile.

An appropriate tariff structure, in the mission's opinion, would aim to yield no less but no more than a reasonable return on the state's investment. The mission does not suggest a particular rate, except to note that it ought to be fixed with an eye to stimulating production and trade through cheap transport rather than reflecting prevailing investment yields in Nicaragua. However, certain high freight rates equivalent to import taxes on luxury items need not be disturbed. Because of traffic uncertainties, the tariffs as redrafted might yield more or less than anticipated. In either case, they should be modified accordingly; decreased in the event of excess profits but increased if there are insufficient profits.

Limiting the FCPN to a reasonable return as suggested would imply renunciation by the government of use of the FCPN as a fiscal tool to bring in a maximum revenue for the Treasury. Admittedly, the potential loss of revenue might be considerable in view of the high freight rates now in force, the FCPN's monopoly status until the road network is greatly enlarged, and the immediate outlook for the growth of Nicaragua's production and trade in a prosperous world economy. But it is dubious wisdom to use a state-owned railroad to maximize treasury revenues in a country where economic development would be immediately and greatly stimulated by cheaper haulage of freight.

Practical reasons as well as policy considerations argue for proportioning the FCPN's tariff structure to the requirements of a reasonable return. The carrier's prospects of retaining a sizeable fraction of its present traffic volume as more and better roads come to be built are largely conditional on a reduction of its freight rates to make them competitive with trucking charges. At present, from what the mission could learn, the ordinary charges for truck-hauled goods on the west coast are of the rough order of U.S. 5¢ per U.S. ton-mile. This is 35-40% cheaper than the railroad's average of U.S. 7.6¢ per ton-mile, a wide differential to divert almost all FCPN freight capable of moving by truck wherever motorable roads are built. It is already causing perceptible diversion wherever the existing roads permit some seasonal truck haulage, for example, exports via San Juan del Sur and trade between the Managua and Granada areas. Unless the rates are reduced the FCPN is likely to lose traffic so heavily and so fast with the gradual emergence of a good road network on the west coast that prompt total abandonment might become a measure of simple prudence to avert large operating losses at the expense of the state.

Assuming, however, that the FCPN does reduce freight rates, the mission foresees no serious impairment of its ability to pay a reasonable return on the necessary investment to rehabilitate and modernize the property. Lower rates would help to bring back, or prevent the loss of a substantial volume of freight otherwise apt to move by truck, thus tending to sustain gross revenues. The new locomotives, new freight cars, new rail cars, and the improved permanent way are bound to cut operating costs to a mere fraction of the present costs per ton-mile. It is also probable that passenger fares can be raised considerably for railcar transport on fast, frequent schedule without adversely affecting the volume of traffic.

Other Reorganization Measures

Finally, in the belief that a railroad should concentrate on carrier work without engaging in extraneous activities, the mission recommends:

(a) Divestment of the FCPN from its nominal ownership of the Managua Light and Power Company (Empresa de Luz y Fuerza Electrica).

(b) Suspension of the FCPN's effort to transform Masachapa into a sheltered ocean port.

(c) Abandonment of the FCPN's transport services on Lake Nicaragua if the line from Managua to Granada is also abandoned.

Conclusion

To sum up, the mission recommends a net investment of $1.75 million to improve the FCPN's means of haulage, contingent on administrative and fiscal reform of the entire property. The mission believes that the usual services which a reorganized and re-equipped railroad would be capable of rendering over the next 10 to 15 years fully justify an expenditure of this size. Moreover, even with lower freight rates we believe that the entire cost can be met out of the carrier's internal revenues, particularly in view of the operating economies the new equipment will make possible. If, as seems likely, there are profits over and above the amount required to bring the carrier back into good shape, these should flow to the state as an additional source of development funds, instead of being diverted to noncarrier purposes or wasted on carrier projects of limited value.

CHAPTER ELEVEN

Construction and Improvement
of Roads

Transport investment to stimulate economic growth will have to concentrate on the construction and improvement of roads. Above all, Nicaragua needs a comprehensive network of main roads on the west coast, supplemented by local meshes of feeder, access, and farm-to-market routes throughout the country. Because of the limited mileage of existing main roads, the bulk of the long-haul trade of the west coast must now be carried by rail. Much, probably most, of it is more suitable for truck transport considering the length of haul, volume of traffic, and type of goods. Existing local roads are for the most part mere trails fit only for beasts of burden so that most local trade moves by oxcart and pack mule, an extremely expensive, slow and inefficient form of transport compared with motor haulage.

I. *NECESSITY OF BETTER ROADS*

For want of good roads, the foreign and internal trade of Nicaragua is burdened with transport charges many times heavier than it need carry. Trucking charges approximate U.S. 5¢ per ton-mile for ordinary loads moving over ordinary routes. Rail haulage, measured by the average charges of the FCPN, costs about U.S. 7.6¢ per ton-mile. Oxcart or pack mule carriage exacts a minimum of U.S. 50¢ per ton-mile. If these rates are applied to an average carload (12 short tons) of FCPN freight moving 45 miles by rail and perhaps 10 miles by farm-to-market trails, the cost comes to at least $100. In contrast, a motor truck operating over good roads all the way could do the entire job for, at most, $35.

Nicaragua needs good roads not only to reduce the burden of

inland transport charges but also to expand the existing capacity of her transport arteries and to open for development new productive areas which are now inaccessible. In its present state, the FCPN is unable to absorb a large volume of additional freight. In the peak season it is already experiencing acute strain so that any large increase in the present peakload is likely to paralyze operations. Further, the FCPN network is limited to west coast regions which are already under intensive cultivation.

Expansion of the carrier's line and tractive capacity is hardly the answer to the problem. In the circumstances of west coast traffic motor transport has inherent advantages over rail transport. As for local haulage, its superiority over beasts of burden is too obvious to need comment. Suffice it to say that if Nicaragua should content herself with improving or adding to existing trails rather than replacing them by genuine roads, her economic growth would be delayed.

II. ROAD-BUILDING PROGRAM

Before considering specific road projects, a brief review of the accomplishments of the past 15 years is in order. Shortly before World War II, there were almost no motorable roads. Today, the beginning of a comprehensive network has emerged on the west coast. It includes the Inter-American Highway with certain branches, the initial stretches of the projected Rama road, the IBRD-financed roads now under construction, and first-class local roads to Masachapa and Poneloya. Within a few years, if the government's plans are carried out, the Rama Road will reach its final terminus on the Rio Escondido. No definite plan for a Chinandega-Corinto road has yet been drafted but a project to make the port of Corinto accessible by road as well as by rail is already under discussion.

Existing main roads, plus those now under construction, represent a total investment of the order of $22 million (not included in this sum are some large but indeterminable expenditures by the United States Army). This is outlay for initial construction alone, with no allowance for the cost of upkeep and repairs to date or for interest payments on borrowed funds. Close to three fifths, or about $12.5 million, is road-building at the expense of the Nicaraguan Government; i.e. outlays financed out of taxes (about $7 million) and by external debt. More than two fifths, or roughly $9.5 million, has been provided by the United States in the form of grants to finance Nicaraguan road-building under the supervision of the U. S. Bureau of Public Roads or by the U. S. Army. These grants have paid for most of the cost of the Nicaraguan stretches of the Inter-American Highway, and the bulk of the cost of the Rama road as far as the route has been carried. A 1940 loan from the Export Import Bank ($2 million) was used to supplement other available funds for the construction of the Inter-American Highway. A 1951 loan from the International Bank ($3.5 million) is being used to build a mesh of high-grade roads fanning, for the most part, out of Managua. These will eventually blanket most of the traffic area now serviced by the FCPN.

III. *RESULTS OF ROAD-BUILDING EFFORT*

The investment to date of $22 million for better roads has yielded a rich return to the Nicaraguan economy. Wherever the mission travelled, there was impressive evidence of development stimulated directly and powerfully by good roads. Where, before the roads, there had been subsistence agriculture at most, there now exist cattle ranches, dairy farms, cotton plantations, and other commercial farming. Whole areas and communities once virtually isolated from the capital, now trade with it daily. Trucks carrying vegetables, fruits, and other produce from hinterlands which previously had no cash crops, now move to towns whose fresh food was formerly limited to what the immediate vicinity could supply. In a few hours autobuses loaded to capacity make trips which used to take a handful of passengers days or weeks.

The Inter-American Highway in particular has already given rise to a good deal of international freight haulage between Managua and El Salvador/Honduras. It is being used for commercial transport instead of pleasure travel in the approximate ratio of four trucks and buses to each automobile.

Expenditure to extend and perfect the road network can fairly be considered as outlay for a highly productive purpose. This means not that roads necessarily merit a higher priority than other basic facilities such as water supply, sewers, schools, hospitals, and electric power, but that, selected with reasonable care, more and better roads will stimulate Nicaragua's economic growth immediately and directly. Road building should therefore go ahead as rapidly as the prior or equal claims of other urgently-needed improvements permit.

Predetermined Road Projects

Much of the actual outlay for road construction and improvement over the next five years is already determined by projects which are under way or committed or which are scheduled for execution as soon as United States grants become available. These include improvement of the Inter-American Highway by agreement with the United States, completion of the International Bank roads, and extension of the Rama Road to a final terminus on the Rio Escondido. Each of these projects, in the mission's judgment, is essential or at least manifestly useful. Each of them would warrant inclusion in the recommended road program on its own merits.

Inter-American Highway

Definite plans to improve the Inter-American Highway, particularly the northern stretches from Sebaco to the Honduras border, have been formulated by the Ministry of Public Works in collaboration with the United States Bureau of Public Roads. The route as it now exists is to be realigned and hard-surfaced, its grades and curves reduced, and permanent bridges installed. The section from the Honduras border to Managua will be made into a high-class road of the same quality as the Managua-Rivas section, and thus fit to carry a heavy volume of interregional and international trade. The total cost to improve the Sebaco-Trinidad-Esteli-Honduras stretches approximates $6 million. One third is to be paid by Nicaragua, and two thirds by the United States.

The United States Congress has recently authorized an appropriation of $8 million a year from mid-1952 through mid-1954 to pay for the United States' share of further work over the entire length of the Inter-American Highway. This is a first step in a larger program for completing the Inter-American Highway to high standards all the way from Mexico to Panama. Assuming that a seven-year program of $56 million is eventually authorized, the mission believes that the U. S. Bureau of Public Roads is prepared to allot $4 million for the Nicaraguan stretches subject to matching funds of $2 million by the Nicaraguan Government.

International Bank Roads

Despite some delay in deliveries of road-building equipment, the main road projects being financed by the $3.5 million from the International Bank in 1951 are in full swing. The entire program should be completed, assuming that equipment is delivered on schedule, by early 1955. It will provide Nicaragua with a road mesh radiating out of Managua into mature areas (Masaya-Granada and Leon-Chinandega) plus some developmental roads into growth areas such as Jinotega and the Tuma Valley. Total costs are of the order of $5 million, including local currency to be provided by the government as well as the dollar proceeds of the International Bank loan.

As of mid-1952 about $3.5 million remained to be expended. Of this amount undisbursed proceeds of the Bank loan approximate $2.5 million. Unutilized commitments of local currency come to around $1 million.

Rama Project

The Rama project is a proposed artery (road-river-ocean) which will serve a triple purpose: provide an east coast outlet for west coast trade, reduce the transport costs of interregional commerce, and open some crop, pasture and timber lands which are presently inaccessible. Equally as important from the government's viewpoint, an east-west route will help to speed the social, political and economic unification of a country now divided into separate regional economies for want of a transport link. To create that link, the existing road which runs 160 kilometers southeast from the Inter-American Highway would be extended 100 kilometers to Rama on the Rio Escondido; the entire route would be constructed or converted to much the same specifications as the best stretches of the Inter-American Highway; Rama would be equipped with a small port to service ocean freighters drawing 15 feet; and a seaway channel to accommodate such craft would be shaped by appropriate drainage at the mouth of Rio Escondido (sandbar at El Bluff and mudbanks in the Bluefields Lagoon).

The economic merits of the Rama project are difficult to assess, since no calculations of the true transport benefits relative to the full investment costs have yet been made. The idea of an east-west route has become an emotionally-charged symbol of Nicaragua's desire to unify her resources and people so that the project is as much political and social as economic. An appraisal of the non-economic factors is outside the scope of the mission's study and our analysis is therefore limited to probable costs and returns so far as they can be assessed from the data available.

Wholly apart from views of national interest, the genuine benefits of an east-west route are hardly open to question. They include 5-10% cheaper transport and thus wider markets for such west coast exports as cotton to Europe and livestock to the Caribbean which now have to move by a round-about ocean route with transshipment across the Panama Canal.

Expansion of east-west trade, now negligible, will be greatly stimulated as trucks and barges come into service on the route. An emergence of cash crops, cattle ranches, dairy farming, and commercial logging can be expected along the 100 kilometer gap which separates Villa Somoza from Rama. In the absence of data on the east coast's productive resources, the traffic potential of the area which the extended road will traverse, and the margin by which future costs for reaching particular overseas markets via the Rama road and the Rio Escondido are apt to decline below present costs, the impact on production and trade cannot be precisely assessed. Nevertheless, output, exports, and interregional commerce will certainly tend to increase when an east-west route comes into service.

Although the benefits are clear, the economic case in support of the Rama project has sometimes been exaggerated. There are serious limiting factors which should not be ignored. For one, the bulk of the west coast's trade is with the Pacific Coast of the United States and South America, the Far East, and other areas more conveniently serviced by Corinto or San Juan del Sur than by the Rio Escondido. Second, with the abandonment of banana plantations and the depletion of timber resources the regional economy of the east coast has long been in decay. Until a far-reaching program of regional development begins to take effect, the east coast will have little capacity to produce more goods for interregional trade. Third, ocean freight rates in Central America are ordinarily determined more by shipowner cartels charging what the traffic will bear that by actual transport costs arising out of distance and speed. Again, the nature, size, and productivity of resources in the area between Villa Somoza and Rama are uncertain. Finally, since the seaway will admit no ships above a 15-foot draft, only relatively small payloads, a few thousand tons per ship, can be lifted by ocean freighters to and from Rama.

According to present estimates, the Rama road built to Inter-American Highway standards over the entire length of 260 kilometers might require $8 million for road construction and improvement, apart from the cost of building and equipping a port and dredging a proper channel. This is much too large an expenditure if Nicaragua had to bear the total cost of the project; much too large, that is, in view of the total amount which the government can afford to spend for public investment. Assuming the necessity of an $8 million road, the Rama project would thus have to be deferred, in the mission's opinion, unless it came largely or entirely as a grant. Fortunately, a serviceable east-west route need not cost as much as $8 million for the road alone. Fortunately, also, the United States Government has expressed its willingness to pay the costs of a $4 million Rama road by recent Congressional action which authorized the allocation of $2 million a year over the next two years for that purpose.

In fact, a satisfactory job of road-building between Villa Somoza and Rama could be done for much less than $8 million. The present road running 160 kilometers from the Inter-American Highway to Villa Somoza is an all-weather, two-lane route, gravel type in certain stretches and crushed stone type in others. It provides year-round serviceability for a sizeable volume of bus and truck traffic despite a rough, uncomfortable surface which is unsuited for high speed travel by automobile. If the 100-kilometer extension to Rama were built to similar specifications, a usable east-west link would be completed at a fraction of the intial cost for a route built to Inter-American Highway standards. Later, with growing traffic, the gravel or crushed stone road could be raised to higher standards (black-top surface, full drainage, permanent bridges, etc.) without much, if any, increase over the outlay required for an immediate first-class road.

Allowing for necessary bridge construction but also for the availability of crushable stone along the route, the mission believes that $4 million should be enough—(i) to build a serviceable all-weather road from Villa Somoza to the Rio Escondido; and (ii) to improve the alignment and drainage of the existing road from the Inter-American Highway to Villa Somoza. The entire route would thus become a two-lane, all-weather road built to simple specifications for bus and truck traffic.

Since the United States is prepared to make a grant for the project, the question arises as to the utilization of funds previously set aside for the construction of the Rama road. The Government has levied a special coffee export tax to accumulate funds for the Rama project. About 80% of the proceeds have been earmarked for the Rama road, and about 20% for access roads into the coffee plantations. By mid-1952, the earmarked funds came to around $2 million.

The mission recommends, first, drawing on the earmarked reserves to pay the full costs of the project other than road construction, i.e. the costs of a port at Rama and of dredging at El Bluff, and second, transferring any remainder to the government's funds for economic development.

Over and above $4 million to come as a grant, certain expenditures will have to be incurred for port construction at Rama and dredging at El Bluff. The Rio Escondido upstream from the Bluefields Lagoon is an adequate channel of 15-20-foot depth. The approaches to Rama, however, are blocked by a sandbar across the narrow exit near El Bluff. Within the past 50 years the bar has built up from a controlling depth of 15 feet or so when Rama was a major port of call for banana ships, to a controlling depth of 10 and a half to 11 feet at present. There are also some mudbanks in the Lagoon athwart the most convenient passages into the river proper. These will have to be dredged if ocean ships are to mount the river as they did in the days of the banana trade.

Neither port construction at Rama nor channel dredging at the river mouth is likely to pose formidable technical difficulties or to require exceptionally large outlays. The mission believes that adequate piers can be installed at Rama for an outlay of about $250,000 and that a 15-foot channel can be dredged across the sandbar and the mudbanks for an expenditure of $500,000.

The aggregate cost of the Rama project is thus of the order of

$4.75 million. Most of this will be cost-free to Nicaragua. A small balance of $750,000 can be financed out of existing reserves without further burden on the Treasury.

Other Main Roads

There is no necessity, the mission believes, to undertake construction of main roads over the next five years other than the projects to which Nicaragua is already committed, i.e. improvement of the Inter-American Highway, completion of the IBRD roads, and construction of the Rama road. It is premature to contemplate construction of a Corinto link to the Managua-Leon-Chinandega route before 1957. Yet a Corinto project, including the conversion of Corinto from a rail to a truck port, may eventually be worth the necessary expenditure. It would be desirable, therefore, for the Ministry of Public Works to initiate the necessary studies of feasibility, cost, and traffic.

Need of Local Road Program

Simultaneously with the main highway program, Nicaragua should give attention to a vital phase of road-building which has been seriously neglected up to now—the construction and improvement of local roads. From 1937 to date, the road-building effort has concentrated almost exclusively on highways. The first job in establishing an effective road system is, of course, linkage of major communities. But feeder, access, and farm-to-market roads must also be built, otherwise most of the potential benefits from good highways will not be realized. The lack of motorable local roads throughout Nicaragua means reduced profit-margins for producers and increased living costs for consumers due to excessive transport charges. Production and trade are heavily burdened at present by the need to use beasts of burden for local haulage. For example, in the Leon-Chinandega district, the charges for carrying raw cotton by oxcart to cotton gins 20 or 30 miles from the farm absorb 10% or more of the sales proceeds. It costs as much, or more, to haul coffee from the Tuma Valley to Matagalpa by pack-mule as to move it thereafter by truck, rail, and ocean freighter to overseas markets. When motor trucks penetrated the Matagalpa-Jinotega hinterlands a few years ago, transport charges for haul-ing cabbages, beans, and other produce to Managua were reduced 80% to 90%.

Nicaragua's need for access roads is not localized. The need is no less urgent on the east coast which has no roads except a few lumber routes than on the west coast.

Between the east coast and the west coast, there is, however, one essential difference. On the west coast, the local roads most urgently needed are feeder routes into the main highways and main railroad stations. On the east coast, the primary need is for penetration roads from the navigable rivers into the surrounding forests beyond the present narrow strip of cultivation. Local roads are necessary on the west coast to improve the productive efficiency of relatively mature areas. What the east coast needs are develop-mental routes to open new areas for agriculture, cattle raising, and forestry.

Recommended Program

The mission thinks that little purpose would be served at present by trying to work out a definite schedule of which regions to equip with good local roads first, but believes it more appro-priate to suggest an effective mechanism and procedure for plan-ning and executing such projects. Specifically, we recommend establishing a specialized instrumentality within the Highway De-partment for creating a proper mesh of local roads in each of the main productive regions. Each region should have assigned to it, we suggest, a mechanized crew whose exclusive and full-time job would be building, improving, and maintaining the local roads. The immediate goal would be local roads traversable by motor trucks during at least the dry season; the ultimate goal, all-weather routes fit for year-round truck haulage.

The mission estimates that the total cost of a five-year effort to provide each of the main productive regions with an adequate set of local roads need not exceed $5.5 million—$1.5 million for equipment, $2.5 million for fuel, lubricants, and other operating supplies, and $1.5 million for labor. This outlay includes routine maintenance for which the Highway Department is presently budgeting the equivalent of $100,000 a year. Part can be covered by drawing on the accumulated reserves—about $400,000—for access roads into coffee plantations. The capital cost thus reduces to $5 million, some of which would be used to purchase equipment whose service life may be longer than five years.

According to the Ministry of Public Works, the terrain, resources, traffic, and administrative structure of the country call for dividing it into nine local road regions broadly as follows: (i) Managua area; (ii) Leon area; (iii) Chinandega area; (iv) Rivas area; (v) Masaya-Granada area; (vi) Matagalpa-Jinotega area; (vii) Chontales-Boaco area; (viii) South Atlantic; (ix) North Atlantic. The estimate of $5 million presupposes that nine regional teams will be established for the five-year program. In practice, some of the teams might not be organized immediately. Some might be able to cover a broader area and some might be able to finish their task in less than five years. The effective cost of realizing the five-year program may thus be less than $5 million; perhaps 20% to 25% less. The required outlay is thus $4 million on the indispensable minimum of the program plus $1 million on the contingent or deferrable work.

The estimates include necessary equipment for nine crews to cost $1.5 million. Fuel, lubricants, and other supplies if each crew works full time would run to about $500,000 a year, and payrolls would approximate $300,000 a year. As for equipment costs, it is assumed that each crew would be outfitted with six trucks, a tractor bulldozer, a motor grader, a pickup, and a DW-10 rubber-tired tractor; that each three crews would share a power shovel and a crusher; that some incidental expenditures would be incurred for rollers, shop equipment, hand tools, etc., and that sufficient spare parts would be bought.

If all nine crews were set up and activated immediately, at the end of five years every agricultural, pastoral, and logging area of present significance could be joined to the highways, the rail lines, or the navigable rivers by some road over which trucks and buses could run during at least the dry season. A scattering of productive areas which are unexploited at present because of their inaccessibility would also be opened for development. Even after the country is blanketed with dry-season local roads, regional crews will be needed to assure the upkeep and repair of the new roads, to improve them to all-weather standards of serviceability, and to extend the network into the further areas. The proposal is therefore for a permanent mechanism, which, initially from mid-1952 through mid-1957 would cost on the order of $4 million to $5 million.

Magnitude of Investment Effort

Adding the expenditures for local roads to those for main roads, the recommended investment program for the next five years approximates $18.25 million. This is a large sum by the yardstick of previous expenditures, current outlays, and Nicaragua's present means for financing development. It compares with a total capital expenditure of the order of $22 million to date for all main roads already built or presently under construction, and with a total budget, for all phases of the Highway Department work, of approximately $1.66 million in 1950-51 and $2.67 million in 1951-52. Applying $18.25 million to the rock-bottom program of aggregate investment which the mission is urging Nicaragua to undertake, roads alone would account for 30% of the expenditure. Applying it to the optimum investment effort which Nicaragua ought to be making if her means suffice, roads alone would absorb 25%.

The United States grants already described will cover much of the cost. Another large part—e.g. projects to be financed out of

1951 IBRD loan or earmarked tax reserves—can be covered without additional taxes or borrowing.

The financial framework of the recommended program is therefore as follows:

Project	US $ 000
Inter-American Highway	6,000
Bank-financed roads	3,500
Rama project (road, port, waterway)	4,750
Local roads	4,000
Total	18,250
U. S. grant (Inter-American Highway) ..	4,000
U. S. grant (Rama Road)	4,000
IBRD loan (west coast main roads)	2,500
Balance to be financed	7,750
Earmarked funds for Rama project	750
Earmarked funds for access roads	400
Additional funds to be raised	6,600

Judging by incomplete data, there are some 4,000-4,500 motor vehicles in Nicaragua, although the true total may be larger. Motor trucks alone number at least 1,300; autobuses upward of 200, and passenger automobiles, 2,500-3,000. The existing fleets are too small for a road network of the scope recommended.

Although the mission has no forecast of motor vehicle needs with growing traffic over the next five years, they are apt to be of an order of magnitude equal to the required road expenditure. About 5,000 motor trucks and 1,000 buses may well have to be imported from mid-1952 through mid-1957 at a c.i.f. cost of perhaps $20 million-$25 million. Considering the profitability of truck and bus operation—truck owners can presently earn as much as $1,000 per vehicle per month before depreciation during the dry season—the necessary funds to multiply the truck and bus fleet are likely to be forthcoming from private sources without excessive strain on the commercial credit mechanism.

Necessary Administrative Reforms

Nicaragua will be unable to get full value from her investment in more and better roads without certain administrative reforms affecting the Ministry of Public Works. Although the Highway Department is well organized, well administered, and staffed by competent, conscientious, and energetic officials, it needs to be protected against the diversion of its equipment, supplies, and labor to non-road purposes for the benefit of other governmental agencies and semiprivate interests. The Department should have full operating control over its equipment, materials, and labor and unconditional powers to restrict their use for purposes outside the Department's proper functions. It should be expressly free from any obligation to do work for governmental bodies, public officials, or private interests except on a contract basis in return for a reasonable fee and it should be expressly empowered to charge fees covering the full cost of the service for any outside work.

To assure a maximum concentration of the Department's resources on the essential task of constructing, improving, and maintaining public roads, the mission recommends that: (a) none of the Department's trucks, tractors, graders, and other equipment for the maintenance of main highways and secondary roads be subject to requisition for work outside its proper functions; (b) the Central Plantel at Managua be limited to repairing and servicing the Department's own vehicles and equipment except as work may be conveniently taken on for other governmental bodies on a fee basis; (c) no outside bodies or officials be empowered to draw on the Department's stock of gasoline, lubricants, and other supplies.

In addition to adequate safeguards against diversion of the

Department's resources, a more systematic programming of road-building is needed. At present, the Department operates on a year-to-year budget except for the carry-over of undisbursed appropriations. It should operate on a five- to 10-year schedule of construction, improvement, and maintenance work meshing with the public investment program as a whole. This schedule should show the proposed outlay for construction of new roads, improvement of existing roads, maintenance of main and secondary roads, municipal street paving, repair shop outlay, and administrative expenses. It should distinguish, within each functional activity, the expenditures for wages, materials, operating supplies, and equipment, and should group capital outlays separately from current expenses.

Although the Highway Department is well organized, well administered, and technically competent, it is not by itself the proper body to decide which communities and areas ought to be joined by main roads, which localities should have access or penetration roads ahead of other localities, or how much ought to be spent on roads to promote particular kinds of agriculture, livestock breeding, and forestry. These are questions which the Highway Department ought to work out in consultation with the Ministry of Agriculture, the Instituto de Fomento, the National Bank, and other competent authorities. The specific projects should be presented to the National Economic Council for further review as part of the total program of public investment.

All the available funds for effectuating this program will presumably be concentrated in a common pool for allocation by strict priority. It follows that earmarked taxes on motor vehicles, gasoline, lubricants or particular export goods to finance road construction and improvement would be inadvisable beyond narrow limits. True, the road program would advance faster if earmarked taxes were brought to bear over the whole range of the Highway Department's work, but it might do so at the expense of other essential public improvements. It is nevertheless administratively sound, in the mission's opinion, to allow certain exceptions in favor of particular road projects. First, the accumulated proceeds of the coffee tax which have already been set aside for the Rama Road might properly be put to use for such of the project as will not be covered by the United States grant. Second, the earmarked reserves for access roads into coffee plantations should be used to finance the improvement of local roads. Third, the owners of real estate tending to increase in value from the improvement of particular roads might properly be asked to bear part of the costs.

Much of the success with which the Department has functioned is the outcome of its close technical collaboration with the United States Bureau of Public Roads. The mission believes that this collaboration ought to be continued and extended, not only to projects for which the United States may be paying part of the cost such as improvement of the Inter-American Highway and completion of the Rama Road but also to projects such as improvement of local roads which will be financed by taxes and borrowings. The mission recommends that the Department explore the possibility of further technical aid from the United States to facilitate road investment effort over the next five years.

CHAPTER TWELVE

Expansion and Improvement
of Port Facilities

If the current workload were the only factor to be considered in determining whether to improve Nicaragua's ports, sizeable expenditures would be difficult to justify. The present flow of goods through any of the ocean ports, even Corinto, is much too small to warrant heavy outlays for new piers, sheds, cranes, or lift-trucks despite the reduced cargo-working charges and the faster vessel turnaround which would result. None of the west coast or east coast ports, so far as the mission could learn, has been a bottleneck to foreign trade in the recent past. During the 1952 seasonal traffic peak none was badly congested or in danger of becoming choked with ships awaiting a berth or with cargo awaiting a carrier. Ocean freight rates might conceivably decline if Corinto and San Juan del Sur were equipped to load and discharge the present volume of cargo with more dispatch. But the chief reasons for the present high tariffs are the small tonnages to be carried and the monopolistic postion of the few carriers who do most of the haulage.

Volume of Traffic

No elaborate analysis is needed to demonstrate that Nicaragua's ocean ports are handling an insufficient volume of traffic to justify expensive installations for berthing ships or expensive equipment for working cargo. In 1950, the latest year for which complete data exist, only 239,600 tons of freight were loaded or discharged at all of the west and east coast ports. Inbound goods aggregated 118,200 tons of which 101,300 were discharged on the west coast. Experts totalled 121,300 tons of which 74,700 moved through west coast ports.

TABLE 1

IMPORTS AND EXPORTS AT PRINCIPAL PORTS—1950
(in thousand tons)

Port	Inbound	Outbound	Total
Corinto	78.2	56.1	134.4
San Juan del Sur	8.7	12.8	21.5
Puerto Morazon[a]	0.1	5.8	5.9
Puerto Somoza[b]	14.3	—	14.3
West coast	101.3	74.7	176.1
El Bluff	5.6	29.2	34.8
Puerto Cabezas[c]	10.7	13.5	24.2
Cabo Gracias a Dios	0.6	3.9	4.5
San Juan del Norte[d]	—	—	—
East coast	16.9	46.6	63.5
Total	118.2	121.3	239.6

[a] River-ocean port for coastal trade with nearby Central American countries, particularly El Salvador.

[b] Open roadstead, more commonly known as Masachapa, which is equipped with pipelines and storage tanks for discharging petroleum products from oil tankers.

[c] Owned and operated by Standard Fruit mainly for the export of pine lumber from a nearby sawmill.

[d] Insignificant amounts; local trade only.

On Lake Nicaragua, the present traffic through Granada, San Carlos, and other communities serviced by the FCPN fleet is so insignificant that a serious question arises whether the port and fleet facilities are worth maintaining at all. The most recent data are for 1950-51. Since then traffic may have declined further in a continued downswing which stems from the recent penetration of much of the area by good motor roads. The FCPN fleet which does all the common carriage on the lake, hauled only 5,370 tons of freight in 1950-51 and transported only 20,800 passengers. Its aggregate revenues from this work were a mere 153,780 cordobas, equivalent to $21,970 of which $12,440 was freight revenue and $9,530 was passenger revenue.

Necessity of Port Investment

Despite the small volume of traffic, the mission is convinced that part of the funds available for development over the next five years may justifiably be invested in some expansion and improvement of port facilities. Cargo traffic through Corinto and 3an Juan del Sur may be expected to expand substantially with further development of west coast resources, particularly as additional areas are provided with cheap, fast truck haulage. The extension of the Rama Road, discussed in Chapter 11, will necessitate port construction at Rama and channel dredging at the month of the Rio Escondido. The potential usefulness of Lake Nicaragua as a transport route for some isolated districts otherwise inaccessible cannot be fully realized without improved landing stages for motor barges, launches, and other small craft. In addition, certain operational factors, such as Corinto's exposure to fire and explosion risks and San Juan's inconveniences as a lighterage port for truck-hauled goods, justify a certain amount of corrective investment apart from the question of traffic volume.

In contrast, investment to improve the port of Masachapa appears to this mission to be a waste of Nicaragua's development funds. An attempt, financed by the earnings of the national railroad, is under way to transform Masachapa from an open roadstead serving oil tankers exclusively into a sheltered port serving freighters as well. The venture appears unsound because there is no need for an additional west coast port; because, for technical reasons, the port cannot be constructed at a reasonable cost, and because the funds this project is now absorbing might be better used to improve the permanent way and rolling stock of the FCPN.

Before considering specific projects the scope of our analysis

should be made clear. Our appraisal is confined to public investment in conditions where some useful purpose would be served
by the expansion or improvement of port facilities. This rules out
certain ports which are privately owned and operated, such as
Puerto Cabezas, the property of Standard Fruit, which is used
mainly by the nearby Nipco sawmill. It also precludes El Bluff
and San Juan del Norte because of the extremely poor export outlook for the east coast areas they service, unless and until some
far-reaching program of regional development should change
the picture.

We recommend the following specific measures:

(a) doubling the present capacity of Corinto while reducing
    its vulnerability to fire and explosion;

(b) increasing the efficiency of San Juan del Sur as a lighterage
    port served by motor trucks;

(c) constructing a river-ocean port at Rama and dredging a
    proper seaway channel across the mouth of the Rio Escon-
    dido;

(d) equipping some of the communities on Lake Nicaragua
    with suitable landing stages for motor barges, motor
    launches, and other small craft;

(e) desisting from additional expenditure to transform Masa-
    chapa from an open roadstead into a sheltered port.

Corinto Project

Corinto is Nicaragua's main ocean port. It is a well-sheltered
natural harbor linked by rail with the richest productive areas of
the west coast. At present it has no road access. Normally, about
75% to 80% of the ocean-borne imports and exports of the west
coast move through Corinto. It is the outlet for the bulk of
Nicaragua's exports of cotton, coffee, sesame, sugar, and other
west coast products. Inbound, it handles both petroleum products
(gasoline, fuel oil, lubricants, etc.) and general cargo (vehicles,
machinery, textiles, iron, steel, etc.). It also clears some inter-

regional trade between the east and west coasts via the Panama Canal.

Although Corinto with a tanker berth, pipelines, and storage tanks, is fairly well equipped to handle petroleum and other liquid cargo, it is poorly equipped to handle general cargo. The main defects are restricted berthing capacity, lack of equipment to work cargo between ship and pier, lack of equipment to work cargo ashore, and a layout of berths which is potentially dangerous. Specifically, the defects are:

(a) There is a single pier, only one side of which can be used for berthing ships because of insufficient depth and transit sheds on the other side;

(b) The pier can accommodate only two deep sea ships at once, although it has some additional space for coastal craft at the shallow, lower end;

(c) The tanker berth is sandwiched between the freighter berth and the accommodations for coastal craft, so that ordinary cargo has to be worked side by side with flammable cargo;

(d) There are no cranes to load and discharge cargo, so that even the heaviest and most cumbersome pieces of freight have to be worked by ships' tackle alone;

(e) There are no lift trucks to move freight on the pier, in the transit sheds, or the railroad yards, so that freight handling ashore is slow and expensive.

As a further limit on operational efficiency, Corinto is laid out exclusively as a railroad port. All goods except petroleum have to be taken to or from the ships in flatcars hauled by switcher locomotives over a short spur of railway track. This track runs the entire length of the narrow pier, and occupies all the working space between the coastal, tanker, and freighter berths to the left and the administration building and transit sheds to the right. It is the only transport artery between the port proper and the warehouses in town. All the warehouses, moreover, are located on a narrow ribbon immediately parallel to the mainline of the FCPN as it traverses the waterfront. There are no roadways of any kind by which goods could be truck-hauled from ship to warehouses or from town to pier; not even paths suitable for lift trucks and similar light apparatus exist.

Despite these shortcomings, and in the face of 25% to 30% more traffic than prewar, Corinto is not congested at present. The average turnaround of the ocean freighters which call at the port is only two or three days. This is neither exceptionally fast nor excessively slow, considering the amount and kind of goods lifted. Nevertheless, if its export traffic continues to grow at the rate of the past 10 years, Corinto may soon become a bottleneck. In 1950 the port handled more than twice the 1941 volume of outbound goods yet almost no new equipment to service ships and work cargo has been installed for 40 years or more. With growing traffic, moreover, the risks of fire and explosion from the proximity of tankers to freighters will greatly increase.

In the mission's opinion, the main job to be done immediately is to install additional berthing capacity for the twofold purpose of accommodating a probable future increase of freighter traffic and separating the tanker and freighter berths in the interest of safety. To accomplish this double objective, the mission suggests that Corinto be equipped with an additional pier, preferably a tanker installation close to the present oil storage tanks. The Ministry of Public Works should draft appropriate plans in collaboration with the FCPN as soon as practicable. In addition, the government should explore the possibility of having the oil companies and other owners of storage tanks bear part of the cost. According to a preliminary evaluation by the Ministry of Public Works, the expenditure of about $1.25 million might be required to build and equip such a pier.

Ultimately Corinto may have to be expanded and improved on a much larger scale. In fact, the existing layout which was designed for railway transport to, from, and within the port area, may have to be replaced by a different and larger layout, specifically designed to permit truck haulage. This would require new piers, sheds, cargo-working equipment, service roads, etc., in substance, a new port. Since such a project would not be necessary until 1957 at the earliest, it has been omitted from the mission's recommended investment program for 1952-57.

San Juan del Sur

San Juan del Sur is a sheltered natural harbor linked to the Inter-American Highway south of Managua by a rail spur and a rough road open only in the dry season. Because of a shallow depth along the waterfront, San Juan del Sur has to operate as a lighterage port. It is laid out, moreover, for railway haulage over the FCPN spur from Rivas although the bulk of the present traffic is truck hauled over the seasonal road. There is a total absence of cranes, lift-trucks, or other cargo working equipment ashore.

Despite these inconveniences, the port has been handling an increasing volume of export-import cargo. Comparing 1950 with 1941 performance, the total movement of freight multiplied four or five times. Before the existing road branching from the Inter-American Highway was reopened several years ago, almost the only export traffic through San Juan del Sur was some export of livestock from the immediate area. Currently, in addition to increased livestock traffic, there is a growing export of coffee, cotton, and other agricultural produce mainly brought in by truck during the dry season. Imports handled by the port are largely wheat flour, newsprint, and iron and steel, also mainly hauled by trucks operating seasonally.

The mission believes that when the IBRD-financed all-weather road from the Inter-American Highway to San Juan del Sur is completed, the port's traffic is apt to multiply far beyond the practical capacity of existing facilities. Expansion and improvement in advance of the traffic upsurge would thus be prudent. The main ultimate need is a deep-water pier where ocean freighters could load and discharge directly. Unfortunately, because no engineering studies have yet been made, the practicability of building such an installation at reasonable cost is an open question. All that is clear at present is that the job is apt to be expensive rather than cheap. The mission is therefore convinced that a deepwater berth at San Juan del Sur need not be given serious consideration for the next five years. Studies to determine its feasibility and costs should, however, be undertaken promptly by the Ministry of Public Works.

For some time to come San Juan del Sur will probably continue as a lighterage port. All rail traffic will stop, however, as soon as the part is linked with the Inter-American Highway by an all-weather road. The traffic workload, moreover, is likely to become a good deal heavier as trucks begin to run over the new road. On this basis, the mission recommends improvement of the existing pier, construction of additional storage space, construction of service and access roads in the immediate vicinity of the port, and the purchase of some light motorized equipment goods for use between the pier and the sheds. Part of this expenditure would have to be at public expense (e.g. piers and roadways) but the rest might be covered by private investment (e.g. warehouses and lift trucks). The mission believes that the public share of the project could be accomplished—or at least as much as might be worthwhile undertaking in the next five years—at a cost equivalent to $250,000.

Rama Port and El Bluff Dredging Project

The need for a river-ocean port at Rama, and of channel dredging at the mouth of the Rio Escondido, arises from the planned east-west route across Nicaragua. The costs of a pier for small ocean freighters at Rama ($250,000) and of a 15 ft. channel across the Bluefields Lagoon ($500,000) have therefore been discussed in chapter 11 in connection with the east-west route and are included in the recommended program of road investment.

Lake Nicaragua Project

A strong case might be made for large-scale transport investment on Lake Nicaragua if a road network were not being constructed which will eventually reach most of the productive areas. The network already includes the Inter-American Highway running south from Managua, which is a trunk artery for the entire western shore, and a branch from Rama road which is a feeder route for part of the northeastern lakefront. If the mission's program of local road-building is put into effect it will soon include a mesh of additional feeder routes on the eastern shore will soon come into being. The roads which have been built to date have already diverted considerable traffic from lake to truck haulage. For example, its workload on the FCPN fleet has dropped from slightly more than 10,400 tons in 1944-45 to slightly less than 5,400 tons in 1950-51. As the roads are extended and improved, almost all the freight is apt to be truck-hauled, no matter how greatly volume may expand, apart from the traffic of certain isolated areas such as San Carlos and Ometepe Island.

In these circumstances, the mission believes that the utmost prudence should be exercised in scheduling additional expenditure for lake ports or lake craft. At the most the government would be justified in constructing some jetties for small craft at a few selected communities such as Granada, San Carlos, and Ometepe Island. These jetties might best take the form of landing stages specifically designed to service motor barges and motor launches rather than steamers, and to give better shelter against winds and storms than some of the present jetties, particularly the Granada pier. ·

The mission is not convinced that a complete new port is needed on the Tipitapa River to clear Managua traffic to and from Lake Nicaragua. The choice appears to be between constructing such a port and using the new jetty recommended for Granada. In either case, there would have to be truck haulage before or after transshipment. Considering that a good all-weather road will soon be in service from Granada to Managua and that Granada ought to be equipped with a new jetty regardless of Managua traffic requirements, the Tipitapa project does not appear urgent. The mission has not therefore included it in the recommended program of 1952-57 investment. If there is sufficient expansion of production and trade along the eastern shore of Lake Nicaragua, a re-appraisal may be needed later.

According to preliminary estimates by the Ministry of Public Works, it might cost about $750,000 to equip the Lake Nicaragua area with the needed landing stages. However, these estimates predicate completion of the Tipitapa project and envisage somewhat more expensive facilities than appear expedient. The mission estimates the necessary expenditure for port facilities on Lake Nicaragua at $375,000.

Masachapa Project

The recommendation to suspend further work on the breakwater and pier at Masachapa and to write off the whole venture as a dead loss, arises from the probability that the costs would be far greater than the realizable benefits. Since the roadstead is completely exposed to heavy storms from the Pacific, its conversion into a sheltered port is apt to require very heavy expenditures, possibly of the order of $15 million to $20 million. Previous installations have been washed away, and so might the new facilities unless engineered with the utmost care. In spite of this, the present work is going forward without engineering studies or control, as a kind of sporadic experiment. Since Corinto and San Juan del Sur can handle the volume of traffic foreseeable in the near future, it is doubtful whether the west coast needs another general cargo port. In any case such a port at Masachapa would be of limited usefulness without large additional expenditures to correct the alignment, grades, and curves of the present concrete road to the Inter-American Highway south of Managua. This road is currently used by tank trucks carrying petroleum from Masachapa, and by heavy-duty trucks carrying cement from the nearby cement plant, but its technical characteristics preclude ordinary trucking of general goods at reasonable rates unless the route is completely rebuilt.

Financing of Investment Effort

The recommended program of port investment for the next five years thus totals $2.625 million if the Rama-El Bluff projects are included. Excluding them the amount is only $1.875 million. Either way the expenditure will be about evenly divided between foreign exchange and local currency, according to a rough evaluation by the Ministry of Public Works. Until engineering studies are made, it is impossible to spell out firm projects and estimates.

Part of the expenditure for an additional pier at Corinto, the largest specific project, could be covered out of the port's operating profits as a state-owned commercial venture. Owned outright by the government, but administered operationally by the FCPN, the port yields a handsome return on the Treasury's equity, according to the latest official accounts, of roughly 750,000 cordobas, equivalent to $107,000. From 1948-49 through 1950-51, earnings after depreciation charges averaged 721,000 cordobas equivalent to $103,000 a year, a return of close to 100%. The port should thus be able to pay at least $515,000 toward its own improvement in the next five years. Also the oil companies with storage tanks at Corinto might be willing to finance some of the required outlay for a new tanker pier located a safe distance away from the present tanker-freighter pier. Assuming the government's intention to expand and improve Corinto as recommended, it might be administratively convenient to treat the cost of the project as a first charge on the port's operating profits, although this would reduce the Treasury's immediate cash dividends on the Corinto investment.

Recommended Administrative Reforms

Some of the present devices and procedures of port administration will have to be modified if Nicaragua is to get the best use from her port facilities. Except for Corinto (State-owned property under FCPN management) and Puerto Cabezas (private property of Standard Fruit), the ocean ports such as San Juan del Sur, El Bluff, and San Juan del Norte are under the operational control of the Customs. On Lake Nicaragua, the FCPN manages the landing stages as well as ships. Rama has no port as yet and thus no port administration.

Since all of the export, import, and internal goods which clear Corinto have to be rail-hauled, there is no immediate need to alter the present arrangements by which the FCPN operates the port as a state-owned public enterprise. Eventually, however, Corinto may become a trucking port as well. In this case, it may be advisable to transfer the management of the port from the FCPN to some autonomous public body. This shift should not be difficult since the state owns the port facilities.

The chief weakness in administration stems from treatment of the port more as a source of Treasury revenue than as an essential public facility to be kept in first-class shape. Upkeep, repairs, and modernization appear to have been long neglected despite substantial operating profits. It would be desirable to concentrate operating revenues, for the next five years, on long overdue maintenance and expansion of capacity. The use of these funds should be formalized in a capital expenditure budget for incorporation into the public investment program. An outside audit of the port's accounts by certified public accountants would also be useful, as would review by qualified specialists of its service charges relative to port management.

The port can be reorganized on public utility lines without disturbing its status as a state-owned commercial venture. Charges for servicing ships and working cargo should be scaled to allow a wide enough margin above operating and depreciation costs to yield a reasonable return. Adequate provision should be made for upkeep, repairs, and renewals. Capital expenditure for renewals, improvements, and additions should be carefully budgeted. There should be full disclosures of receipts, expenses, reserves, and capital disbursements, calculated by sound accounting methods.

Except for Corinto and Puerto Cabezas the ocean ports are managed at present by local customs officials as an incidental part of their duties. This is inconsistent with efficient port administration and ought to be corrected by appointing a well-qualified, full-time manager for each port. While he might for convenience be attached to the Customs Service, his job would be to check the operation of ships and piers, sheds and warehouses, cargo and equipment. The mission particularly recommends this form of management for San Juan del Sur and Rama. Creation of a formal port authority would not be necessary, provided there is a competent port manager who works full time on the job.

On Lake Nicaragua, the situation is complicated by the FCPN's ownership of railway lines (Granada-Managua and San Jorge-San Juan del Sur) as well as a common carrier fleet. As long as the FCPN controls lake haulage and rail services to and from the lake, it is desirable that it continue to be responsible for landing stages. This suggestion is based on the assumption that the present defects of FCPN administration will be corrected. Ultimately, with the growth of main and local roads, the FCPN's lake fleet, the Managua-Granada line, and the San Jorge-San Juan del Sur line may all have to be abandoned. In that event it might be desirable to appoint a single manager for all the landing stages on Lake Nicaragua.

The mission considers it premature to propose a national port authority with complete responsibility for all public ports, in view of their highly localized character, the close meshing of Corinto with the FCPN as a rail carrier, and the insufficient volume of present or impending traffic to justify an elaborate administrative structure. Eventually, such an authority may have to be created in the interest of a coordinated investment effort, optimum routing and clearance of traffic, and effective regional development. The immediate problem is to draft a long-range program for the expansion, improvement, and modernization of the ocean, lake, and river ports as a whole. Our recommendation for Corinto, San Juan del Sur, Rama, and the Escondido seaway are intended as a starting point for such a program. The mission urges that the Ministry of Public Works be authorized to start this work at once.

CHAPTER THIRTEEN

Other Transport Facilities

This chapter considers the Lake Nicaragua fleet, the ocean-going merchant marine, and airfields for internal service.

Lake Nicaragua Fleet

The FCPN-operated lake fleet carries so little freight and so few passengers that if commercial profit-and-loss alone had to be considered, the operation ought to be suspended. The annual operating deficit, 209,000 cordobas per year from 1948-49 through 1950-51, is as large as the entire investment in ships, landing stages, and repair facilities—213,000 cordobas after ex-depreciation as of mid-1951. The losses are likely to continue indefinitely and may even increase as more and better roads come to be built, particularly feeder roads on the eastern shore.

Where truck haulage is already practicable—e.g. along the Inter-American Highway on the western lakefront, and along some spurs to the Rama Road in the northeast corner—there has been a steady and continuing diversion of traffic from lake craft to motor trucks. In the past 10 years, the volume of freight carriage by the FCPN fleet has shrunk 50%. With the additional feeder roads recommended by the mission, the entire volume of inbound, outbound, and local trade will probably be truck-hauled all the way from initial pickup to final delivery, except to and from certain isolated communities. Truck transport is cheaper, faster, and more reliable than barge transport in most of the Lake Nicaragua area. As trucking routes reach more districts, fincas and towns, more of the region's external traffic can be picked up and delivered directly without intermediate and expensive trans-shipment across the lake and the lake fleet will become increasingly dispensable. Finally, a good mesh of roads to connect lake

Nicaragua with Managua, San Juan del Sur, Rama and other marketing and supply centers outside the area will ultimately interconnect much of the area.

Existing transport services on the Lake are an indispensable service for Omotepe Island, San Carlos, and a few other places which cannot be reached by road at all or have no convenient road access. They will therefore have to continue, despite operating losses equivalent to a state subsidy, until some better means of transport can be devised. Certain developmental considerations also argue against immediate suspension of the FCPN service; for example, the availability of the lake craft may help to stimulate commercial agriculture in areas which would be too costly to penetrate by new roads for the present.

The mission does not believe that the FCPN ought to be indefinitely burdened with an unprofitable operation. As long as the railroad lines to the lake ports remain active, however, there are administrative advantages in having the carrier bear the cost of a state-subsidized service. But in the event these lines have to be abandoned after completion of the Granada and San Juan del Sur roads now under way, there would be little or no purpose in FCPN ownership or management of the lake fleet.

The mission believes that the appropriate solution would be the gradual replacement of the FCPN craft by modern motor barges and launches to be owned and operated by private carriers. This shift can be effected without too much difficulty by vigorous governmental assistance in the form of low-interest loans, tax exemptions, and temporary subsidies to encourage private entrepreneurs to enter the business of hauling freight and passengers on Lake Nicaragua. As an added stimulus, prompt action should be taken to eliminate the vexatious police controls, petty taxes and other administrative measures which now obstruct the growth of commercial traffic on Lake Managua as well as on Lake Nicaragua. Meanwhile, the FCPN should begin to work out definite plans for selling or scrapping its present vessels as alternative means of transport become available. It should also promptly suspend its present effort to salvage, rehabilitate and recondition certain craft long out of service.

In short, the mission's ideas of a proper policy for the lake fleet would be ultimate withdrawal of the FCPN, private investment by independent carriers, and certain administrative reforms requiring no investment.

Ocean-Going Merchant Marine

Although the bulk of the ocean-borne trade is carried by foreign ships, some of it moves in Nicaraguan-flag vessels. The craft which do the work are a few small coasters owned and operated by a private corporation, *Marina Mercante Nicaraguense,* more commonly known as Mamenic. They run in regular service out of Corinto: (a) to Bluefields and other east coast ports via the Panama Canal; (b) to nearby ports in other Central American countries; and (c) occasionally, to west coast ports in the United States and South America.

In the mission's opinion, whatever expenditure might usefully be made for modernizing and expanding the Mamenic fleet should come entirely from private sources. It would be unsound for the state to help finance the effort by loans, equity capital, guarantees, or otherwise. First, intercoastal and nearby foreign freight amount to so little at present that new facilities to do the job better cannot reasonably be considered one of Nicaragua's more pressing needs. Second, the completion of the Rama road prolonged by a seaway down the Rio Escondido is likely to reduce much of the present need for intercoastal shipping shipping via the Panama Canal. Finally, the improvement of the Inter-American Highway by the various Central American countries in collaboration with the United States is likely to channel more of Nicaragua's interchange of goods with her immediate neighbors along trucking routes rather than shipping lanes.

It might be argued that the Mamenic fleet ought to be enlarged for deep sea transport between Nicaragua and the overseas world. If this argument is taken to imply that part of the necessary financing should be provided by the state, the mission dissents. Nicaragua's overseas trade is much too small, in our opinion, to justify public investment to create a Nicaraguan fleet large enough to carry some prescribed fraction, say 50%, of the traffic. Nor is it clear that a Nicaraguan fleet of the size required to haul half the traffic could or would charge lower rates than those now in force.

We do not mean that Nicaragua ought to refrain from the creation of a large merchant marine in any and all circumstances. On the contrary, we believe that a plausible case can be made for the eventual creation by Nicaragua jointly with other Central American countries, of a regional fleet similar to the Grancolombiana fleet of Venezuela, Colombia and Ecuador. From time to time there has been a good deal of talk, even some preliminary discussions, about the advisability of such a venture. To date, however, no definite plans have emerged or are in sight. Until and unless they are worked out, it would be premature to envisage a big expansion of the Nicaraguan merchant marine except as a private venture at Mamenic expense.

Airfields for Internal Service

All common carriage by air within Nicaragua is by a semi-private enterprise, *Lineas Aerias de Nicaragua,* more commonly known as Lanica. It operates scheduled flights for the general public, and charter flights for some isolated mines, over a triangular Managua-Puerto Cabezas-Bluefields route, with several intermediate stops. The aircraft are mainly of the DC-3 or C-46 type.

The main drawback is the restricted scope of the network. For example, such communities as Corinto, Chinandega, Granada, San Carlos, Cabo Gracias a Dios, Matagalpa, and Jinotega have no readily accessible service and thus no regular convenient means of air transport. The situation will be partially alleviated when a mesh of good roads radiating out of Managua is completed. Satisfactory service, however, will also require construction or improvement of a few airfields at several places which now lie outside the Lanica network, e.g. San Carlos. These should be simple grass strips, fit for DC-3s at most, near main towns which have only emergency strips unsuitable for scheduled flights or no strips at all.

The cost of constructing a few such strips is estimated at about $100,000. Since the new fields would be an operational facility for a single common carrier, Lanica might well pay part or all of the cost.

CHAPTER FOURTEEN

Postal, Telephone, and Telegraph Services

Internal communications are under the control of the Armed Forces *(Guardia Nacional)* which administers them through an operational entity known as *Communicaciones*. Functionally, Communications corresponds to the PTT administrations of continental Europe which operate postal, telephone, and telegraph services. It has, however, no financial autonomy or even working funds of its own. Instead of being retained to pay working expenses, the operating receipts are turned over to the Ministry of Finance, which in turn pays for wages, supplies, equipment, etc. as formally authorized in the national budget.

Communicaciones runs at a heavy deficit, subsidized by the

TABLE 1

COMMUNICACIONES BUDGET 1951-52
(thousand cordobas)

Service	Expected Receipts	Budgeted Expenditures
Post Office	554[a]	1,010
Telegraph System	430	1,841
Telephone System	550	687
Unassignable	—	1,443[b]
Total	1,534	4,981

[a] Excludes receipts from sale of collectors' stamp by Philatelic Bureau and of tax stamps to finance the National Stadium.

[b] Includes administrative salaries and overhead; retirement pay and medical benefits; rentals of leased properties, and upkeep and repair of facilities.

state. For each dollar collected from telephone subscribers, telegraph messages, and the sale of stamps, more than three are spent
for salaries, upkeep, rentals transport costs, and other working
expenses. The 1951-52 budget, for example, estimates receipts
at approximately 1.5 million cordobas against expenditures of
5.0 million cordobas.

Post Office

Each large community in Nicaragua has its own post office; but
there are no branch offices of consequence even in the largest
towns. Nor are there mail boxes so that anyone who wishes to
send a letter must take it to the nearest post office. Stamps are on
sale only at post offices; frequently some of the largest offices are
out of stamps for hours on end. There are no pre-stamped en-
velopes or postcards and no use of postal meters. In Managua
and possibly a few other large towns, mail is delivered to homes,
government bureaus, offices and hotels by a postman but in the
countryside there is no delivery at all, either free or paid. Any-
body who lives on a farm must go to town to get his mail. Private
boxes for receiving mail can be hired at main post offices such as
Managua and are in wide use as a more reliable way of getting
mail than waiting for a postman to bring it.

Telephone Service

Telephone service for the general public is limited almost
entirely to the west coast. A few of the larger towns on the west
coast have local exchanges serving private subscribers as well as
governmental offices, but most smaller communities ordinarily
have a handful of phones for the whole town, usually at the
Post Office, the Tax Bureau, the Guardia Nacional, or the municipal office. Frequently the Armed Forces have the only instrument
in town. Here and there, particularly near Managua, a few large
fincas have a telephone line to the nearest community. A network
of land lines joins all the main communities of the west coast.
Interregionally, there are radio-telephone circuits between the east

and west coast but these are for official use only. Side by side with the Communicaciones land lines over much of the west coast, are the FCPN's land lines used in the carrier's operations, particularly for train control. These lines carry telegrams as well as telephone calls.

The Communicaciones facilities for transmitting local and trunk telephone calls are old and badly worn. The switchboards are of the most antique type, manual boards with hand-operated plugs and cords. The instruments are ancient, worn apparatus of every variety and make—American, German, Italian, Japanese. Normally the land lines for trunk calls can handle only one message at a time so that a single call in progress between Managua and Corinto, for example, blocks all other calls over the entire circuit. Local calls in Managua are carried by overhead wires in bad disrepair, made of inferior materials and poorly insulated. They are hung in such a way that storms, wind, and other external forces cause recurring interruptions of service.

Partly but not entirely because the facilities are so poor, making or receiving a telephone call is a torturous and uncertain affair. In Managua it takes so long to put through a local call that the governmental bureaus, diplomatic missions, business firms, and many private subscribers often prefer to send a telegram or a note by hand. In calls between Managua and other towns, prolonged waits before the trunk line is clear are the general rule. Frequently it may be 24 hours before a circuit is free.

Telegraph Service

Unlike the telephone system, telegraph service extends to all parts of the country. Land lines interlace the whole west coast, an interregional line stretches between Managua and Bluefields, and radio-telegraph circuits link the east and west coasts. The telegraph lines are separate from both the telephone lines and the FCPN's network. All west coast communities of any size and some east coast towns as well have telegraph offices where messages can be brought for transmission and from which messages are delivered by carriers. When a message is local, the office transmits a kind of special delivery letter instead of sending a telegram proper.

The telegraph facilities are obsolescent and greatly in need of repairs. The messages have to be hand-tapped on slow-speed keys, and are sent along badly maintained lines of limited carrying capacity. There are no teletypewriters, multicommunication devices, or other modern apparatus for the fast transmission of a heavy flow of messages. With all its faults, however, the system functions more satisfactorily than the telephone system. One evidence of this is the wide-spread habit of sending telegrams instead of making telephone calls for local communications.

Extent and Nature of Market

Since the postal services penetrate all parts of the country, they reach the whole literate population. The nation-wide network of telegraph lines and radio-telegraph circuits is also usable by the Nicaraguan people as a whole. Telephone service, in contrast, is limited to a small fraction of the public. According to rough estimates by the Communicaciones management, there are about 1,500 residential, professional and commercial subscribers in Managua, and perhaps 1,200 more in the rest of the country. In addition, about 500 so-called "official" clients, mainly government offices and government officers in Managua, get free telephone services.

Much of the internal traffic by post, telephone, and telegraph moves free of charge to the users, and much of the rest, at nominal charges which make it virtually free. The government offices, as in some other countries, send internal letters, transmit internal telegrams, and make internal telephone calls without payment. So, too, do many other users who would be paying clients elsewhere; government officials, diplomatic missions, newspapers in most phases of their work, and some influential private persons. Those who have to pay, at least in the case of telecommunications, pay cheap rates indeed, if quality of service is ignored. In Managua the telephone subscribers have the right to an unlimited number of local calls for which they are billed 12 cordobas a month (equivalent to $1.71) for residential service, and 15-25 cordobas a month (equivalent to $2.40-$3.57) for professional and commercial service. The basic rate on internal telegrams is 40 centavos (equivalent to U.S. 5.7¢) for five words sent during the day, plus 100% surcharge if sent at night. Toll calls by telephone are also cheap.

About 10-15% of the internal mail, 65-70% of the internal telegrams, and 15-20% of the internal telephone calls are carried free of charge as "official" traffic. These ratios are derived by adding free traffic valued at commercial rates to actual revenue from stamps, messages and calls. From 1948 through 1950, only three fifths of the work done by Communicaciones brought in revenue while two fifths was unpaid labor.

TABLE 2

COMMUNICACIONES: REVENUE AND OFFICIAL (FREE) TRAFFIC

1948-50

(thousand cordobas)

	1948	1949	1950
Telephone			
Revenue	321	486	543
Official	110	114	116
Total	431	600	659
Telegraph			
Revenue	281	302	378
Official	746	762	724
Total	1,027	1,064	1,102

TABLE 2 (Continued)

Parcel post, cables, and radio			
Revenue	61	54	82
Official	31	15	24
Total	92	69	106
Post Office			
Revenue	466	421	462
Official	67	70	55
Total	533	491	517
Total			
Revenue	1,129	1,263	1,465
Official	954	961	919
Total	2,083	2,224	2,384

Necessary Administrative Reforms

In the mission's opinion, the free and low-cost services which cause Communicaciones' heavy losses are the outcome of traditions of special privilege combined with unbusinesslike methods of operation. They do not appear to express a deliberate policy of providing PTT services below cost as a developmental stimulus or a social welfare measure. Rather, free postage, free telephone, and free telegrams have come to be regarded as a vested right of certain groups. Because no tradition of commercial operation exists, there is no pressure on the Communicaciones management to charge rates roughly commensurate with the cost of rendering service.

Communicaciones is thus a heavily subsidized enterprise for reasons of social inertia alone, and not because the government has a conscious, coherent policy of stimulating delevopment, facilitating trade, or equalizing income through cheap PTT services. The results are harmful to the national economy in three ways. First, funds which could be used for sewers, water supply, hospitals, and other badly needed facilities, are diverted to subsidizing PTT users who need no subsidies. Second, the beneficiaries of these privileges tend to overuse them so that the telephone and telegraph systems in particular have become so overloaded that prompt, reliable service is out of the question. Third, Communicaciones itself is deprived of operating revenues which could be usefully applied to maintenance, modernization, and expansion of the property.

Considering the serious harm which results from the present setup, the mission believes that Communicaciones ought to be commercialized by:

(a) Eliminating all free services to PTT users, including government departments, public officials, the press and diplomatic personnel as well as private persons. In the case of government departments, this will necessitate budget appropriations to pay for their postage, telephone calls, and telegrams.

(b) Raising telephone and telegraph rates to a level where the telecommunications services can pay their own way and yield a reasonable return on the investment;

(c) Reviewing postal rates to ascertain whether and how far they can be increased without weakening the campaign against illiteracy, impairing public administration, or unduly burdening low-income groups.

Top priority should be given to commercialization of the Managua telephone system. Eliminating free service and imposing higher tariffs here are imperative to relieve a state of such congestion that putting through any call is a genuine accomplishment. The root cause, simply stated, is an intolerable load on line and switchboard capacity because of swelling traffic in response to cost-free or very nominal cost service. This state of affairs is bound to recur, even where additional capacity is installed, unless the users of the Managua telephone system are made to pay substantial fees for its use.

Although commercializing the work of Communicaciones would trim operating deficits and thus release funds for public investment as a whole, this is not the only reason for recommending it. First, the telephone system, the telegraph network, and the post office would all be able to function more efficiently, if they were relieved of the burden of working for clients who need not economize on mail, calls, and messages. Second, Communicaciones would have additional revenues to finance maintenance, renewals, and improvement from charges to be paid by clients. Third, the government would have a clear idea of the communications costs of individual departments.

The kind of commercialization the mission proposes is a compromise between PTT practices in continental Europe and public utility practices in the United States. There is no reason, in view of the profitable operation of public telecommunications elsewhere, why telephone and telegraph services in Nicaragua should not be expected to pay their own way. However, post offices the world over trim their charges to particular groups of users on grounds of public welfare. In conformity with this practice, postal rates in Nicaragua might properly be scaled to recover the largest fraction of working expenses consistent with any government policy to subsidize certain sectors and activities by cheap mail.

In the mission's opinion, providing postal, telephone and telegraph services to the general public is a function distinct from military defense, and should be carried on under civilian control and management. Reorganized as a civilian entity, Communicaciones might best take the form of a public corporation with enough operational and financial autonomy to permit it to work in a businesslike manner. The final decisions on the magnitude of the investment effort, the character of the rate structure, the regions serviced to be serviced, the groups and sectors to be subsidized will, however, have to be made by the government. Apart from such issues of broad national policy, the Communicaciones' management should have power to administer internal affairs over a broad range. It should have its own working funds fed by operating receipts, out of which to pay salaries and other current expenses. It should be empowered to prepare a capital expenditure budget, as well as a current expenditure budget for clearance and approval by the competent authorities. Within the limits of the approved budget, it should be able to order equipment, buy supplies, set wage scales and hire and dismiss personnel. Subject to appropriate review by the government, it should also have authority to fix service charges.

There is no need, in the mission's judgment, to disturb the present arrangements by which Communicaciones brings together the postal, telephone, and telegraph services under the same administrative control. This is the normal practice of most countries, like those of Europe, where the telephone and telegraph systems are state-owned. It offers certain conveniences to the general public—for example, all PTT services under a common roof and the sharing of administrative overhead tends to reduce working expenses. Nevertheless, for efficient administration, each PTT activity requires specialized personnel—executive, technical and clerical. We suggest therefore that each service be set up as a separate division or branch within the administrative framework of a reorganized Communicaciones.

It is particularly important that Communicaciones acquire the habit of applying strict and thorough accounting controls to all phases of its work. The controls it now uses consist of budgetary bookkeeping to make sure that expenditures conform with appropriations, auditing procedures to determine cash revenues and the value of free services and policing safeguards to prevent the misappropriation of cash, stamps and supplies. Some of the most basic accounting tools are lacking. There is neither a balance sheet nor an income-expense statement for the telecommunications properties. No accounts are kept of the government's equity in telecommunication plant and equipment, no traffic statistics are prepared other than the aggregate revenues, actual or presumptive, of each PTT service as a whole, and no attempt is made to assess the specific costs of providing particlular types of service to particular groups of clients.

Unless proper methods of accounting are brought to bear, Communicaciones will be unable to devise an effective operational budget to shape and control its work. The present budget, like that of other public enterprises in Nicaragua, is essentially a proposed list of salaries side by side with revenue forecasts. It looks ahead to future performance but never behind to past performance. Instead of functional analysis to clarify a complex operation, there is the predicted payroll and a sketchy idea of expected receipts.

A brief glance at the 1951-52 budget as submitted to Congress may be instructive. In Table 3 the appropriations request is restated as functionally as possible.

TABLE 3

Budget for Communicaciones, 1951-52
(thousand cordobas)

Purpose	
Salaries—	
Administrative	570
Post Office	620
Telegraph System	1,841
Telephone System	687
Regional inspectors	103
Total	3,821
Welfare—	
Retirement pay	24
Medical services	30
Total	54

Maintenance and repair of facilities   600
Rentals of leased properties   91
Payments to international air carriers   264
Payments to internal air carriers   42
Transport of rail   84
Foreign services   24
                                           _____

Grand total   4,980

Simplified slightly for postal receipts, the revenue forecasts run as follows:

TABLE 4

ESTIMATED COMMUNICACIONES REVENUES, 1951-52

Post Office (Sale of stamps)
    Philatelic   735.0
    Ordinary   319.0
    Special types   462.0
                                          _____

    Total   1,516.0

Telegraph
    Public services   377.8
    Unspecified   93.6
                                          _____

    Total   471.4

Telephone
    Public services   76.8
    Subscribers   468.5
    Unspecified   4.6
                                          _____

    Total   549.9

The first aim in operational budgeting by the new management should be increased expenditure on maintenance to make good previous arrears and keep the properties in good shape. Much of the present inefficiency of the PTT services, particularly the tele-communications services can be traced to neglect of maintenance.

This is largely the result of inadequate appropriations. Under the present setup, where Communicaciones has to rely on appropriations by Congress for all its spending power, the allowable outlays for upkeep and repair are much too small. The 1951-52 budget authorizes only 600,000 cordobas (equivalent to $85,700) for all the post offices, the entire telephone system, and the entire telegraph network. The mission recommends not only an increased rate of expenditure but also a pattern of budgeting in which maintenance would be a first charge on operating revenues. Where necessary, state appropriations should supplement these funds.

Adequate budgeting of maintenance ought to go hand in hand with advance programming of renewals, modernization, and expansion. The programming should be systematic and continuous, not a mere improvisation of projects as they become urgent. After long years of neglect during which the Managua telephone system was allowed to deteriorate badly, the government is now prepared to modernize the property. No attention is being given, however, to the possible need of increased trunk line facilities for long-distance calls, to making good the maintenance arrears of the telegraph system, or to equipping the post office with better means of handling mail.

If there is no systematic programming of capital expenditure at present, it is mainly because Communicaciones is neither organized for the work nor held responsible for getting it done. Assuming a public corporation run on public utility lines, the preparation of a capital expenditure budget would follow naturally. This is one of the strongest administrative arguments for reorganizing Communicaciones as the mission recommends.

Capital Investment and Operational Procedure

To provide fast and reliable means of communication, additional capital investment to modernize and expand capacity will be needed, particularly in the telecommunications field. Procedural reforms to improve the quality of service, especially in the postal system, are also urgent.

Some of the major defects in the postal system can be corrected without incurring expense; others require an increased labor force rather than capital outlay; and the remainder might be allowed to continue, without too much harm, until the time comes when the government can afford to increase its spending on public amenities. There is therefore no need to include the post office in the recommended program of public investment for the next five years. The faults of the postal service so far as they stem from lack of equipment are not a developmental block of the kind to justify immediate large state expenditures.

For this service the mission recommends a program of action rather than a pattern of investment. The correctives which cost nothing should be applied at once. In this category are speedier and more accurate techniques for collecting, sorting and distributing mail, and more efficient emission of stamps through the sale of prestamped letters and cards. The correctives which cost something should be brought into play as rapidly as the financial position permits. These include equipping Managua with mail boxes, employing more mail carriers, re-equipping some of the larger post offices, and extending postal delivery to the rural areas as farm-to-market roads are built. Part of the costs could be met out of the increased earnings apt to result from the abolition of free mail, the growth of postal traffic, and better operating efficiency. Most, however, would probably have to be met by state appropriations, which might or might not have to be subsidies in support of an essential public service.

The official project to modernize and expand the Managua telephone system is a soundly conceived response to an essential need. It can be made to pay its own way from increased earnings if Communicaciones is commercialized on public utility lines. Under the proposal, the manual switchboards would be replaced by automatic switchboards and the handphones by dial instruments. Switchboard capacity would be expanded to service 5,000 clients instead of 2,000 as at present and line capacity and the number of instruments would be increased correspondingly. The overhead lines now in use would give way to underground cables made of better materials. The total cost, as estimated by qualified technicians, is roughly $1.69 million, mainly foreign exchange.

The mission believes that modernization and expansion of the Managua telephone system should be followed by action to improve the interregional network—e.g. by multiplying the land-line circuits for trunk calls along the west coast and by setting up radio-telephone circuits for east-west transmission of public calls. Because of the pressure of other developmental needs of higher priority, no project of this kind has been included in the immediate budget of recommended public investment. The mission believes, however, that a prompt start should be made on the studies necessary to work up a definite project to be carried out when Nicaragua's finances permit.

Telegraph System

The telegraph system would also benefit by some technical modernization, for example, faster sending and receiving equipment, teletype facilities, and multiplex apparatus. But there is no urgent need to invest large sums for this purpose immediately, particularly since the public is now getting better telegraph than telephone service. If the telegraph system is overloaded, a basic cause is a heavy load of traffic which would be sent by phone if calls could be made promptly and reliably. Another is the lavish transmission of messages by clients who do not have to pay for the service. Modernization and expansion of the Managua telephone system will relieve much of the pressure on the telegraph network. Suppression of free telegrams and phone calls will bring added relief.

The immediate outlook is a big shift from telegraph to telephone as soon as proper telephone facilities become available. Notwithstanding the factors which now make the use of telegrams preferable to that of phone calls where practicable, effective demand for telephone service is increasing faster than effective demand for telegraph service. This is a local expression of a worldwide tendency, not something unique to Nicaragua. As the flaws which impair telephone service are corrected, the revenues of the telegraph system will become increasingly vulnerable to traffic diversion.

TABLE 5

COMPARISON OF TELEPHONE WITH TELEGRAPH TRAFFIC
(thousand cordobas)

Measure	1948	1949	1950	Ratio of 1950 to 1948
Realized revenues from paying clients:				
Telephone	321	486	543	1.7
Telegraph	281	302	378	1.6
Foregone revenues from official clients:				
Telephone	110	114	116	1.0
Telegraph	746	762	724	0.9
Realized plus foregone revenues:				
Telephone	431	600	659	1.5
Telegraph	1,027	1,064	1,102	1.1

The modernization of Nicaragua's telegraph system is thus a project to be approached with caution. Nevertheless, maintenance arrears have accumulated which ought to be made good in the interest of minimum operating efficiency. This is another priority task for the new management of Communicaciones. Most or all of the cost can be covered out of increased earnings from the suppression of free messages, the imposition of higher rates, and the improved serviceability of equipment.

CHAPTER FIFTEEN

Summary of Recommended Investment Program for Transport and Communications

The transport and communications projects which the mission recommends for execution in the next five years would require a total outlay of close to $23.8 million. Of this, about $18.3 million is needed for construction and improvement of roads, $3.8 million for railways, ports, and airfields, and $1.7 million for telecommunications.

TABLE 1

ESTIMATE OF REQUIRED INVESTMENT
IN TRANSPORT AND COMMUNICATIONS—1952-57
(thousand U.S. dollars)

Project	Amount
Roads[a]	18,250
FCPN	1,850
Ports	1,875
Telecommunications	1,690
Airfields	100
Total	23,765
Local roads: (contingent expenditure)[b]	(1,000)[c]

[a] Includes Rama port and El Bluff dredging
[b] Contingent (assuming availability of funds) on need to incur expenditure
[c] Excluded from total as shown above.

Much of the outlay will be cost-free to the Nicaraguan Treasury. Two thirds of the cost of the Inter-American Highway and the entire cost of the Rama Road will be covered by United States grants; the entire cost of the FCPN projects can be charged against the carrier's earnings; part of the costs to improve Corinto and to build airstrips may be assumed by private enterprises; and part of the cost of the Managua telephone project will, under the mission's proposal, be offset by induced earnings. These reductions add to $10.4 million, leaving a net cost to the government of $13.4 million or 56% of the gross cost.

TABLE 2

ESTIMATED COST TO THE GOVERNMENT
OF TRANSPORT AND COMMUNICATIONS PROGRAM—1952-57

(thousand U.S. dollars)

Project	Amount
Roads[a]	10,250
FCPN	—
Ports	1,560
Telecommunications	1,520
Airfields	75
Total	13,405

[a] Includes Rama port and El Bluff dredging.

The Treasury's need for additional funds over the next five years will be less, probably about 25% less, than the net cost to the government. First, both the Rama port and the El Bluff channel can be financed out of reserves earmarked for the Rama Road which already exist. Second, part of the cost of the local roads can also be financed out of reserves earmarked for access roads into coffee plantations. Third, the foreign exchange cost of the IBRD roads under the 1951 loan agreement will be financed out of the undisbursed proceeds of that loan. Subtracting the available reserves for the Rama port and El Bluff channel ($750,000) the available reserves for local roads ($400,000) and the remaining balance of the IBRD loan (about $2.5 million), the Treasury burden will be around $9.8 million.

TABLE 3

ESTIMATED IMPACT ON TREASURY
(thousand U.S. dollars)

Project	Amount
Roads[a]	6,600
FCPN	—
Ports	1,560
Telecommunications	1,520
Airfields	75
Total	9,755

[a] Includes Rama port and El Bluff dredging.

Of $23.8 million to carry out the total program, roughly $16 million might be foreign exchange for imported equipment, materials, supplies, and technical know-how, and almost $7.8 million might be local currency expenditure, mainly for labor. These are mere orders of magnitude, not close estimates within narrow margins of error. Assuming, however, that Nicaragua does go ahead with a $20 million-$25 million program made up of the kinds of projects recommended, it is estimated that around two thirds of the outlay will be in foreign exchange, and one third in local currency.

Roughly three fifths of the foreign exchange expenditure will create no immediate pressure on the Nicaraguan balance of payments; e.g. all the purchases abroad arising from the IBRD roads, all those arising from the Rama Road as well, and part of those arising from the Inter-American Highway, modernization of the FCPN (offsetting proceeds from sale of scrap) and expansion of

TABLE 4

COMPARISON OF FOREIGN EXCHANGE WITH LOCAL CURRENCY COSTS
(thousand U.S. dollars)

Project	Foreign Exchange	Local Currency
Roads[a]	12,375	5,875
FCPN	1,390	460
Ports	935	940
Telecommunications	1,265	425
Airfields	10	90
Total	15,975	7,790

[a] Includes Rama port and El Bluff dredging.

Corinto port facilities (possible inflow of private capital). Allowing for these factors, the strain on the balance of payments would be $6.6 million, or only 40% of the foreign exchange costs.

TABLE 5

ESTIMATED NEED FOR ADDITIONAL FOREIGN EXCHANGE
(thousand U.S. dollars)

Project	Amount
Roads	3,375
FCPN	1,290
Ports	620
Telecommunications	1,265
Airfields	10
Total	6,560

Similarly, much of the local currency expenditure would not call for any immediate effort by the Treasury to raise additional funds through taxes, borrowing or both. Taking into account the existence of earmarked reserves for part of the Rama project and

TABLE 6

ESTIMATED NEED FOR ADDITIONAL LOCAL CURRENCY
(thousand U.S. dollars)

Project	Amount
Roads	3,600
FCPN	—
Ports	940
Telecommunications	255
Airfields	65
Total	4,860

The aggregate dimensions of the recommended investment program are thus as follows:

Measure	Thousand Dollars
Gross outlay	23,765
Net cost to government	13,405
Immediate burden on Treasury	9,755
Foreign exchange costs	15,975
Net cost to government	7,770
Added burden on Treasury	4,595
Local currency costs	7,790
Net cost to government	5,635
Added burden on Treasury	5,160
Net strain on balance of payments	6,560
Rama port and El Bluff channel (financed from existing reserves)	375
Certain local roads (financed from existing reserves)	300
FCPN project (carrier-financed)	1,290
All other projects (Treasury-financed)	4,595

for certain types of local roads, the FCPN's ability to finance rehabilitation and modernization out of internal earnings, the likelihood of some induced earnings from the Managua telephone project, and the possibility that some of the airfield investment might be carrier-financed, the local currency costs of $7.8 million reduce to a Treasury impact of only $4.9 million.

Turning to the individual sectors, the recommended program can be summarized as follows:

Roads: Improvement of the Inter-American Highway to perfect the north-south route across Nicaragua; completion of a Rama Road with incidental port and seaway facilities to create an east-west route; completion of the IBRD roads now under construction, to expand the highway network on the west coast; and a five-year drive to provide Nicaragua with local meshes of feeder, access, and farm-to-market routes. Total costs: $18.3 million of which $8 million would come as a United States grant.

FCPN: Rehabilitation of the permanent way; replacement of steam locomotives by diesel-electrics; replacement of passenger coaches by auto-rail cars; procurement of freight cars; and re-equipment of repair shops. Gross cost (to the carrier, not the government): $1,850,000, reducing to a net cost of $1,750,000 with allowance for scrap credit.

Ports: (except Rama). Construction of additional berthing facilities at Corinto, improvement of pier for lighters, and of service roads for trucks at San Juan del Sur; and installation of landing stages for small craft on Lake Nicaragua. Gross cost: $1.9 million reducing to a net cost (to the government) of $1.5 million.

Telecommunications: Modernizing and expanding the Managua telephone system at a gross cost of $1,690,000 which might be cut back to $1,520,000 through induced immediate earnings.

Airfields: Construction of a few simple grass strips for DC-3s operating on internal flights at a total cost of $100,000 of which perhaps 25% might be covered by private investment.

Tables 7 to 10 give a breakdown of the investment program for transport and communications by project and cost.

TABLE 7

COMPARISON OF FOREIGN EXCHANGE WITH LOCAL CURRENCY COSTS
(thousand U.S. dollars)

	Foreign Exchange			Local Currency		
	Total	Immediate Burden on Treasury	No Immediate Burden on Treasury	Total	Immediate Burden on Treasury	No Immediate Burden on Treasury
Roads						
Rama road	2,500	—	2,500[a]	1,500	—	1,500[a]
Port of Rama	125	—	125[b]	125	—	125[b]
Seaway channel	250	—	250[b]	250	—	250[b]
Rama project	2,875	—	2,875	1,875	—	1,875
Inter-American Highway	4,000	—	4,000[a]	2,000	2,000	—
IBRD roads	2,500	—	2,500[c]	1,000	1,000	—
Local roads	3,000	2,700	300[b]	1,000	900	100[b]
Total	12,375	2,700	9,675	5,875	3,900	1,975
FCPN						
Permanent way	340	—	340	435	—	435
Motive power	425	—	425	—	—	—

Rolling stock	500	—	500	—	—	—
Repair shops	125	—	125	25	—	25
Total	1,390	—	1,390[d]	460	—	460[d]
Ports						
Corinto	625	310	315[e]	625	625	—
San Juan del Sur	125	125	—	125	125	—
Lake Nicaragua	185	185	—	190	190	—
Total	935	620	315	940	940	—
Telecommunications	1,265	1,265	—	425	255	170[f]
Airfields	10	10	—	90	65	25[g]
Total	15,975	4,595	11,380	7,790	5,160	2,630

[a] Expected grants from the United States.
[b] Earmarked reserve funds.
[c] Undisbursed proceeds of 1951 loan from IBRD.
[d] Expected carrier earnings plus proceeds from sale of scrap.
[e] Possible investment by foreign oil companies.
[f] Expected earnings from Managua telephone project; property now run at a loss.
[g] Possible investment by private air carrier.

TABLE 8

RECOMMENDED PROGRAM OF PUBLIC INVESTMENT—1952-57
(thousand U.S. dollars)

Class of project	Gross Outlay	Net cost to Government	Immediate burden on Treasury
Roads			
Rama road	4,000	—[a]	—
Rama port	250	250	—[f]
El Bluff dredging	500	500	—[f]
Rama project	4,750	750	—
Inter-American	6,000	2,000[a]	2,000
IBRD roads	3,500	3,500	1,000[g]
Local roads	4,000[h]	4,000	3,600[f]
Total	18,250	10,250	6,600
FCPN			
Permanent way	775	—	—
Motive power	425	—	—
Rolling stock	500	—	—
Repair shops	150	—	—
Total	1,850	[b]	—
Ports			
Corinto	1,250	935[c]	935
San Juan del Sur	250	250	250
Lake Nicaragua	375	375	375
Total	1,875	1,560	1,560
Telecommunications	1,690	1,520[d]	1,520
Airfields	100	75[e]	75
Total	23,765	13,405	9,755

[a] Reflects expected grant from the United States equal to full costs (Rama road) and two thirds total cost (Inter-American Highway).

[b] Reflects carrier's ability to finance project out of internal earnings. FCPN is state-owned but pays no cash dividends to state, despite large operating profits.

[c] Reflects possibility that foreign oil companies might bear part of the project cost.

[d] Reflects induced earnings from Managua telephone projects; property now run at a loss.

[e] Reflects possibility that semi-private air carrier might pay part of the project cost.

[f] Reflects availability of earmarked reserve funds.

[g] Reflects availability of undisbursed proceeds of previous loan.

[h] Reflects theory that part of total program costing $5 million might be deferred if financial exigencies so dictate.

TABLE 9
LOCAL CURRENCY COMPONENT OF RECOMMENDED PRORGAM
(thousand U.S. dollars)

	Gross Outlay	Grants, Earmarked Internal Earnings, and Local Private Investment	Strain on Treasury Resources
Roads			
Rama road	1,500	1,500[a]	—
Port of Rama	125	125[b]	—
Seaway channel	250	250[b]	—
Rama project	1,875	1,875	—
Inter-American Highway	2,000	—	2,000
IBRD roads	1,000	—	1,000
Local roads	1,000	100[b]	900
Total	5,875	1,975	3,900
FCPN			
Permanent way	435	435[c]	—
Motive power	—	—	—
Rolling stock	—	—	—
Repair shop	25	25	—
Total	460	460	—
Ports			
Corinto	625	(500)[d]	625
San Juan del Sur	125	—	125
Lake Nicaragua	190	—	190
Total	940	(500)	940
Telecommunications	425	170[e]	255
Airfields	90	25	65
Total	7,790	2,630	5,160

[a] Expected grant from the United States.

TABLE 9 (Continued)

[b] Balance of earmarked reserves over amounts required to pay foreign exchange costs.

[c] Balance of expected earnings, totalling about $1.5 million, over amount required for foreign exchange costs.

[d] Expected earnings which are payable to Treasury under present regime; if used for port project, they would reduce Treasury revenues by the same amount.

[e] Expected earnings from Managua telephone project; property now runs at a loss which has to be subsidized out of Treasury resources.

TABLE 10

FOREIGN EXCHANGE COMPONENT OF RECOMMENDED PROGRAM
1952-57
(thousand U.S. dollars)

	Gross Outlay	Grants, Previous Loans, Scrap Credit, and Foreign Private Investment	Strain on Balance of Payments
Roads			
Rama road	2,500	2,500[a]	—
Port of Rama	125	—	125
Seaway channel	250	—	250
Rama project	2,875	2,500	375
Inter-American Highway	4,000	4,000[a]	—
IBRD roads	2,500	2,500[b]	—
Local roads	3,000	—	3,000
Total	12,375	9,000	3,375
FCPN			
Permanent way	340	15	325
Motive power	425	25	400
Rolling stock	500	50	450
Repair shops	125	10	115
Total	1,390	100[a]	1,290
Ports			
Corinto	625	315[d]	310
San Juan del Sur	125	—	125
Lake Nicaragua	185	—	185
Total	935	315	620
Telecommunications	1,265	—	1,265
Airfields	10	—	10
Total	15,975	9,415	6,560

[a] Expected grants from the United States.

[b] Undisbursed proceeds of 1951 loan from IBRD.

[c] Estimated proceeds from sale of scrap.

[d] Assumed investment by foreign oil companies.

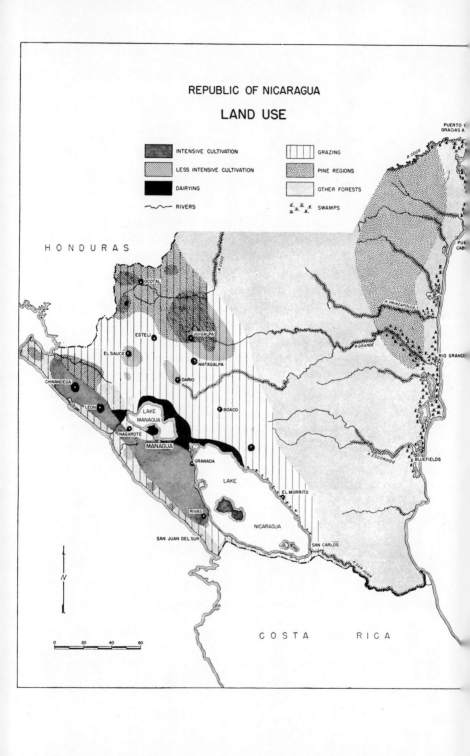

CHAPTER SIXTEEN

The Natural Regions of the Country

Introductory Note

The report of the FAO Mission to Nicaragua, published in 1950, contained a broad survey of the agricultural and forestry resources of Nicaragua. The International Bank mission did not therefore attempt an over-all agricultural study. Instead, this section of the report has confined its study to specific problems and recent developments important to the proposed investment program not already covered in Parts I and II.

I. *THE WESTERN PLAINS REGION*

This region is made up of volcanic plains ranging from sea level to several hundred feet elevation. The rainy season[1] usually begins in May, or a little earlier, and normally ends in October. According to the limited number of gauge readings available, there is considerable variation in the rainfall within this region as the following examples of annual mean and range values show.

Managua (inland—200 feet elevation). 1932-1948: mean, 45.20 inches; range, 16.02 inches in 1946 to 70.36 inches in 1932. Over 45 inches were listed in nine of the 17 years on record.

San Antonio (western). 1903-1949: mean, 82.58 inches; range 41.87 inches in 1939 to 187.73 inches in 1924. Over 83 inches were listed in 20 of the 47 years on record.

Granada (on Lake Nicaragua—196 feet elevation). 1877, 1883-1884, and 1897-1949: mean for 56 years: 58.57 inches;

---

[1] Rainfall and similar data from FAO Report. Additional data on coffee have been provided by Mr. J. Phillip Rourk of the United States Embassy, Managua, in his unpublished study, "The Coffee Industry of Nicaragua," 1949.

range from 15.35 inches in 1946 to 93.67 inches in 1897; over 45 inches were noted in 51 out of the 56 years on record.

Rivas (between sea and Lake Nicaragua—elevation 160 feet). 1932-1948: mean, 59.39 inches; range, 31.14 in 1946 to 89.91 in 1933; over 45 inches were recorded in 14 of the 17 years on record.

The volcanic ash soils of this region are naturally fertile. A full description cannot be made on the nature of the soil because of insufficient data, but FAO reports that heavily cropped soils near Managua were found to be "extremely low" in nitrate (two parts per million) and "high" in available phosphate (100-150 p.p.m.), soluble potash (400 kg. per hectare) and replaceable calcium (700 p.p.m.). On the average the pH ranges from 6.0 to 7.0; it goes up to 8.0 in limited areas near Rivas and on western Ometepe where the soil contains calcareous material.

The better farming areas are in the Departments of Leon, Chinandega and Rivas. Sixty per cent of the population of the country is concentrated in these areas, which are the most developed of the country. Except where *Hyparrhenia rufa* (Jaragua grass), introduced from Africa, grows, or other grasses have been planted, the grazing is of relatively poor quality. Despite this, a considerable number of livestock, principally cattle, are raised in the Departments of Chinandega, Leon, Rivas and Chontales.

Agricultural production is concentrated on corn, sorghum, sesame, rice, beans, cotton, sugar and livestock. The largest sugar producing estate and mill in the country, San Antonio, is located in this region. While examples of good to fair farming can be found, the general average of crop agriculture and animal husbandry is mediocre to very poor. Little of the land is irrigated.

The main communications are limited to the railway running from Managua to Granada on the one side and from Managua to Corinto, Puerto Morazan and El Sauce on the other; and to the Inter-American Highway extending from Managua to Rivas on the south, and northward to Sebaco and the border with Honduras. The main new roads under construction will go outward from Managua to Chinandega and Granada. Lateral or feeder roads are of poor quality, many of them being dust baths in the dry season and mud-and-water rivers during the wet weather.

The main lines for development of the area are:

1. The construction of feeder and farm-to-market roads leading into the main highways and railroad stations.

2. Improvement of farming practices, with emphasis on soil improvement, better crop rotation, a more careful selection of seed, the development of mechanical farming of arable land, and more scientific handling of livestock.

3. Planned long-range extension of cotton areas after due consideration has been given to world market prospects, and to the availability of additional land within the developed portions of the region, and of suitable land within portions not yet opened up.

4. Cultivation of additional crops including peanuts, castor beans, dwarf sorghum (by mechanical means), hard fibers and—at a later stage when retting practice is better understood—kenaf *(Hibiscus cannabinus)*. It might also be feasible to extend coconut production in suitable sites near the coast.

5. Irrigation of land around Lake Nicaragua, in order to grow more sugar and rice.

II. *THE MANAGUA-CARAZO UPLANDS (SIERRAS)*

This comparatively small sierra and upland plateau region ranges in elevation from about 1300 to 4000 feet. In the Department of Managua coffee is grown from approximately 1300 to 3500 feet, while in the Department of Carazo the range is about 1600 to 2300 feet.

The region includes the district of "Los Pueblos," geographically a continuation of the Sierra country but differing from it in that the steep Managua uplands merge, in part, into a comparatively flat plateau in the Departments of Carazo and of Masaya.

The region has a dry season of about five to six months in

which there is little or no rainfall, although there is a certain amount of precipitation in the form of mists. The rains usually commence about mid-May and end about mid-November but not infrequently the season will continue until the end of December. Generally the wettest months are June, September and October.

From the published records for the Hacienda San Francisco (San Marcos-Diriamba) 1925 to 1949, the following facts are derived: mean rainfall 71.37 inches, range 36.19 inches in 1946 to 146.85 in 1933: 45 inches and upward were recorded for each of the 25 years, except 1930 and 1946. There are no data on humidity and evaporation.

Temperature records are not available, but it is probable that there is a decrease of roughly three degrees F. for each 1000 feet of elevation. There is never any frost. In relation to the mean annual figure of about 83 degrees for Managua, the range in temperatures, according to range of elevation in this upland region, would be from about 73 to 79 degrees F. The range is greater between day and night than between the wet and the dry months. From February to April there are strong, gusty winds.

On the whole, the climate is cooler and somewhat more humid than that of the western plains region, as might be expected from the elevation. This is reflected in the vegetation, which, while of the type of mixed deciduous hardwood climax of the western plains, possesses specific and physiognomy characteristics that place it in a different faciation of the mixed deciduous hardwood forest climax. During the dry period many forest species lose their foliage and the herbaceous vegetation shrivels but, even so, the vegetation on the whole is greener and fresher looking than at a lower elevation in the western plains region.

The soils are of volcanic origin and originally were quite fertile; they are loose, porous and well drained. In the Department of Managua, almost all the coffee estates are on slopes ranging from about five to over 15 percent, whereas in the Department of Carazo it is estimated that only about half the estates are on such steep slopes. The remainder are on level to very slightly sloping ground.

Where the soil is not protected by vegetation and is exposed to severe insolation (heat-light-high evaporation complex), cracking of the surface occurs to a width of several inches and often to a depth of several feet. Exposure of the surface of the slopes in the Department of Managua results in some soil movement and erosion.

Despite the fact that some regions have been planted to coffee since about 1860, and many others for upwards of 50 years, the soils still show comparatively high fertility. It seems clear, however, that there must have been some loss in both depth and fertility where the steeper slopes have been cultivated, especially where systematic removal of all weed growth under coffee has taken place over a number of decades. Leaching of nutrients and slip of surface soil have clearly occurred and must still be taking place.

This is essentially coffee producing country. The industry has gradually grown over the last 90 years to a reported 37,000,000 trees. Elevation, climate and soils all are suitable for the production of coffee. About two-thirds of the coffee of the country is produced in this region.

Statements of yield vary considerably according to the estate, precise locality, the age of the trees and the nature of the treatment accorded them. The average yield per tree for this region has been estimated at about 0.6 pounds, in contrast with about 0.4 pounds per tree for the Central Montane region described later. Some estates, however, record averages from one to 1.5 pounds per tree with some stands bringing in as much as two to four pounds per tree.

From discussion with the growers in the region, it appears that practically all the acreage capable of producing coffee is already planted to this crop. Since extension is impossible, therefore, it is clear that emphasis should be laid on the improvement of production from existing plantations. Such improvement may be gained along the following main lines:

(a) Gradual removal of nonproductive trees and their replacement by new plants;

(b) Careful attention to the provision of more congenial conditions of light—reducing shade, where it is too heavy,
   but not to a point that would produce severe insolation.
   Insolation is liable to stimulate production for a while
   but may in time exhaust the trees. Further, it may do harm
   to the soil when is is exposed to heat, light and wind
   for too long a period and in too great a degree.

(c) Considerably more attention to pruning and development
   of pruning methods best suited to the local sub-varieties
   and environmental conditions;

(d) Further introduction of moderate cultivation and weeding,
   and the provision of organic and inorganic fertilizers.

The labor supply is reported to be barely sufficient for coffee
harvesting because of competing crops in other regions; however,
the workers are reasonably competent owing to their long experience with the production of coffee.

While a few staple crops are grown, and some cattle are kept
on the estates and by the small landowners, coffee is likely to
continue to be almost the only local industry.

III. *THE CENTRAL MONTANE REGION*

This region includes the Departments of Matagalpa, Jinotega,
Madriz, Nueva Segovia and part of Esteli, in northeastern Nicaragua. As the region is situated in the range of mountains forming
the continental divide, most of the streams and rivers flow into
the Caribbean Sea and there are numerous small but swift-flowing
mountain streams. The elevation ranges from about 1,500 feet
to about 5,500 feet. Coffee, which up to the present is the chief
industry, can be grown at about 2,000 to 5,000 feet, preferably
from 2,200 to 3,500 feet.

The topography is rugged. Mountain peaks attain heights of
4,500 to 5,500 feet, alternating with comparatively small lowland
valleys and plateaus. Fairly extensive llanos or plains exist in
the Department of Matagalpa, commencing some 25 miles east
and southeast of the town. Climate, soil and elevation are con-

ducive to coffee production. Similar plain areas occur in the Department of Jinotega.

Some indication of the roughness of the general terrain may be obtained from the fact that 80 to 90 percent of the coffee is grown on land and of over 15 percent slope, and the remainder on slopes of five to 15 percent. Very little coffee is grown on level land.

The climate is typical of highland country in the tropics, that is, of country known locally as "tierra templada"; cool, humid to very humid, with little seasonal range in temperature but quite marked diurnal range. No satisfactory meteorological records exist but from various references and from the appearance of the natural vegetation, the following description of the area is probably reasonably accurate.

Rainfall is somewhat greater than in the Managua-Carazo Sierras but the rains are usually of a lesser intensity. Heavy downpours of a torrential nature occur occasionally. The rainy season commences about mid-May, but toward the northern portions of the region light rains may be experienced even in February, March and April. From the FAO report it appears that the months of June to October may be described as having a 100% frequency of wet conditions, November about 95%, December about 90%, January about 80%, February about 60% or slightly less, March about 20%, April about 25% and May about 90%.

No temperature, humidity or evaporation data exist, but on the basis of a drop of about three degrees for every 1,000 feet increase, the mean annual temperature may range from 69 degrees to about 77 degrees F. At about 4,000 feet the night temperature may be as low as 50 degrees F. Frost is never experienced.

The very high humidity appears to preclude successful growing of coffee above 5,000 feet.

The soils are reported to differ greatly from those of the Managua-Carazo region. In general the metamorphic rocks of the Matagalpa highlands are deeply weathered, resulting in a light reddish brown clay subsoil, with a relatively shallow layer of loamy topsoil, sometimes no more than several inches in depth at the higher elevations in the region. The soils have developed from the decomposition of ancient volcanic and sedimentary rocks. They are considered to be sufficiently suitable in terms of physical and chemical characteristics for the successful production of coffee, but are not equal, for this purpose, to the soils of the Managua-Carazo region.

The steepness of the slopes can be expected to cause serious erosion of cultivated soil during the rainy season. To a substantial extent, this loss is compensated for by the fact that top shade of considerable density and little ground cultivation are significant features of coffee growing in this region. Wherever careless cultivation is practiced, whether in coffee growing or in annual field cropping, there are marked signs of local soil deterioration, washing and erosion.

The vegetation is made up, in the higher portions of the region in any event, of an evergreen subtropical—tropical forest climax, mixed in species and as yet little known in terms of economic timber productivity. In physiognomy these forests are similar to equivalent high-level mixed evergreen forests of the tropics of the old world.

At lower elevations, fire and agricultural activities have wrought considerable damage to these forests, and much of the country is in the successional stages of secondary grassland and tree-and-grass savanna.

Within the area, which has as yet been little studied, there occur stands of *Pinus oocarpa,* a valuable coniferous timber. The density and extent of these stands have not been established. Unfortunately the pines are annually devastated by uncontrolled fire started by local inhabitants grazing their cows, with consequent gradual but sure reduction of the regeneration stages of the conifer. Prompt and active steps alone can avert ultimate loss of these potentially valuable coniferous forests.

Coffee production began about 1885, but the period of greatest expansion was delayed until about 1910. Thus a considerable proportion of the estimated 27,000,000 trees are less than 30 years of age. This is even truer in the Departments of Jinotega, Madriz and Nueva Segovia, where coffee production is more recent than in the Department of Matagalpa.

Some points of interest regarding coffee in this region are:

(a) The prevailing view is reported to be in favor of growing the crop under lower light intensity than in the Managua-Carazo region, with tall forest shade of several layers being preferred.

(b) Practically no pruning is done, the coffee being permitted to develop into tall spindly trees. The difficulty of pruning on steep slopes and the suspected loss in crop resulting from the development of poor growth in the slope side of the tree are given as reasons against pruning.

(c) No fertilizers are used. There is little or no cultivation, apart from freeing the young plants from creepers and tall growth.

All of these points require further investigation and study with a view to improving coffee growing techniques in the region.

As has been noted already, the mean yield per tree is said to be about 0.4 pounds per annum. This is very low considering the favorable rainfall and other climatic factors and the general nature of the soils. Improved cultivation practices should raise this average in the course of time.

In addition to coffee, which amounts to about one third of the country's production, scattered annual crops and some cattle are raised in the region, particularly at the lower elevations. Torsalo fly is a troublesome pest of all livestock in the region and ticks (Ixodidae) are abundant. Treatment with "Toxophene," is advocated by the Servicio Tecnico, and is proving a useful means of controlling both the fly and the ticks.

The main agricultural needs or prospects of the area are:

(a) Development of additional feeder or lateral roads leading to the road from Matagalpa to Tuma, (constructed with

IBRD funds) and opening up of areas suitable for coffee extension.

(b) Determining the nature, extent and distribution of the areas suitable for expanded coffee cultivation and also for wheat and black wattle *(Acacia mollissima)* production.

(c) Mixed farming at the lower elevations should be investigated to determine the possibility of raising cattle and of growing corn, sorghum, sesame, and perhaps castor beans. At suitable points cotton production might be developed. Small scale sisal growing should also be considered.

(d) Protection of the *Pinus oocarpa* against fire, where the larger, more compact, and more valuable stands occur, should be organized after a proper survey has been made of the distribution of the pine. In due course some effort should be made to provide some simple silvicultural thinning if fire-protected sites become densely regenerated.

(e) As so little is now known of the evergreen subtropical-tropical forests either as to extent, stocking or potential economic use, their assessment should be organized as staff and funds become available.

IV. *THE EASTERN PLAINS REGION*

This region comprises over half the total area of the country and is made up of the low slopes and plains which are bounded by the Atlantic. The region has a wide range of soils, from alluvial types along the numerous larger rivers, to shallow gravelly soils and clay-loams of low natural fertility.

There is a dearth of published or manuscript information on the soils of this region. Some data have been collected by the Servicio Tecnico, through their work at El Recreo, Cukra Hill and elsewhere in the region.

The country is dissected by numerous rivers—some of them of appreciable length, width and volume—and countless streams.

The prevailing vegetation is tropical evergreen hardwood forest of very mixed composition. These forests are estimated to cover nearly 20 million acres of which about one quarter is believed to be of a superior type. These figures must be considered very rough estimates since no adequate surveys have been made.

The northeastern portion of the country contains stands of *Pinus caribaea* of varying density, dimensions, economic values and regeneration potential. The pine flats of the Zelaya Department are estimated to occupy about 1.5 million acres of land below 600 feet elevation; about 40 to 50% of this area is covered with pine stands. No systematic survey has been made.

The Eastern Plains have never been thoroughly explored. Apart from the five main rivers which permit a certain degree of navigation—the San Juan, the Escondido, the Rio Grande, the Prinzapolca, and the Rio Coco—and some local roads built by private enterprise in the vicinity of Puerto Cabezas, there are at present few means of transport. The road planned from a point on the Inter-American Highway toward Rama on the River Escondido should, in time, prove a useful means of developing some of the country tapped by the road and by the Escondido. At present agricultural activity exists within several miles of the main rivers; beyond this there is little or no human habitation. The human population is the lowest per unit in Nicaragua.

The rain is heavier here than elsewhere in the country, with the fall extending over nine to 12 months of the year. Examples of two centers give some impression of the amount and distribution of the fall: Bluefields (coastal): on a basis of 23 years of record: 1926-32: 1934-49: Annual mean fall, 151.68 inches: range 61.19 inches (1936) to 200.11 (1927); Cukra Hill Experimental Station on Rio Escondido: 1945-50: range 132.05 inches (1946) to 155.71 inches (1945).

Temperature, humidity and evaporation data are lacking, but it may be stated that there is little range in temperature between the drier and the wetter months; the humidity range is slightly more marked, the values being somewhat less in the months of February, March and April, in years when the rainfall is markedly reduced. To judge from evaporation data for the stations at San Carlos at the very southern extreme of the region and on Lake Nicaragua, the evaporation is very much less than in the drier Western plains region.

Up to the present the principal activity in this great region has been the exploitation of hardwood timber, principally Mahogany *(Swietenia macrophylla)*. This has been carried on within reasonable distançe of some of the principal rivers, which have been used for floating the logs down to the Atlantic. More recently there has been some exploitation of the *Pinus caribaea* in the Department of Zelaya.

There has been some production of rice, beans and other staple foods. At one time bananas grew quite abundantly but hurricane and disease have caused the production and export of bananas to fall off, until today comparatively little tonnage is exported from the region.

Experimental work is carried on by the Servicio Tecnico at its station at El Recreo, on the River Escondido, about 70 miles up its course and about 30 to 35 miles directly inland from the coast. Here a wide range of plants, including rubber *(Hevea)*, African oil palm, tropical fruits, abaca, and medicinal plants have been studied to test their suitability for economic production. The Cukra Hill station of the Servicio Tecnico has also been experimenting with rubber, African oil palm, abaca and pepper.

The following is a brief summary of the most important lines of development needed in the region:

1. Extension of the African oil palm industry.
2. Development and extension of cattle farming, along with establishment of pastures of sown and transplanted grasses on the site of secondary forest.
3. Improvement in cacao growing and extension of the acreage.

4. Survey protection and systematic exploitation of *Pinus caribaea* in Zelaya.

5. Survey of hardwood forest resources, especially mahogany, and gradual introduction of controlled exploitation and replanting of the more valuable timbers.

6. Possibly, at a later stage, limited production of abaca on suitable soils.

7. Controlled production of Ipecacuanha, following studies being made at El Recreo.

8. The introduction of pepper *(Piper nigrum)*.

9. Increased production of tropical fruits for domestic consumption.

10. Improved production of staple foods such as rice, beans and other crops.

CHAPTER SEVENTEEN

Agricultural and Forestry Production

There has been little direct government technical assistance to agricultural development, production techniques employed are frequently primitive and labor productivity low, yet agricultural production has achieved notable diversification, particularly over the past four years.

More than 35 products are grown commercially, others are raised for home consumption, and still others have been tested and found suitable for the soils and climate. In addition, livestock and timber production and their by-products are important activities closely associated with crop growth.

The total value of agricultural and forestry production was estimated by the Central Statistical Bureau at 416 million cordobas (US$83 million) in 1950. The 1951 value has been estimated as 637 million cordobas (US$91 million). (The sharp increase in the cordoba value was very largely a reflection of the effective devaluation of the cordoba at the end of 1950).

The expansion of production in cotton, sesame and sugar cane has been closely geared to increased credit allocations by the National Bank for these crops. In 1951-52, for example, nearly 80% of the agricultural credits of the National Bank were allocated for these three cash crops, extended mainly to a few hundred of the larger producers.

The range of agricultural products is shown in Table I indicating the value of principal agricultural exports in 1939, and since 1945. In 1951 there were seven agricultural and forestry products (including cotton and cotton seed as a single product) with a value of over a million dollars each in exports. What is more noteworthy is that, while the price of coffee has nearly doubled in the past three years, giving it in consequence a very heavy weight in export values, the percentage of coffee in total

292

value of agricultural exports showed a decline from 54% in 1945 to 50% in 1951. The increasing diversification of production is a feature of the economy which gives a basis for the expectation of continued expansion in the agricultural sector.

The major products for export include coffee, cotton, sesame, sugar, rice, cattle and timber. Other important crops, primarily for domestic consumption, include sorghum, beans, yucca, tobacco, bananas, cacao, cheese, lard, milk, vegetables and a wide variety of tropical fruits. Very rough estimates prepared by the Central Statistical Bureau for its national income study, are appended in Table 1 which indicates the value of total production for export and for domestic consumption. Table 2 gives the area planted and estimated volume of production of selected crops.

Coffee traditionally has been the principal cash crop. Exports of important crops such as cotton, sesame, sugar and rice have expanded considerably since the war, although production of staple foods such as corn and beans has also increased, and the former has become an important export item. Cotton has become a mechanized crop in the past two years.

Imports of agricultural products are confined for the most part to animal products, fruits and vegetables not grown locally, and wheat and wheat flour. The east coast also has to import canned meats, fruits and vegetables, because it lacks adequate communications with the west coast.

I. CROPS AND LIVESTOCK

Coffee

Coffee has long been the most important crop in Nicaragua. Unfortunately, almost no attention has been given to improving methods of cultivation, production per tree, or the quality of the bean.

In the Managua-Carazo region, plantings are confined mainly to the high plateaus with little slope, which facilitates cultivation. Here the "Vaughn" system of pruning is widely used. The limbs

TABLE 1
VALUE OF AGRICULTURAL AND FORESTRY EXPORTS
(dollars)

Crop	1939	1945	1946	1947	1948	1949	1950	1951
Sesame	—	361,781	852,654	2,185,040	3,614,121	4,126,263	1,514,611	2,479,498
Cotton	253,478	—	145,070	198,269	237	211,719	1,842,520	5,457,405
Rice	—	535	948,351	806,736	788,113	1,619,248	301,990	1,484,021
Bananas	654,356	81,412	193,294	335,783	659,293	827,929	613,453	496,853
Cacao	50,177	30,214	131,829	170,694	98,649	98,127	49,321	107,778
Coffee	2,639,981	3,667,952	4,316,433	5,332,724	8,457,122	4,361,969	17,331,044	18,449,845
Corn	—	70,125	297,559	72,815	896,553	195,862	538,710	1,049,009
Cotton seed	24,772	12,000	31,005	—	—	31,044	203,972	113,038
Sorghum	—	—	—	—	47,758	—	—	184,705
Beans	1,036	48	197,393	11,926	125,454	70,375	58,984	122,976
Cattle	186,670	40,705	265,775	1,016,369	1,198,926	1,202,079	291,314	1,141,461
Chicle*	—	17,464	12,559	9,277	55,437	101,392	189,495	230,840
Rubber	27,937	846,836	381,179	209,306	—	183	3,427	129,627
Ipecacuanha	76,126	171,311	758,094	411,990	212,214	325,104	292,002	639,456
Timber	363,200	674,438	1,009,235	1,751,799	1,332,978	1,390,603	1,742,159	1,986,974
Sugar	83,600	—	565,147	—	160,034	399,720	714,236	1,411,360

*Includes both Goma de Nispero (chicle) and Goma de Tuno.
Source: Memorias del Recaudador General de Aduanas.

TABLE 2
VALUE OF AGRICULTURAL AND FORESTRY PRODUCTION, 1950
(thousand dollars)

Product	Value of Exports	Value of Local Consumption	Total Value
Sesame	1,514	—	1,514
Cotton	1,842	1,032	2,874
Rice	302	3,080	3,382
Bananas	613	1,960	2,573
Cacao	49	690	739
Coffee	17,331	1,800	19,131
Corn	539	9,799	10,338
Cotton Seed	204	220	424
Sorghum	—	2,876	2,876
Beans	59	3,980	4,039
Meat	291 (cattle)	7,053	7,344
Chicle	190	—	190
Rubber	3	98	101
Ipecacuanha	292	na	292
Timber	1,742	6,851	8,593
Sugar	714	1,066 (cane)	1,780
Cheese	20	892	912
Butter	16	378	394
Lard	—	2,905	2,905
Hides and Skins	86	611	697
Charcoal	—	1,305	1,305
Poultry	—	1,278	1,278
Fish	—	248	248
Eggs	—	1,759	1,759
Milk	—	3,236	3,226
Fruits and Vegetables	—	2,120	2,120
Potatoes	—	785	785
Tobacco	—	2,200	2,200
Other Products	102	1,829	1,932
Total	25,909	60,051	85,951

Note: Cordoba values converted to dollars at 1950 exchange rate of 5 cordobas to US$1.

TABLE 3

CULTIVATION AND ESTIMATED PRODUCTION OF SELECTED CROPS (WEST COAST ONLY) 1945-46 — 1950-51

AREA PLANTED (*Manzanas*)

Product	1945-1946	1946-1947	1947-1948	1948-1949	1949-1950	1950-1951
Sesame	na	11,410	26,579	42,347	20,694	25,345
Cotton	na	na	na	1,178	21,314	23,945
Rice	16,844	12,468	14,682	22,001	22,114	22,986
Corn	110,314	41,040	122,765	109,337	140,215	160,513
Beans	22,544	19,918	25,370	25,112	37,742	38,576
Sorghum	na	na	38,537	31,941	47,995	52,998
Sugar Cane	na	na	10,217	17,021	19,738	20,273
Potatoes	na	na	na	na	140	414
Yucca	na	na	na	na	1,519	2,965

TABLE 3 (Continued)

PRODUCTION

Product	1945-1946	1946-1947	1947-1948	1948-1949	1949-1950	1950-1951	Unit
Sesame	na	114,673	189,513	280,322	167,947	184,769	Quintal
Cotton	na	na	na	9,420	107,375	111,904	Quintal
Rice	252,660	123,691	134,971	200,911	280,428	319,014	Quintal
Corn	661,530	373,526	592,967	520,978	613,699	784,916	Fanega
Beans	74,766	55,121	69,646	70,067	119,395	117,518	Fanega
Sorghum	na	na	349,453	281,318	407,640	342,370	Fanega
Sugar Cane	na	na	302,675	519,112	558,718	497,037	Ton
Potatoes	na	na	na	na	2,586	35,996	Quintal
Yucca	na	na	na	na	26,520	138,874	Quintal

1 Manzana = 1.74 acres
1 Quintal = 101.4 pounds
1 Fanega = 310-330 pounds, varying by crop

are trained downward in an umbrella effect so that the beans grow on the upper side of the stems and are easily reached by the pickers. Considerably more work is involved in caring for the plants in this manner, but production records of the best plantations indicate that the effort is worthwhile.

In general, the growers of this area are the most progressive to the high plateaus with little slope, which facilitates cultivation. merits of clean cultivation and cover crops, the use of organic and chemical fertilizers, and the degrees and types of shade. There is now a definite trend away from clean cultivation, but a good cover crop has not yet been found, and thus far fertilizer trials have been inconclusive. A marked tendency has been noted to do away with top shade. In one case at least, shade was being removed entirely, exposing the trees to full sunlight.

The little experimentation now in progress is being conducted by a few planters, each working according to his own ideas, and without the help and guidance of qualified and trained coffee specialists. These planters are to be commended on their recognition of the need for improvement and their desire to improve, but at the same time they should be cautioned about drawing conclusions too soon. There is considerable danger that the full effects of a particular experiment may not show up for several years. The tendency for some growers to reduce shade drastically may hold serious consequences for the future production and life of the trees.

Although there are experimental coffee farms in neighboring countries, information developed there rarely finds its way into Nicaragua. Neither the government nor the Coffee Growers' Association have adequate means of obtaining the latest information on developments elsewhere in Central America.

The coffee association, composed of the major coffee growers, is supported by a small export tax on coffee. The association is concerned more with the general economic aspects of coffee growing than it is with specific recommendations and measures to increase yields and production. If properly reorganized and supported by grants from its members, the association could play an important role in aiding the industry. It would be the most logical organization to collect all available information on coffee growing and to inform its members of new developments. Any coffee experts placed on the staff of the Servicio or the Instituto should establish several experimental coffee farms to test new developments and, in cooperation with the association, to demonstrate for the benefit of growers the most modern techniques.

Coffee yields per tree are considerably higher in the nearby countries of El Salvador, Guatemala, and Costa Rica. Because of the similarity of soils and climates, there is no reason to suppose that Nicaraguan yields cannot be improved to at least the neighboring levels.

The principal matters requiring both technical investigation and practical trials include:

1. The best shade relations according to region, site, slope and age of stand.
2. The most satisfactory methods of pruning in terms of production and costs of operation.
3. Soil cultivation, cover crops, weeding intensity, nutrition and conservation.
4. Variety trials to obtain the kinds of trees most suitable by region, and particularly by locality within the region.
5. Testing of insecticides before general use, and studies of incipient physiological, virus and fungus diseases.

Recent work in Guatemala indicates that a legume may be grown as a cover crop to enrich and protect the soil and this may have some bearing on the reduction of shade requirements. Pests and diseases are not serious yet, but there is a need for an inspection and advisory service to call the growers' attention to incipient diseases and pests apt to present economic problems if left uncontrolled.

Recent experience with the use of benzene hexachloride insecticides makes it desirable to check the effect of chemical treatments on the bean (taste and color) before any particular chemical is recommended for routine use. Indiscriminate use of BHC without adequate testing caused rejection of some amounts of coffee because of the musty flavor developed through its use.

Rice

In a short period of time, Nicaragua has changed from an importer to an exporter of rice. Further expansion is still possible by opening up new lands, improving cultivation practices, and by irrigation.

To date, plantings have been confined entirely to upland varieties using little mechanical equipment. Present varieties lodge badly and prevent the use of combines for harvesting.

Yields may be increased considerably, and perhaps even doubled, by changing to irrigated cultivation. This would mean a shift of production to new areas with a good supply of water, such as those bordering Lake Nicaragua which can be irrigated with low lift pumping. However, further detailed studies of the soils are needed. Only varieties which can be cultivated and harvested with mechanical equipment should be considered, since the goal is to increase both yields and production without increasing labor requirements. For this reason, paddy type cultivation, with its high labor needs, cannot be recommended, even though yields are higher than for either upland or irrigated rice.

Sesame

Sesame production requires large amounts of hand labor for planting, harvesting, and threshing. Production costs can be lowered by using varieties amenable to a greater use of power equipment. One variety, developed in Venezuela, is now under test; other varieties should be placed under test and development work started, in order to provide the farmers with new seed as soon as possible. This should be an important additional task of the Servicio Tecnico.

Sorghum

Sorghum is widely grown in the drier sections of the country and some planting is to be found on most subsistence farms. The type in use is long-stocked, and does not yield as much as varieties cultivated elsewhere.

Sorghum is well adapted to the needs of some regions, since it has good resistance to drought and grows well on into the dry season. The crop will need improvement through the introduction or development of new varieties, adapted to mechanized harvesting, with capacity for regrowth after cutting, and with improved yields. Tests of varieties from other countries should be made by the Servicio Tecnico.

Wheat

Wheat has been grown on a limited scale for many years in the highlands near Jinotega and San Rafael del Norte. Since wheat and flour imports are substantial, both the mission and the government were interested in verifying reports that additional lands eixsted which were suitable for the expansion of wheat production and which could be worked with mechanized equipment.

Field investigation as far as Yali failed to confirm these reports. If such lands exist, they are at present too isolated to be considered as potentially useful in the near future. Explorations should be continued and if suitable lands are found, wheat production should be expanded to fill one of the essential needs of the country. Further expansion cannot be recommended under present circumstances.

Bananas

There are no large banana plantations such as are found in other Central American countries. Bananas are grown on small farms located along two principal rivers, the Escondido and Coco. Exports are moved from the east coast of Nicaragua to Florida ports by small, fast, unrefrigerated ships. In recent years, banana exports have been decreasing in importance in the over-all economy.

The banana provides the sole source of cash income for many people of the region, but transportation difficulties, variations in the size of shipments, and other factors have made this a rather precarious crop. The best lands stretch along the river banks so that large plantations cannot be developed easily. At the present time, there is no control of disease and yields are low. The bananas that are shipped are generally second-class fruit.

In order to improve the quality of the bananas, the growers must spray and fertilize. Since the farms are small, no single grower is able to afford the necessary equipment, although the cooperative system used in Jamaica might be applicable to Nicaragua. A study should be made of this system and the equipment used, to see if some improvement can be made over the present situation.

A recent attempt was made by one of the large foreign fruit companies to establish a plantation in the Chinandega area, using irrigation. Originally the plan was to purchase the fruit from the farmers at around $0.50 per stem. This offer was rejected as being too low, and the company leased land to establish their own plantations. Lack of capital and supplies have delayed this venture, and its future is uncertain.

In the opinion of the mission, the reintroduction of large plantation operation in bananas will not provide the opportunity for bettering the living standards of the Nicaraguan farm worker that the diversified farming, recommended in the investment program, will offer.

Cacao

Cacao is grown on both the east and west coasts of Nicaragua, although the major production comes from the west. The west is not well adapted to cacao production because of its prolonged dry season, and new plantings should be concentrated on the east coast. Costa Rica's east coast is already production large quantities of cacao under climatic and soil conditions similiar to those found in eastern Nicaragua where unlimited land areas exist for expansion.

The cacao market outlook is favorable because of the lowered production in other countries caused by disease and insect damage. At present the cacao of Nicaragua appears free from any serious pests.

Livestock

Cattle are now used as work animals as well as meat and milk producers. Before much improvement can be made in animal husbandry, each farmer must choose whether he is going to raise dairy or beef cattle. Although all cattle are raised on the same basic principles, the type of animals selected and feeding practices will vary with the choice.

In both cases a carefully planned and directed breeding program is needed to bring about the development of good milk producers, and of beef cattle which can be fattened on a minimum of feed.

General observations during field trips indicated that the proper feeding and handling of livestock is not widely known. Even poor types of cattle can be brought to maturity more rapidly when adequate feed is available. Rotational grazing, an adequate supply of clean drinking water, and provision of hay and ensilage during the dry season are essential if beef production is to be made profitable on the west coast. For milk production, these same observations apply. In addition, some quantities of grains and proteins must be fed to sustain milk flows during the dry season.

It is believed that dairy production should be very largely concentrated on the western plains, near the larger centers of consumption, and with easy access to export markets. Beef operations should be shifted as much as possible to the eastern side of the country where better pasture conditions prevail. In the high rainfall areas on the east coast, pastures are green the year around, and it will not be necessary to make hay and silage. The forages of this area are deficient in protein and perhaps in some essential minerals, and a protein and mineral supplement feed will be required to fatten cattle rapidly. Protein is available in Nicaragua in the form of oil cakes and can be transported easily to the cattle areas. Minerals must be imported but the amounts required are small and will place no appreciable burden upon the country's foreign exchange resources.

The program for the improvement of the cattle and dairy industry is not easy, and results will not be apparent for some time. Its implementation will require continuous work and pressure by the Ministry of Agriculture, the Servicio Tecnico, and the Instituto de Fomento. The Servicio Tecnico should maintain demonstration herds, but even more important, it should have extension programs to aid farmers in instituting their own animal selection, breeding and feeding programs; to show them how to make hay and ensilage and how to store these products; to teach them the elements of veterinary medicine and how to recognize certain diseases and how to control insect pests; and, finally, to teach them the basic principles of sanitation in dairy production. Credits of the Instituto de Fomento for cattle production should be closely supervised by the Instituto to assure the adoption of these practices.

II. FORESTRY PRODUCTION

A useful description of the forest areas is contained in the FAO report of 1950. The main purpose of this chapter is to emphasize the problems encountered, and to suggest means for their solution.

Major differences in rainfall and soil conditions have resulted in two general classes of forests; evergreen or rain forest to the east of the continental divide, and deciduous forest to the west.

In the western region are included the best farming areas of Nicaragua. Forest areas are scattered and are being reduced rapidly as lands are cleared for planting, through wasteful cutting for fuel, or uncontrolled burning. Timber of good size and quality is becoming increasingly difficult and expensive to find and log. Little sawn lumber is exported from the west coast, since it finds a ready local market.

The eastern forest region covers perhaps 50% of the area of Nicaragua and is divided into two sectors, the Zelaya pine flats to the north and the rain forest to the south. Exploitation has been confined to the readily accessible and valuable types of woods, which are cut wholly for the export market.

Land Ownership and Government Control

Little is known of the actual ownership of the lands of the eastern region. Maps of the region are completely lacking and the national lands have never been surveyed except for very limited areas. Much land is occupied by squatters without permit, often on lands privately owned. Frequent disputes over boundaries result from the fact that there are no official maps.

Most logging concerns on the east coast obtain concessions from the government to cut timber from large blocks of land. The government has passed legislation to limit the size of trees cut, and to tax exports of logs and sawn lumber. Revenues are intended to provide for tree replanting, but there is no evidence that the objectives have been attained. There is in fact little or no control over concessionaires, especially in the outlying regions, and they are free to operate with little regard for sound forestry practices.

Limiting the diameter of trees cut may help to protect the valuable species such as mahogany, but such legislation does not take into account the age or health of the trees. In the pine areas, some trees are now over 60 years old and are still under the minimum diameter. Many of these will never reach the legal diameter since they are past their prime and are now diseased.

In establishing a forest service, legislation must be provided to permit cutting small trees in order to maintain healthy forests. Thinning will have to be practiced in a successful reforestation program. If properly carried out, the removal of small trees will not reduce the amount of timber which can be cut from a given area. Instead it may encourage faster growth of the remaining trees and bring about an increase in production.

Major Problems

In considering what should be done to conserve and develop the forest resources, the discussion will be limited to the east coast region and to the northern pine sector of the west coast near Ocotal and Somoto. The problems of these regions are more urgent than those of other areas of the west coast.

The most serious problem is that of uncontrolled burning of grass in the pine forests. The inhabitants of the Zelaya pine flats burn the grass two or three times a year to improve pastures for their cattle. This practice has prevented all natural regeneration and, in consequence, no young trees replace those now being cut. A few small areas which are naturally protected from fire prove that natural reseeding can take place.

The loose gravel soil of the Zelaya pine flats is suitable only for pine. The grass is sparse and does not provide good pasture. Unless some action is taken to control the fires in this region, it will soon be finished as a lumber producer.

One of the first steps to be taken is the organization of a Forestry Service under the direction of an experienced forester. As soon as this is accomplished, at least three demonstration plots should be established in the Zelaya pine area to show the benefits of controlling fires. These plots should be laid out with watch towers, fire roads, and sufficient manpower and equipment for fighting fires, replanting and thinning. Within a few years the demonstration should be far enough advanced to convince private landowners of the benefits of such a program and to persuade them to adopt similar measures in cooperation with the government.

At first, the size of the service and the amount of work undertaken will have to be kept within reasonable limits. However, as the staff gains experience and training, similar plots should be established in the Ocotal-Somoto region.

Another serious problem is the complete lack of information and knowledge of the large hardwood forests. Mahogany and a few other trees have been exploited for many years. These are becoming increasingly more difficult and expensive to log, since the readily accessible trees have long been cut. There have been no timber surveys so it is not known how much mahogany remains, while the properties and potential uses of other species are unknown and unexplored.

A survey of the forest lands should be started as soon as possible in order that the country may know its forest resources. Such a survey would be greatly facilitated by aerial photographs to serve as a basis for the maps needed.

At the present time, the United States geodetic survey is undertaking a mapping of the whole country. After the first order triangulation is completed, aerial mapping is to be carried out. This survey is to be so exact that it is estimated that from 10 to 15 years will be required to finish this work. However, the urgent need for maps of certain areas cannot be delayed until this work is completed. Mapping should be carried on by the government on a section-by-section basis, through aerial photographs of particular areas under study, while taking care to tie this mapping to fixed and known points.

Such a proposal might be criticized on the grounds that the degree of accuracy is not high. It should be emphasized that there are no maps at all in existence now, and it will be of more benefit to obtain working maps of sufficient accuracy for field reconnaissance and reporting, than to wait for perfect results.

A further task of the Forestry Service should be to study the

existing legislation governing lumbering and, with the cooperation of the lumbering companies, to prepare new and rational
legislation in order to develop forestry on a sound basis.

The mission believes that, in view of the progress made in the
past few years under unfavorable technical conditions and with
an uncoordinated and rather haphazard program, a well-planned
agricultural and forestry program, coordinated with national investments in transport, health and education, should result in
considerable agricultural growth over the next five years. At
present, less than a quarter of the arable land of the country is
devoted to productive use. Increased mechanization, soil conservation and the opening up of new land, are major parts of
the agricultural investment program outlined in Part I.

CHAPTER EIGHTEEN

Special Agricultural Problems

Land Use

Agriculture is generally conducted on an extensive basis, with a low yield per acre. Little effort has been made to conserve or improve the soils and the introduction of mechanical equipment has brought increasingly serious soil erosion. In part, this situation exists because of the favorable land to population ratio, with large areas of good land remaining to be exploited. Another factor is the very limited degree to which technical knowledge of soil conservation has been disseminated in the country.

Present arable lands under cultivation are in two distinct groups; coffee, and general farming and cattle raising. There has never been a cadastral survey, and information from the current agricultural census was not available to the mission. The information herein presented is based very largely on personal observation.

The smaller coffee plantations contain up to 100 manzanas (about 100,000 trees), while an average plantation consists of 200 manzanas (about 200,000 trees). Additional lands are often held in reserve for future expansion, or are used for food production for the plantation.

Lands used for general farming range from perhaps 50 to 200 manzanas for a small farm, and from 400 to 500 manzanas for an average farm. Large farms occasionally exceed 10,000 manzanas, but the average is in the neighborhood of 3,000 to 4,000 manzanas. The large farms usually combine general crops with cattle raising. Cattle ranches normally will fall within the large farm grouping since in some areas as much as 10 manzanas may be required per head. Farms under 50 manzanas are generally subsistence farms which support one or more families. Above this size, farms will usually provide cash income beyond minimum family needs.

In the lesser developed regions, the so-called "Milpa" system is widely used. Usually, those using this system are not landowners but squatters on government land or occasionally on private land.

As a general rule, lands other than subsistence farms are held for investment or speculative purposes. Few large owners live on the land and direct day-to-day operations. Instead, they live in town and leave the management to poorly paid majordomos. Some owners prefer to rent their land for cash and thus are relieved of any management problems.

The agricultural investment program, outlined in Part I, calls for the opening of new lands for coffee and other crops, cattle raising, African oil palm and small-scale land colonization. In order to carry out this program and meet these goals, careful attention must be given to the lands selected for each purpose. The complete lack of basic information makes it essential that land-use studies be made prior to a final recommendation for the use of a particular region.

The objective of a land-use survey is to collect basic information relating to the natural resources of a region, locality or site. Depending on specific conditions, subjects needing study would be the climatic, geologic and soil features, the natural or induced vegetation, the crop and animal population distribution, the nature of the water resources, and the existing and possible future lines of transport and communications. This information should be integrated in order that definite recommendations can be made on the potentialities of a given region.

In the first instance, personnel experienced in land-use surveys will have to be recruited abroad. At least four to five specialists will be needed, depending upon the region covered. These should have at least the following qualifications:

(a) An ecologist trained in land-use survey and with good field experience. He should also possess a professional and practical knowledge of arable and livestock agriculture and, if possible, of forestry;

(b) An experienced soils man, with extensive field experience and a good ecological and agricultural background;

(c) An agronomist with experience with a wide variety of crops;

(d) An engineer with training and experience in soil and water conservation;

(e) A livestock specialist with experience in the tropics and knowledge of the production of supplemental crops.

To this group of specialists will have to be added an adequate supporting staff of draughtsmen and surveyors.

The most urgent land survey studies needed are:

(a) Location of lands for the extension of coffee plantings;

(b) Irrigation possibilities of the western plains region for rice and sugar production;

(c) Survey of forest areas, especially of *Pinus caribaea* and *Pinus oocarpa,* for their protection and regeneration, in cooperation with the Forestry Service;

(d) Surveys on the east coast (in localities within reasonable distance of navigable rivers) of the possibilities of production of cacao, African palm oil, cattle, pepper and exportable tropical fruit;

(d) Survey and planning for opening of the more remote western plains and regions for the production of food crops, livestock and fiber crops.

Credit

Bank credit is for the most part limited to short term loans on a few major cash crops, although medium-term credits for agricultural machinery have been given recently by the National Bank. No credit is available for the purchase of land, buildings, or cattle or to make major improvements.

Credit for agricultural machinery is a very recent development, associated with an International Bank loan. Prior to this, credits were extended by machinery dealers rather than by banks.

The security requirements for crop loans from the bank are so strict that they eliminate small farmers. Only a few hundred of the major producers of five or six cash crops have adequate credit facilities. The normal and accepted practice is for the large landowners to obtain bank loans and relend the funds to small farmers, often at usurious rates of interest. The creditor frequently requires that the crops of small farmers be sold to him, and not always at the most advantageous price.

Crop loans are restricted to a percentage of the estimated crop value, but this percentage is usually high enough for the large farmers to cover all production costs. Thus, a borrower is able to carry on his operations without risking any of his own money. This has often been a contributing factor to inflation, since there is no incentive or need to build up working capital. Profits are rarely reinvested in the land which produced them. Instead they are used to purchase additional land or to finance non-agricultural activities.

Obviously there is great need for revision of the agricultural credit structure to provide credits (a) to the small farmer, (b) for medium- and long-term capital improvements, and (c) to correct past abuses of the crop loan system.

The Instituto de Fomento, described elsewhere, will be the principal agency to accomplish these reforms. Supervised credits of all types can and should be made available to small farmers, as well as medium- and long-term credits to projects covered in the framework of the five year development program.

Markets

The majority of exports go to the United States, but exports to neighboring Central American countries are increasing and may be expected to continue to do so because the demand is for the type of product indigenous to Nicaragua. This trade will be greatly facilitated by the extension of the Inter-American Highway to Costa Rica. Trade with Europe has been small since the war, but shows signs of expansion.

Production of several crops is approaching the point where the traditional markets may no longer be able to absorb the output. The projected expansion in production of other crops, especially animal products, will also require the development of new markets, since Nicaragua's capacity to produce is many times greater than her domestic needs. Exports are now handled by local agents, usually acting for foreign buyers, and by the Government's Compania Mercantil del Ultramar. These organizations are geared to supplying goods upon requests from foreign agents, but they are not organized for seeking out new or expanded markets.

An organization must be set up now to promote Nicaraguan products. It is important that government commercial attaches be placed in key countries to maintain continuous promotional activities. These representatives must be furnished with accurate and up-to-date crop forecasts in order that they may know the products that must be pushed. More important, they must know of possible crop shortages so that no commitments are made which cannot be filled promptly and in full.

Another feature of current marketing practices is the farmer's complete lack of information on daily prices in foreign markets. A few of the larger farmers obtain weekly quotations from abroad, but the average farmer has no knowledge of price trends abroad. At the present time sales from the farm, at least for the smaller farmer, are generally governed by the need for cash rather than by current market conditions. Many buyers, knowing this, set prices arbitrarily and often with little relation to the current market price. Crop prices fluctuate over a wide range during the year, partly for this reason, partly because of the lack of crop storage facilities, and partly because the crop speculator is often a creditor of the farmer.

As a public service, the government or the Instituto de Fomento should regularly obtain quotations and post these prices in the towns and villages. The newspapers also should publish daily market quotations and other guides to the farmer.

Labor

Agricultural labor is generally inefficient, with low output per man hour. The climate is undoubtedly a contributing factor, but perhaps the major factors are the lack of incentive to produce more, and failure to provide workers with proper tools. Wages run from three to five cordobas per day for ordinary labor, although piece-work rates for coffee and cotton picking this past season sometimes provided earnings as high as 15 cordobas per day. Although daily rates are low, the rate per unit of production is relatively high, and, without improvements in production methods, probably cannot be greatly lowered.

Low production per man hour is closely associated with the general problem of poor agricultural techniques: (a) failure to maintain soil fertility, (b) failure to provide proper tools to labor, (c) lack of knowledge of developments in methods and crops taking place in other countries.

The labor supply is generally adequate although local shortages occurred during the recent coffee and cotton harvests, when the highest cotton crop on record had to be harvested simultaneously with the coffee crop. Increases in production called for in the development program will require additional labor, partly from the untapped female labor force. A greater use of mechanical equipment will increase labor productivity and reduce prospective labor shortages.

Mechanized Farming

Most of the tractors used in agriculture have been imported since 1946. At present it is estimated that there are more than 600 in the country which are used exclusively for agriculture. For the most part they are used for cash crops, mainly cotton.

As a general rule, none of the tractor owners are fully utilizing their machinery. Tractor-drawn equipment, for example, is used almost exclusively for plowing and cultivation, while harvesting is still done manually. Corn and cotton are often planted by tractor, but sesame is planted by hand. In some cases, the wrong type or size machine is hitched on to a tractor. Inefficient use of expensive equipment means a low return on investment and higher production costs.

Corn pickers, corn cutters or field ensilage choppers, combines for rice, sorghum and sesame, flame weeders for cotton, and rotary hoes are implements which can be effectively used in Nicaragua to reduce hand labor requirements. Harvesting equipment will prevent losses due to spoilage in the field or shattering during hand threshing. The failure to use such equipment is due to the lack of knowledge that such equipment exists, to failure to introduce crop varieties designed for mechanized farming, and to inadequate credit facilities.

The lack of knowledge may be overcome by a vigorous sales and educational campaign on the part of the machinery manufacturers and dealers. To further the educational effort and to prevent the promotion of equipment not suited for local conditions, the Ministry of Agriculture, through the Servicio Tecnico, should maintain and use a complete line of mechanical equipment for test and demonstration purposes. Throughout the year, "Field Days" should be sponsored to demonstrate the proper use of equipment appropriate to the seasons.

In the case of rice, sorghum and sesame, the Servicio Tecnico should institute an active program to introduce or develop new varieties suitable for combining. Such varieties are known in other countries but may need adaptation to local conditions.

Soil Conservation

The rapid increase in the use of mechanized equipment, with its deeper and cleaner cultivation, has accentuated the twin problems of erosion and depletion of soil fertility. The soils of the best regions are light, loose, volcanic soils, easily eroded by rains and winds, and generally deficient in available nitrates.

The government, with the funds available under the development program, will be able to aid in the prevention of further erosion. A major part of the task will be in the education of the farmers to the need for contour and strip farming. The Servicio Tecnico should assume an important part of this work by active demonstrations, and by providing technical help in laying out contour lines. A small amount of work has been done in the past but not on a scale comparable to the needs of the country. The erosion problem is serious and deserves immediate attention.

The depletion of soil fertility is not as serious a problem as straight erosion, but it is taking place and on an increasing scale. Crop yields are still relatively good, but only because new lands being opened are helping to maintain the average. The system of planting two crops per year is hard on the soil, since crop rotation is not practiced. The common custom is to grow two crops each year of corn, or sesame and corn, sesame and cotton, or corn and cotton. Only a few farms are known to be trying a rotation system, using cow peas as a first crop and turning them under before planting the second crop.

Chemical fertilizers have not been used to any extent but a few trials have been made on acreage devoted to sugar cane. Cane yields were increased an average of 10%. Tests are continuing to determine the best formulation. For annual crops, there seems to be little need for chemical fertilizers at the present time. Nitrate deficiencies may be corrected by the selection of a rotation system using legumes to build up the nitrogen content of the soil.

The Servicio Tecnico, should undertake a more vigorous program to explain the value of building up the soil. Demonstration fields should be planted in each of the communities to show how crop yields may be increased through proper soil care.

Crop Storage

Estimates of annual crop losses due to spoilage or insect damage are placed at 20 to 40% of the total crop. Losses due to spoilage are highest from the first crop, which matures during the rainy season. Second crop losses are small because of dry weather during harvest. First crop corn, for example, is frequently left on the stock in the field because the husk offers good protection from the rain.

The new grain storage plant now being built in Managua will help to reduce this enormous loss, since the grain can be dried and kept free from insect infestation during storage. This new plant will be able to handle only a small percentage of the total crop of corn, rice and beans. Under the mission's development plan, four to five small plants would be added in the major production centers. While these will be able to dry grain, they will be unable to store more than small amounts.

The question of crop drying and storage must be considered at the farm level in order to eliminate the largest share of crop losses. Some areas may find the answer in cooperative driers but for others, small farm driers must be developed or adapted. Work along these lines is underway in Costa Rica and has progressed to the point where trials should be made in Nicaragua to select the best design for modification to local conditions. The mission believes that the Servicio Tecnico should undertake the technical phases of the work and conduct the necessary field tests. The financing of these driers or storage units should be one of the first tasks of the Instituto de Fomento.

CHAPTER NINETEEN

Summary

I. *THE PRESENT STRUCTURE OF THE FISCAL SYSTEM*

The present fiscal system of Nicaragua is ill adapted to adjust to rapid economic changes. Inequitable as well as inelastic, it has developed haphazardly over the years. No systematic effort seems ever to have been made to simplify the tax system by unifying multiple taxes levied on the same product, to remove from the statute books taxes that have proved to be uncollectible or, for one reason or another, are no longer collected. No attempt has been made to calculate the net yield to the Treasury of various taxes after collection costs. Most important, there is no evidence of a systematic effort to tax these categories of individuals or businesses which, in spite of the recent substantial rise in income, have remained almost entirely exempt from taxation. Moreover, almost no effort has been made to use fiscal policies to stimulate the economic progress of the country.

The most striking features of the fiscal system are:

(a) an almost exclusive reliance on indirect taxes and on duties falling primarily on consumption;

(b) the absence of an income tax;

(c) insignificant direct property taxes; and

(d) the absence of any progressive features in the tax system.

Internal revenue is obtained from a large variety of taxes, some of which, such as taxes on liquor, sugar, tobacco and cattle slaughter, have been levied for a century or longer. The heavy reliance on import duties for revenue purposes increases the proportion of indirect taxes. Since the end of the war, import and excise taxes combined have averaged 85% or more of the total net revenue of the government. This percentage declined slightly to 82% in 1950-51 after the imposition of the coffee export tax of $3.00 per quintal.

Many other indirect taxes, such as stamp taxes, are also borne by consumers. The resulting tax burden is heavily regressive. Even the property tax, traditionally progressive elsewhere, is practically proportional, while the property transfer tax is strictly proportional. Rudimentary attempts to graduate taxes (such as scaling taxes on admission tickets according to price) are too insignificant to be of any consequence.

Taxes on alcoholic beverages and tobacco are the main single sources of revenue from ultimate consumers. Prior to 1949-50 these two taxes yielded two thirds of all consumption taxes proper, while taxes on sugar, meat (in the form of a slaughter tax), soft drinks and matches (collected through the match monopoly), accounted for the remainder. In contrast, luxury items and other goods consumed primarily by the higher income groups are not subject to excise taxes.

The tax on alcoholic beverages alone has provided more than half of the yield of all excise taxes combined. The share of liquor and tobacco taxes has been declining—from 86% of all excise taxes in 1945-46 to 77% in 1950-51—but only because of the introduction of new excise taxes on soft drinks in 1948-49 and on admissions in 1945-46. Tax rates on alcoholic beverages and on tobacco were increased in 1950-51.

While excise taxes proper account for only about one third of total tax revenue, practically the entire burden of import duties and taxes, which in recent years accounted for half or more of tax revenue, was borne by consumers. A significant segment of business (foreign mining and other concessions) is exempt from import duties and some related taxes as well; thus, between 12% and 20% of dutiable merchandise entering the country was imported by concessionaires without payment of customs duties. In view of the composition of imports and the structure of domestic commerce, there can be little doubt that practically all import charges are ultimately passed on to consumers.

Taxes which cannot be clearly allocated either to business or to consumers consist mainly of the proceeds from the sale of fiscal stamps and stamp paper. Part of this revenue represents taxes on the gross receipts of wholesale and retail stores, on their payrolls, and on gross receipts of movie theaters and of other entertainment. By 1950-51, the revenue raised through such mixed taxes had declined to less than 5% of total tax revenue.

Business taxes are insignificant, averaging in recent years half of 1% of total revenue.

The property, property transfer and inheritance taxes are the only direct taxes in Nicaragua. These three taxes combined have yielded an almost identical sum during the fiscal years from 1945-46 to 1950-51, despite the sharp increase in the price level during this period. Neither rising prices nor increased volume of foreign trade, nor the rise in the tax rate and the removal of the tax exemption on owner-occupied dwellings seems to have had any effect on the yield of the property tax—the most important of the three—prior to 1949-50. In the last two fiscal years there was a modest increase in yield but the relative contribution of all three property taxes to total tax revenue declined from 5.9% in 1944-45 to 3.4% in 1950-51.

Export taxes, which come closest to being an indirect tax on income (at least of producers of export crops) increased less than other tax revenues through 1948-49. The imposition of a tax on coffee exports brought a moderate increase in export tax yield in 1949-50, and in 1950-51 raised the share of export taxes to 8.8% of total tax revenues.

The export tax on gold did not yield more than half a million cordobas until 1950-51; in that year, the lumber export tax brought in 260,000 cordobas after having yielded less than 50,000 in preceding years. Other miscellaneous export duties levied by the Customs Administration increased gradually, with the value of exports, from 0.6 million cordobas in 1944-45 to 1.7 million cordobas in 1950-51.

Miscellaneous taxes, including some which have been abolished in recent years, have yielded in the last six fiscal years only about half of 1% of total tax revenue.

Government revenue other than taxes, mainly profits of government-owned enterprises, is extremely small. Prior to the last fiscal year it averaged a little over 630,000 cordobas, or not much more than 1% of total net revenue.

Reimbursements and payments for services sold and goods resold by the government are not available for meeting ordinary government expenditures, except to the extent that resales involve a profit. They have been, therefore, excluded from the above analysis of government revenues.

The Main Weaknesses of the Fiscal System

The present tax system is inequitable because, in spite of the profusion of taxes, large segments of the population and of the business community are, in effect, totally exempt from taxation. Since there is no general income tax, income from the rental of real estate or farm land is not taxed at all. The large agricultural producers and the cattlemen, who hold a large part of the wealth of the country and receive a substantial share of the national income, pay only the nominal property tax. Professional people are also subject only to such taxes as might apply to them as owners of real estate or other property. Merchants are subject to a two per 1,000 tax on their gross sales (with the exception of certain types of goods) and on their payrolls. Although the law exempts only the small merchants (with annual sales of less than 5,000 cordobas or $710[1]), many merchants above the exemption limit evade payment of this tax, and others underdeclare their gross sales volume.

---

[1] In this report, a conversion rate of seven cordobas to one dollar has been used throughout.

The present tax system is made even more inequitable by the fact that, while consumption taxes are collected at the source (on the import or production level), large groups of taxpayers evade payment of all or most direct property and property transfer taxes.

It is generally believed that, even after upward revision of owners, yearly declarations by local Assessment Boards and the Revenue Administration, real property is commonly assessed at as little as one fifth, and even one tenth, of its real value. As a result, the total value of property declared to the tax administration is substantially smaller than the estimated national income, although normally it would be at least five times as large.

Two figures will suffice to illustrate the extent to which the property tax—the only direct tax of any consequence—is evaded:

(a) During the 1951-52 fiscal year, only 5,200 citizens out of a population of about 1.1 million were assessed for owner-occupied homes valued at 3,000 cordobas ($450) or more.[2] Their average annual tax bill amounts to only 17 cordobas ($2.38).

(b) The total number of persons and business firms in the country paying property taxes is less than 13,500.

Under prevailing circumstances, it is scarcely surprising that the recent attempt to collect a nominal head tax (*impuesto proletario*) resulted in failure.

The number of new taxes superimposed on existing taxes has been constantly growing. As the revenue needs of the government have increased, new taxes or surtaxes have been added, frequently on products or transactions already taxed. Apparently this has been done because the machinery for collection was already in existence.

Taxes on movie theaters and other entertainment are a good

---

[2] An average old house sells in Managua for about 30,000-50,000 cordobas.

example of multiple taxes on the same taxable income. They are collected by the same administration, but in different ways:

(a) a 5% tax on gross receipts (*Ley de Papel Sellado y Timbre*);

(b) a tax for the school milk fund (*Fondo Pro-Desayuno*) (three different rates, according to the price of tickets; *Ley del 11-8-44*); and

(c) a tax for municipal improvements (only two rates, but for different price brackets than the school milk fund tax).

The first tax is collected by affixing fiscal stamps on a declaration of gross receipts, while the other two are collected in cash. In addition, in Managua three different municipal taxes on admissions are collected.[3]

Fiscal practices such as these involve considerable inconvenience to the taxpayer and unnecessary paper work for the tax administration. Moreover, they result in an unduly complicated tax system. The official list of taxes collected by the Revenue Administration specifies more than 150 different taxes, fees and fines, while the list of transactions and documents subject to the stamp tax includes 237 items, some of which involve 11 different rates. The yield of these taxes, partly because of wholesale evasion, is in many instances so small that the cost of collection either absorbs a very large proportion of the gross yield or even exceeds it.

The inelasticity of the present tax system arises from the government's dependence upon import taxes for its main source of revenue. Returns from these taxes increase only in proportion to the increase in quantities imported. The yield of excise taxes, the second largest single source of revenue, has also proved over the years to be extremely inelastic. No significant increase from this source is possible without further depressing the already low

---

[3] Another example is taxation of gasoline. There are now in effect eight different taxes on gasoline, in addition to import duties, consular fees and two municipal taxes (in Managua).

standard of living of the majority of the rural and urban population.

The doubling of tax revenue within the short period of five years has about exhausted possibilities for any significant increase in government revenues from the existing types and methods of taxation. Even allowing for the increase in the price level, the sharp increase in revenue over the last five years was possible only because of a succession of good crops and other favorable circumstances. This rise resulted partly from the automatic increase of revenues depending on the volume of foreign trade, and partly from an increase in rates of existing taxes and duties (both in the form of surtaxes and of additional taxes on top of existing taxes). Special taxes placed on the net profits of coffee and cotton producers late in 1951 were stopgap measures made necessary mainly because old tax sources were unable to yield the additional revenue needed to launch the development program.

The present tax system has reached the point where it has become an obstacle to the economic development of the country. The regressive effect of a system consisting nearly exclusively of indirect taxes, most of them falling directly on consumption, depresses the standard of living of the great bulk of people—which in Nicaragua is nearly identical with farm workers and subsistence farmers—without enabling the country to improve its production and transportation facilities. Any new taxes on consumption or on business transactions would only add to the existing list of low-yielding taxes, without in any way solving the long-range problem of increasing government revenue for financing a program of economic development.

The absence of direct income taxes and of any form of progressive taxation has not resulted in channelling the bulk of the large savings of the higher income groups into productive investment. As a matter of fact, Nicaragua is a striking illustration for the view that even substantial immunity from taxation of personal and business income does not automatically create favorable conditions for physical capital formation. Positive fiscal action is needed to prevent a large part of profits from being channeled into unproductive investment, thus adding to inflationary pressures.

Because of laxity in enforcing existing laws, most of the existing taxes yield only a fraction of what they should yield. Underassessment, evasion and fraud are generally admitted. Under such circumstances, any attempt to increase government revenues significantly merely by finding new objects of taxation or by increasing tax rates will be largely doomed to failure. Significant additional sources of revenue can be made available to the Treasury only by introducing taxes which will fall upon groups of the population now largely immune from taxation. First among such taxes is a general income tax, the foundation stone of all modern tax systems.

II. *SUMMARY OF RECOMMENDATIONS*

The Main Objectives of Fiscal Reforms

In making recommendations for a reform of the tax system, we propose the following major objectives:

The budget of a country determined to develop its national wealth and to raise its standard of living must be, to a large extent, a development budget. Up to the present time, development expenditures have absorbed at best not more than 15% of net government expenditures.

Any further mobilization of domestic financial resources for economic development requires thorough reorganization of the fiscal system and establishment of taxes whose yield will increase automatically with the economic growth of Nicaragua. As both the development program and the fiscal capacity of the country are likely to grow gradually, it will be essential to endow the new fiscal system with enough flexibility to yield high revenues in years of favorable crops and world prices. In other years the goal should be to collect minimum revenues that will permit carrying forward a long-range program.

The Revenue System

The reforms of the revenue system recommended by the mission include:

(a) the introduction of new taxes on net income;

(b) an increase in rates and improvement in collection of the property tax;

(c) a review of all other sources of internal revenue and of the customs tariff, with the triple objective of reducing the burden of indirect taxes, of abolishing taxes whose collection costs are disproportionately high and of simplifying the tax system by consolidating different taxes and duties on the same object.

The first two recommendations represent the heart of the proposed reform. Implementation of the third recommendation will contribute materially to increasing the efficiency of the fiscal system and to decreasing the inconvenience to the taxpayer. Because it embraces a number of specific measures, some of them concerned with relatively minor taxes, it requires more elaboration than the other two.

Introduction of an Income Tax. A general tax on individual and corporate net income will tap fiscal resources which so far have been completely neglected. Income tax rates should be progressive; they should be set high enough to yield a substantial revenue, but not so high as to encourage wholesale evasion.

The Property Tax. The property tax should be rigorously enforced. The present rates should be revised upward and assessments should be raised to realistic levels. At the present time this tax is yielding only a small fraction of its potential revenue. It should become one of the major sources of revenue of the government.

The property transfer and inheritance taxes should be modified to include features of a capital gains tax. One of the main purposes of the capital gains provisions should be to discourage speculation in real estate.

Other Taxes. Export taxes should be, as far as possible, integrated with the income tax. Separate taxes on a few main export products should be maintained, at least until income taxes begin to yield a substantial revenue. Export tax rates should be reviewed each crop year in relation to average production costs and export prices. The rate structure should be designed to capture part of any windfall profits from increases in world prices not offset by increased production costs, and from particularly abundant domestic crops.

Import taxes including the various surtaxes as well as the tax on the weight of imports (*bultos*) should be, as far as administratively possible, amalgamated with import duties.

The tariff should be reviewed thoroughly with the following main objectives;

(a) establishment of new classifications for materials and products not listed. The tariff has not been subjected to any general revision since 1918;

(b) integration of import taxes and surtaxes with customs duties;

(c) reduction of duties on consumption goods and on those capital goods which are not already duty free;

(d) determination of the extent to which rebates or even exemptions could be given on imports of staple foods and gasoline to the east coast area (Department of Zelaya) to compensate for the transport disadvantages of that area.

The task of reviewing the tariff is so large that the mission was not in a position to make even a cursory survey. This review should be undertaken as promptly as possible, as its completion will take considerable time. It will require the services of an experienced technician.

The relative contribution of consumption taxes to the budget should be decreased. The sugar tax should be repealed immediately and other possible reductions in excise taxes, in particular those falling upon the lowest income groups, should be examined. The slaughter tax, the tax on soft drinks and on matches should be the first taxes considered for reduction. Outright appeal of several excise taxes rather than a pro rata reduction in all of them by the equivalent amount will achieve a greater saving in collection costs.

The number of transactions subject to fiscal stamp duties should be drastically reduced. As far as possible, these taxes should be merged with other taxes on the same transaction.

The tax system of a country is greatly impaired when taxes which are on the books are not actually collected. Taxes which prove ill-conceived or uncollectible for some valid reason should be repealed or promptly amended. Those with small and declining yield should be consolidated with other taxes or repealed. Only those taxes for which the costs of collection bear a reasonable ratio to average yield, should stay on the books and their collection should be rigorously enforced.

Nontax government revenue should be increased by the sale of government lands in areas where construction of roads and other improvements increase land values. Income from the lease of government lands should also be increased.

The communications services should be reorganized as an autonomous agency and operated along the lines of a business enterprise. It should be placed outside the general budget and collect its revenues directly. The rate structure should be reviewed in order to make the communication service self-supporting.

Consideration should be given to liquidating other business activities of the government, including the match monopoly.

These recommendations are treated at greater length in Chapter 14. Various alternatives as well as the difficulties that may be encountered in introducing the reforms are also noted.

The Revenue Administration

The success of the tax reform program will hinge on the efficiency and impartiality of the revenue administration. For the period of reorganization, and in particular while tax rolls for the property tax are revised and machinery for administering the personal and corporate income taxes is being established, the appointment of a foreign technical tax adviser to the Minister of Finance is recommended.

Within the internal revenue administration, a separate division should be created to handle assessment and collection of the property tax. Another new division should be created to deal with the proposed personal and corporate income taxes. It will probably be expedient to organize the work of the local revenue offices along similar lines.

The administration of the property tax should be reorganized by:

(1) requiring filing of returns with the revenue office within whose territory the property is located. This will permit checking and auditing by officials in a position to make visual inspection and examine local property and other records.

(2) consolidating returns at the main office;

(3) giving local revenue offices the power to assess property not declared by the taxpayer, and not just to review assessment of the property listed on returns (*manifiestos*); and

(4) enacting provisions for tax foreclosure of property on which payment of taxes is in arrears.

The need for a revenue office in each department (and the number of additional fiscal agencies now in existence) should be examined. A greater concentration of personnel which makes it possible to increase the functional division of work might result in more efficiency.

The Customs Administration should be placed under the Ministry of Finance.

All taxes should be collected exclusively by regular employees of the Ministry of Finance and use of free-lance collectors, compensated by a percentage of revenues collected, should be discontinued.

The practice of negotiating lump payments in lieu of taxes should be discontinued. Such practices are an indirect recognition that the existing system of multiple taxation of the same object is irrational and cannot be administered economically. Rather than circumvent it indirectly by making separate settlements with individual taxpayers, taxes for which such settlements are now permissible should be reviewed and recast to make their collection practicable. Negotiating lump sum settlement with individual taxpayers (except where necessary to avoid protracted litigation) destroys the principle of equal tax treatment of all citizens. It also offers additional opportunities for possible fraud.

Efficient methods should be devised to audit the local internal revenue and customs offices regularly—not just when shortages or fraud is suspected—and frequently.

The possibility of using modern mechanical equipment for billing and posting should be studied. In reorganizing the revenue administration the possibility of central billing (from one single office) for all income and property taxes should be studied.

CHAPTER TWENTY

Government Expenditures and Sources of Revenue

I. *GOVERNMENT EXPENDITURES*

The following analysis covers the six fiscal years since the end of the war, 1945-46 to 1950-51. Because of the purpose of this study, it was deemed unnecessary to go back farther. A more historical approach would require considerable research and a large volume of statistical computations to assure comparability.

In 1950-51, 6.9% of net budgetary expenditures were required to service and amortize the public debt. The cost of collecting revenue, including customs duties, and other expenditures of the Ministry of Finance absorbed an additional 16.9%. The legislative, judicial and executive branches of the government including general administration, accounted for 14.2% and the Defense Department for an additional 16.2%. This left (after allowance for foreign relations and the communications service) 15.4% for education and public health and 21.8% for all economic and development activities (under the ministries of public works, economy,[1] agriculture and labor). The share of all these activities in the total was in 1950-51 substantially the same as five years earlier (see Table 2).

In Table 1, net government expenditures are shown annually for the six fiscal periods since the end of World War II. In Table 2, the percentage distribution of government expenditures is shown for the same period.

---

[1] The Ministry of Economy, organized in 1948-1949, had in 1950-51 a modest budget of less than 1.1 million cordobas (1.4% of total net expenditures).

331

TABLE 1

NET GOVERNMENT EXPENDITURES, BY FISCAL YEARS, 1945-46 TO 1950-51[1]

(thousand cordobas)

	1945-46	1946-47	1947-48	1948-49	1949-50	1950-51	1950-51 as a % of 1946-47
1. Legislative	1,290	1,328	1,146	1,530	1,547	1,656	124.7
2. Judicial	1,524	1,589	1,805	1,773	1,733	1,886	118.7
3. Presidency	1,811	2,346	1,301	1,079	1,101	2,236	95.3
4. Interior	3,557	4,275	4,813	4,839	4,142	4,398	102.9
5. Finance	5,505	9,413	10,609	13,830	10,409	9,688	102.9
6. Customs Administration	1,769	2,161	2,789	3,151	2,067	2,349	108.7
7. Foreign Relations	2,025	2,393	2,521	3,467	3,072	4,096	171.2
8. Defense	7,767	7,564	10,244	11,989	11,394	11,548	152.7
9. Education	5,662	6,819	7,122	7,880	6,406	7,875	115.5
10. Public Health	1,220	1,222	2,081	2,398	1,352	3,129	256.1
11. Agriculture and Labor	1,382	1,250	1,263	1,417	1,415	1,913	153.0
12. Economy	—	—	—	70	1,425	1,053	—
13. Public Works[2]	10,227	8,052	8,301	11,392	6,755	12,582	156.3

14. Communications[3]	997	1,455	1,485	1,972	2,202	2,013	138.4
15. Not allocated[4]	3,377	219	90	90	236	—	—
16. Public Debt[5]	1,749	2,157	3,200	2,263	4,222	4,931	228.6
17. Total	49,862	52,243	58,770	69,140	59,478	71,353	136.6
18. Total as shown in closed accounts	59,850	68,643	71,181	82,892	64,016	76,514	111.5

[1] Based on final accounts, the following adjustments have been made:

a. Expenditures of the Customs Administration are entered net.

b. The cost of matches is eliminated from Finance.

c. Refunds from the United States Government are eliminated from Public Works.

d. Finance is split between Finance and Public Debt.

e. Communications are separated from Public Works prior to 1949-50; Radio Nacional is included with Communications throughout.

[2] Public Works slightly overstated and Communications understated because holdover appropriations (remanentes) could not be broken down and are allocated entirely to Public Works.

[3] Receipts of the communications service netted out against expenditures. The figures in this line represent the implicit deficit of the communications service as a whole.

[4] Servicio General de Administracion.

[5] Includes payments to Banco Hipotecario to service and amortize the Bank of America loan.

TABLE 2

Percentage Distribution of Net Government Expenditures, Fiscal Years, 1945-46 to 1950-51

		1945-46	1946-47	1947-48	1948-49	1949-50	1950-51
1.	Legislative	2.6	2.5	1.9	2.2	2.6	2.3
2.	Judicial	3.1	3.0	3.1	2.6	2.9	2.6
3.	Presidency	3.6	4.5	2.2	1.6	1.9	3.1
4.	Interior	7.1	8.2	8.2	7.0	7.0	6.2
5.	Finance	11.0	18.0	18.1	20.0	17.5	13.6
6.	Customs Administration	3.5	4.1	4.7	4.6	3.5	3.3
7.	Foreign Relations	4.1	4.6	4.3	5.0	5.2	5.7
8.	Defense	15.6	14.5	17.4	17.3	19.2	16.2
9.	Education	11.4	13.1	12.1	11.4	10.8	11.0
10.	Public Health	2.4	2.3	3.5	3.5	2.3	4.4
11.	Agriculture and Labor	2.8	2.4	2.1	2.0	2.4	2.7
12.	Economy	—	—	—	0.1	2.4	1.5
13.	Public Works	20.5	15.4	14.1	16.5	11.4	17.6
14.	Communications	2.0	2.8	2.5	2.9	3.7	2.8
15.	Not allocated	6.8	0.4	0.2	0.1	0.4	—
16.	Public Debt	3.5	4.1	5.4	3.3	7.1	6.9
17.	Total	100.0	100.0	100.0	100.0	100.0	100.0

Components may not add to total because of rounding.

The analysis is based on adjusted rather than on the original figures given in the final accounts (*liquidacion*). Corresponding adjustments were made on the revenue side of the budget.

Budget expenditures as shown in the final accounts are inflated by inclusion of refunds and reimbursements which do not represent the actual cost of government services.

For instance, for some reason, the theoretical amounts of duties on free imports of foreign concessionaires were until recently included in customs receipts and corresponding amounts were shown as "refunds" under expenditures. Similarly, deposits required of importers and exporters were included in customs receipts; to the extent that they exceeded duties and taxes actually paid, they appeared under expenditures as "reimbursements." Also, receipts from the sale of postage stamps and collection of the various charges for telegraph, telephone and radio services are shown as government receipts. To obtain the net expenditures of the communications service, receipts have been deducted from the expenditure shown in final accounts.

Expenditures include also the amount of dividends returned to the government-owned railroad. Since these are not actually collected, the whole transaction is only an accounting fiction inflating both sides of the budgetary accounts. Finally, expenditures include the cost of matches resold by the government monopoly and also funds provided by the United States Government for the construction of the Inter-American Highway (reimbursements by the Public Roads Administration being shown under receipts).

Adjustments for these various gross items reduce the actual expenditure budget of the national government considerably, as can be seen by comparing the two last lines in Table 1. During the last five years, gross government expenditures averaged 72.6 million cordobas, while net expenditures averaged only 62.2 million, or 14% less. The following brief analysis of the structure of the budget is based on net figures, after adjustment of the several gross items mentioned above. The various categories were regrouped in order to make possible comparisons over the entire six-year period.[2]

Net government expenditures have increased since the end of the war by more than one third.[3] This increase was considerably higher than shown in the gross figures of closed accounts (36.6% against 11.5%). From 1946-47 to 1950-51 expenses increased about 10% for the legislative and judicial branches, the presidency and the general administration (which together now account for about one seventh of total expenditures). The greatest increase was for the Public Health Department which in the last year has greatly expanded its activities, partly in cooperation with international programs. Foreign Relations ranked next (except for the public debt service), reflecting not only the participation in United Nations and related activities and international conferences, but

---

[2] The following deductions were made from the figures of the final accounts:
1. Reimbursements and refunds by the Customs Administration.
2. Imputed payments to the railroad.
3. The cost of matches purchased by the Ministry of Finance for resale.
4. Refunds from the United States Government for road construction.
5. Receipts of the communications service were netted out against expenditures.

No further adjustments were made (for some minor gross items, such as medicines and other products imported by the government for resale) in order to reduce the amount of computing work involved. The original figures of the final accounts are given in the last line of Table 1. The original data were rearranged as follows:
1. The public debt service was segregated from the budget of the Ministry of Finance; payments to the Banco Hipotecario to meet the service on the Bank of America loan were classified as public debt service;
2. The communications services (post, telegraph, and telephone) were separated from Public Works in which they were included prior to 1949-1950; Radio Nacional (a government-operated domestic radio communications network) has been included with the communications service throughout.

[3] In 1945-46 the expenditure of 3,377,000 cordobas (supplemental budget) could not be allocated by departments; for this reason, increases for individual departments were related to 1946-47 rather than to the first year shown in the table.

also increased costs of a rather widespread diplomatic representation. The increase in expenditures of the Defense Department—over 50%—was among the largest. Actually, the amounts shown under Defense Department do not include all military expenditures. Some military units, such as the urban police of Managua and the "finance guard" (*Resguardos de Hacienda*) are carried in the budgets of the Interior and the Finance Department, respectively, although their functions are apparently not much different from other army units which perform gendarmerie functions. Other military expenditures are carried in the budget of the presidency.[4]

If the two units carried in the Interior and Finance Ministries were shifted to the military budget, it would increase by nearly one third. Actual military expenditures amounted in 1950-51 to at least 20% rather than to 16.2% of the total expenditures. If expenditures included all members of the Guardia Nacional, the military budget would be even higher because there are smaller units of the Guardia Nacional, or even individual guardsmen, attached to other administrations as guards, chauffeurs and the like.

In contrast, the budget of the Ministry of Education—in a country where 70% of the population is illiterate and where the efficiency of the entire public administration suffers from lack of trained personnel—increased percentagewise less than the budget as a whole. The increase in public works was much larger than for the net budget as a whole, but the increase of 56.3% shown in Table 1 overstates the actual rise since a considerably larger proportion of the road building program was financed by the United States government in 1946-47 than in 1950-51. Total expenditures of the Public Works Department, excluding the share of the United States Government, increased only 6.2%.

---

[4] There is more justification for including Radio Nacional with the communication services than in military expenditures (as has been done in recent budgets) although its personnel forms part of the National Guard, as does—nominally—that of the Customs Administration.

The budget of the Ministry of Agriculture and Labor also increased 53%.

The budget of the Finance Ministry represents the largest single departmental expense. In the tables, the budget of the Finance Ministry was broken down between administrative and public debt expenditures; as can be seen from Table 1, the latter have increased considerably more than the former.

II. *THE SOURCES OF GOVERNMENT REVENUE*

It is no mean task to obtain a clear picture of the Nicaraguan tax system, as the tax laws are not codified, nor is there any systematic printed collection of administrative or court decisions in tax and customs cases.

The Ministry of Finance has not published an Annual Report since 1944-45, but it is understood that reports for subsequent years are under preparation. In the meantime, in preparing this report, it was necessary to draw upon such data as were available at the Accounting Office (*Tribunal de Cuentas*) and on information supplied by various officials of the Ministry of Finance.

In order to analyze the sources of fiscal revenue and the nature of the changes which have taken place in recent years, it is necessary to regroup (and in some cases, to break down) various categories of receipts summarized by the Accounting Office in its annual fiscal accounts. The detail of the adjustments made is given in the technical note appended.

Since reimbursements and payments for services sold and goods resold by the government are not available for meeting ordinary government expenditures (except to the extent that such operations involve a profit), the analysis is focused on net government revenue consisting of tax revenue and genuine non-tax revenue (profits of government-owned enterprises).

Between 1945-46 and 1950-51 net government revenue more than doubled (increasing from 41.0 million to 84.1 million cordobas). This is a considerably sharper increase than that shown in the original liquidaciones (compare lines 3 and 7 in Table 4).

This result was achieved nearly exclusively by increasing the already heavy burden borne by consumers. Increases in net tax
revenue took place in each year, but they were of modest proportions in two of the years (1947-48, when the coffee crop was poor,
and 1949-50, when it was disastrous).

The increase in government revenue since the end of the war
has resulted from large increases in the yield of excise and import
taxes. Thus, in 1946-47 import taxes alone increased by the same
amount (9 million cordobas) as total taxes. In 1948-49 when
tax revenue rose by nearly 8 million cordobas, import and excise
taxes accounted for the entire increase. In 1950-51, import taxes
rose by 45%. Altogether, of a total increase of net tax revenue
of 42 million cordobas between 1945-46 and 1950-51, around 34
million were obtained from higher excise and import taxes.

Excise taxes on alcoholic beverages and tobacco are the main
sources of government revenue. The share of these two sources
of revenue declined from 86% of all excise taxes in 1945-46 to
77% in 1950-51 because of the introduction of new excise taxes
on soft drinks and admissions, even though tax rates on alcoholic
beverages and on tobacco were increased in 1950-51. Previous to
the last fiscal year, the tax on alcoholic beverages alone provided
more than half of the yield of all excise taxes combined (see
Table 3).

Other important excise taxes are those on sugar, soft drinks,
cattle slaughter, gasoline, and matches, all of which fall, directly
or indirectly, on the broad masses of consumers.

While excise taxes proper accounted for only about one third
of total government tax revenue, there is no doubt that practically
the entire burden of import duties and import taxes, which in
recent years accounted for half or more of tax revenue, was borne
by consumers. A significant segment of business (foreign concessions) is exempt from import duties (and some related taxes
as well); thus, between 12% and 19% of dutiable merchandise

entering the country was imported by concessionaires without payment of customs duties.[5]

In each year prior to 1950-51, import and excise taxes combined (lines 5 and 6 in Table 3) amounted to more than 82% of total net revenue.

Property taxes, including property transfer, gift and inheritance, have yielded an almost identical sum during the first five fiscal years covered, in spite of the increase in the price level. The property ("capital") tax accounted in recent years for about three quarters or more of the yield of all types of property taxes.

The property tax rate is extremely low, one per 1,000 for owner-occupied dwellings and six and a half per 1,000 for all other property, with an exemption of 3,000 cordobas, or about $430. These rates represent a consolidation of three separate taxes previously levied on property.

The yield of the property tax in 1950-51 was 2.3 million cordobas, or 2.8% of total tax revenue, even though in that year it included a head tax of three cordobas. The head tax was not, however, generally collected and is now in abeyance. Neither rising prices, nor increased crops, nor the rise in the tax rate and the removal of the tax exemption on owner-occupied dwellings, has caused the yield of the property tax to rise during the first four postwar years.

Export taxes come closest to being an indirect tax on income, at least on producers of export crops. Through 1948-49 they increased less than other tax revenues. The yield of export taxes was first increased moderately by a coffee export tax in 1950-51 which yielded 4.6 million cordobas. As a result, the share of export taxes in that year rose to 8.8% of total tax revenue.

The export tax on gold is 0.5% of the official value of $35 per ounce, although Nicaraguan gold is sold on the free market at

---

[5] In addition to duties, specific and ad valorem, imports are subject to the payment of consular fees (a flat 5% on f.o.b. value), a 5% "basic tax," a 5% general ad valorem import tax and two separate taxes on the physical volume of imports.

premium prices. Only in 1950-51 did it yield more than half a million cordobas. In the same year the lumber export tax rose to 260,000 cordobas, after having yielded less than 50,000 in each of the preceding years. Various export duties levied by the Customs Administration have increased gradually, with the value of exports, from less than one million cordobas in 1945-46 to 1.7 million in 1950-51.

Business taxes are truly insignificant. Annual license fees are paid by various categories of manufacturing and trade establishments. In addition, banks pay a special tax to meet the cost of the office of Superintendent of Banks. All direct business taxes combined average only half of 1% of total tax revenue.

Business pays, however, the bulk of taxes collected in the form of stamp duties. Fiscal stamps must be affixed to a large variety of documents, such as receipts, bills, contracts, diplomas, etc., while certain applications and briefs must be written on stamp paper. While part of the revenue from the sale of fiscal stamps and paper is obtained from consumers, the bulk is paid by business. In particular, two business taxes are payable in fiscal stamps. One is the tax of two per 1,000 on the gross value of sales and on the amount of salaries paid by all wholesalers and retailers with an annual gross volume of 5,000 cordobas and more. The other is a 5% tax on gross receipts of movie theaters and other public entertainment. It is likely that a large part of the total receipts from the sale of fiscal stamps represents payment of these two business taxes, and that a large proportion of the balance is paid by business firms for various legal papers, receipts, and other documents. Receipts from fiscal and paper are included, together with a number of small taxes which cannot be clearly allocated either to business or to consumers as "mixed taxes" in Table 3. In 1950-51, the revenue raised through mixed taxes was about 4.5% of total tax revenue, including fees for automobile license plates introduced in 1948-49.

Miscellaneous taxes, including some which were abolished during the period covered, yielded also only about 0.5% of total tax revenue. The most important items in this group are two taxes paid by municipalities, one to meet the cost of local courts and the other that of the office in charge of auditing municipal finances. Actually they represent transfer to the national government of a small fraction of municipal tax revenues.

Government revenue from sources other than taxes is extremely small, averaging prior to the last fiscal year, a little more than 630,000 cordobas, or not much more than 1% of total net revenue. Such revenue consisted of dividends received from the Bank of Nicaragua (which paid into the Treasury only a relatively small part of its net profits) and the profit of the harbor of Corinto, operated by the government-owned Ferrocarril del Pacifico de Nicaragua.

The Nicaraguan budget and reports of the Accounting Office include two additional sources of revenue:

1. Reimbursements for cash outlays not chargeable to the budget (see Table 4, line 5) and

2. Gross receipts of the government-operated communication service (postal, telegraph, telephone, radio) and from the resale of merchandise by the government either to collect excise taxes as in the case of matches, or to supply medicines and various products to farmers at fair prices (line 4). In addition, in the years prior to 1949-50, receipts included amounts to be refunded or reimbursed by the Customs Administration (included in line 7).

Total gross government revenue, including sales and reimbursements, (Table 4, line 6), increased from 44.9 million cordobas in 1945-46 to 89.1 million in 1950-51. This increase is considerably sharper than the rise shown by the unadjusted official data in line 7 of Table 4, which for the earlier years include and for recent years exclude refunds by the Customs Administration.

Receipt of the communication service and miscellaneous sales (including those of matches) represented the bulk of the difference between gross and net revenue. Only in 1946-47, when reimbursements from the United States for the construction of the Inter-American Highway were particularly heavy, did re-

TABLE 3

GOVERNMENT NET TAX REVENUE[1]

FISCAL YEARS 1945-46—1950-51

(thousand cordobas and % of total tax revenue)

Type of Tax	1945-46	%	1946-47	%	1947-48	%	1948-49	%	1949-50	%	1950-51	%
1. Property Taxes	2,026	5.0	1,946	4.0	2,005	3.8	1,988	3.3	2,368	3.9	2,776	3.4
2. Export Taxes	1,428	3.5	1,539	3.1	1,863	3.6	1,313	2.2	2,115	3.5	7,241	8.8
3. Business Taxes	256	0.6	254	0.5	278	0.5	286	0.5	303	0.5	328	0.4
4. Mixed (business and consumption) Taxes	1,993	4.9	2,219	4.5	2,397	4.6	2,499	4.3	2,782	4.7	3,749	4.5
5. Import Taxes[2]	19,836	49.1	29,261	59.4	27,869	53.7	33,678	56.5	30,737	51.4	44,658	53.9
6. Excise Taxes[3]	14,618	36.2	13,811	28.1	17,210	33.1	19,522	32.7	21,281	35.6	23,691	28.6
7. Miscellaneous Taxes and Fees	251	0.6	187	0.4	321	0.6	362	0.6	238	0.4	381	0.4
8. Total Net Tax Revenue	40,408	100.0	49,217	100.0	51,943	100.0	59,647	100.0	59,824	100.0	82,824	100.0

[1] Including taxes transferred to autonomous funds (Rentas Pignoradas). Because of rounding, some columns do not add up to totals.
[2] Including additional contributions of the Customs Administration.
[3] Including the estimated fiscal revenue of the match monopoly.

TABLE 4

GROSS GOVERNMENT REVENUE[1]

FISCAL YEARS 1945-46 TO 1950-51

(thousand cordobas and % of total gross revenue)

Type of Revenue	1945-46	%	1946-47	%	1947-48	%	1948-49	%	1949-50	%	1950-51	%
1. Total Net Tax Revenue[2]	40,408	90.0	49,217	84.2	51,943	90.0	59,647	90.8	59,824	93.9	82,824	92.9
2. Profits of Government owned Enterprises	608	1.4	620	1.1	836	1.4	539	0.8	545	0.9	1,320	1.5
3. Total Net Revenue	41,016	91.4	49,837	85.3	52,779	91.4	60,186	91.6	60,369	94.8	84,144	94.4
4. Miscellaneous Sales (including matches)[3]	3,429	7.6	3,391	5.8	3,174	5.5	2,691	4.1	3,077	4.8	3,897	4.3
5. Reimbursements	462	1.0	5,201	8.9	1,768	3.1	2,827	4.3	253	0.4	1,039	1.2
6. Total Gross Government Revenue	44,907	100.0	58,429	100.0	57,721	100.0	65,704	100.0	63,699	100.0	89,080	100.0
7. Government Revenue According to Liquidacion[4]	53,025		68,024		66,391		74,926		65,377		90,046	

8. Difference Between
   Lines 7 and 6   8,118   9,595   8,670   9,222   1,678   966

[1] Including taxes transferred to autonomous funds (Rentas Pignoradas). Because of rounding, some columns do not add up to totals.

[2] For detail, see Table 3.

[3] Estimated at two-thirds of the receipts from the sale of matches.

[4] Includes, in addition to the line above, dividends of the government-owned railroad, which all are automatically returned to the railroad, and amounts to be refunded by the Customs Administration.

imbursements and payments for goods and services combined amount to as much as 14.7% of total gross revenue. Reimbursements alone came to 8.9%; in the other years, they fluctuated irregularly between 0.4 and 4.3% and miscellaneous sales between 4.1 and 7.6% of gross government revenue.

While not a form of taxation, the foreign exchange control system in operation since the beginning of 1951 has, in effect, placed considerable additional revenue at the disposal of the government. The total amount of revenue raised through exchange surchanges has been substantial. If the foreign trade situation continues favorable, and after the 1950 foreign trade debt has been liquidated, revenue from exchange surcharges will became available for development and other budgetary purposes.

NOTE TO TABLES 3 AND 4

The figures in Tables 3 and 4 (lines 1 through 6) include all cash receipts of the national government, including (1) assigned and shared taxes, (2) extraordinary receipts (*ingresos no previstos* —mainly reimbursements from the United States Government for Inter-American Highway construction and transfers from reserves accumulated by the Customs Administration, and (3) municipal revenue transferred to the national government (a relatively minor item).

Starting from the final accounts of the Accounting Office, the main adjustments made involved:

1. Netting out receipts of the Customs Administration which, prior to fiscal year 1950-51, were given in the liquidacion in the gross form (i.e. including reimbursements for overpayment and the theoretical amounts of import duties on imports of foreign concessions exempt from such duties).

2. Adding to customs receipts, from reserves accumulated by the Customs Administration payments into the general fund (*sobrantes de reservas aduaneras*). Since a breakdown of the origin of these reserves is not available, and since during the period

covered more than 90% of net customs revenue consisted of import duties, the entire amount of these reserves was assigned to import taxes.

3. Under Miscellaneous Revenue (*Rentas Diversas*) the liquidacion of the Accounting Office lumps together a wide variety of registration, license and monthly business taxes with some minor nontax revenue.[6] Also, in the earlier years, some items were included in this section which in subsequent years are shown under other headings.

Most, but not all items included in "Miscellaneous Revenue" are listed in a *"Catalogo Oficial de Ingresos Fiscales"* compiled in 1948.[7] This catalog lists more than 150 individual items. Some of them are not taxes or fees, but rather prices charged for the sale of various government documents, and charges for the telephone, telegraph and radio service and for the sale of matches. Various police and other fines are also included.

The various items included in Rentas Diversas after transfer of some items to other headings have been allocated as follows:

(a) Sales of products and services.

(b) Business taxes (included in Table 3, line 3).

(c) All other miscellaneous taxes and fees (included in Table 3, line 7).

Business Taxes and Fees

This group includes:

(a) Business registration fees on various categories of drugstores, importers, laboratories, soft drink plants, breweries, tobacco factories, medicine wholesalers and retail outlets and pro-

---

[6] The monthly *Recapitulacion* of the Tribunal de Cuentas lumps together most of the individual fees and minor taxes.

[7] The present analysis takes into account changes subsequent to September 24, 1948. The Catalogo also lists some categories of internal revenue which are listed separately in the liquidacion (such as property transfer and slaughter taxes as well as several taxes and fees grouped there under the heading of Sanitary Fund).

ducers and sellers of alcohol, aguardiente, liquor and perfume. Some of this revenue is estimated in the budget under the heading *Impuesto sobre licencias para comerciantes.*

(b) Monthly taxes paid by some of the establishments listed above.

(c) Registration fees for patents, trademarks, registered designs and patent medicines.

(d) Taxes on mining, prospecting, and on working of mining and lumber properties.

(e) A tax on railroad freight.

Miscellaneous Taxes and Fees

In this category are included:

(a) License fees on boats, firearms, dogs, vehicles (revenue from auto license plates is shown separately) and flashlights.

(b) Miscellaneous taxes on consumption, such as taxes on admissions, and foreign medicines.

(c) Miscellaneous fees and taxes which affect individuals as well as business such as taxes on sailing permits and fees for mail delivery and notorization of documents.

In recent years, all business taxes and fees combined, included in Rentas Diversas, yielded about 100,000 cordobas a year. All other miscellaneous taxes and fees averaged only about half of this amount.

4. The receipts from the sale of matches were broken down between the cost of matches (based on the price paid by the government) and net fiscal revenue (estimated as the difference between the sales price to distributors of matches and the cost price). It was estimated that the fiscal revenue represents one third of the gross item listed in the liquidacion under matches. The remainder was assigned to "miscellaneous sales."

5. Several minor reclassifications were made to preserve comparability of the various categories over the entire period covered.

6. Dividends received from the Ferrocarril del Pacifico de

Nicaragua, which are an accounting fiction and do not represent actual cash receipts, were excluded.

The effect of excluding refunds and reimbursements of the Customs Administration and railroad profits was to lower total gross government receipts in the fiscal years 1945-46 and 1948-49 by between 12% and 15%. The difference was much smaller in the two recent fiscal years (see Table 4, line 8).

III. *THE STRUCTURE OF THE TAX SYSTEM*

The Nicaraguan tax system is unnecessarily complicated for a small country. Fortunately, a number of the more undesirable features can be removed without reducing significant sources of revenue. For instance, while the list of transactions subject to stamp duties requires 23 pages of close print, only a few of the provisions of the Law on Stamp Paper and Duties (Ley de Papel Sellado y Timbre) are important.

Some of the complications are the result of the independent status of the Customs Administration. In order to obtain full benefit from any increase in import levies, instead of raising import duties, import taxes collectible by the Internal Revenue Administration were introduced on some products. With the placing of the Customs Administration under the complete control of the Ministry of Finance this problem will disappear and a full integration of import duties with import taxes and consular fees will become possible.

Another complication arises from the fact that the respective taxing powers of the national and municipal governments are not defined. Thus, real property is taxed both by the national government and by municipalities. There is a clear tendency for municipal governments to impose taxes on items or transactions already taxed by the national government. For instance, movie theaters and other entertainment in Managua are subject not only to a 5% national tax on gross revenue, but to an identical municipal tax as well.

The system of assigned and shared taxes, special funds and earmarked taxes creates unnecessary complications in Treasury accounting and withdraws from the control of the Minister of Finance and of Congress considerable sums of tax revenue.

The imposition of assigned taxes to meet the cost of special projects has been a direct consequence of the meagerness of the regular government revenues in recent years. Thus, assigned taxes were levied on numerous consumption goods and on admissions in order to finance welfare work among prisoners, the construction of a hospital in Managua, and such organizations as the Tourist Office, the National Sports Commission and the Coffee Growers' Association.

The number of these assigned taxes has grown considerably in recent years. The liquidacion for the fiscal year 1950-51 lists 15 different assigned taxes.[8] No fewer than six different assigned taxes are levied on a single product—gasoline.

Five of the assigned taxes are shared between two special funds. Half of the proceeds of four of these taxes is covered into the general fund and is earmarked, in equal part, for two different purposes. Furthermore, two important nonassigned taxes (the 5% import tax and the property transfer, gift and inheritance tax) are shared between the general fund and a special fund.

There are two assigned taxes—for the school lunch fund, *Fondo Pro-Desayuno Escolar,* and for the construction of the National Stadium—which are covered directly into the general fund. In addition, one tax (the coffee export tax of $3.00 per quintal) is covered into the general fund, but is earmarked for two different purposes. The larger part of the proceeds (80% for the Rama Road) is segregated in a special account at the National Bank, while the smaller (20% for the road building program) is merged with other revenue. (The special semipostal stamp for the con-

---

[8] One of them, for the victims of *Cerro Negro,* is no longer levied, but another earmarked tax on admissions (for civic improvements) has been imposed in the meantime.

struction of the National Stadium should also be considered as an earmarked tax covered into the general fund.)

With the exception of the 5% import tax, the yield of the various assigned taxes has been on the whole meager. In 1950-51 the import tax in addition to channelling 2.3 million cordobas into the general fund yielded 3.4 million cordobas assigned to increase the capital of the Mortgage Bank. Fourteen different taxes (or shares in taxes), some of them collected by two different administrations, yielded a total of 1.2 million cordobas in 1950-51; the revenues from the individual assigned taxes ranged from as little as 8,877 cordobas (Communications Week) up to 179,000 (share in the property transfer tax).

The different ways in which the several assigned and shared taxes are earmarked for specific purposes or transferred to autonomous organizations may be summarized as follows:

(a) Some are transferred to autonomous organizations which are under various degrees of government supervision. The budgets of these organizations—for example, the local Welfare Boards (*Juntas de Asistencia Social*)—are appended to the national budget, and audited by the Accounting Office. No final accounts are, however, submitted to Congress.

(b) Some are transferred to autonomous organizations whose budgets are not even submitted to Congress (for example, the National Sports Commission—*Comision Nacional de Deportes*).

(c) Some are assigned to special accounts segregated on the books of the National Bank from the general fund of the Treasury (Rama Road Fund).

(d) Some are assigned to earmarked accounts, not segregated on the books of the National Bank, but specifically recognized in the expenditure budget.

(e) Some receipts are earmarked in the budget for a specific purpose. There is, however, no visible relationship between the yield of such taxes and the particular expenditures which they are supposed to finance. Thus, when surtaxes on liquor, tobacco and beer were introduced in 1950, it was specified that the proceeds were to be used to meet the expected deficit. If no deficit should occur, the receipts were to be used, in equal shares, for the construction of schools and of sanitary units. The year ended with the highest surplus in the history of the country but there is no evidence that the amounts earmarked for schools and sanitary units are being spent for the purpose designated in the law.

(f) Some taxes originally imposed for a specific purpose are not used for that purpose, such as the tax on insurance premiums. When this tax was imposed in 1944, the revenue from this source was earmarked for public education. The mission was informed that currently the proceeds of this tax are not assigned to any specific purpose.

In spite of the complexity and intricacies of the tax system, the fiscal system is less complicated than that of some other Latin American countries. For instance, departments have no separate taxing power, so that there are only two layers of taxation. Moreover, collection of some local taxes (in Corinto, Bluefields, and some other ports) by the Customs Administration reduces the number of collecting agencies.

Because of the high degree of centralization of the government structure and the relatively small number of individuals and businesses likely to be subject to the direct taxes recommended, the problem of creating an efficient tax administration in Nicaragua is one which requires only time and determination.

IV. THE INCIDENCE OF TAXATION

Basic statistical data for a study of the incidence of taxation in Nicaragua are lacking. This much, however, is clear: individuals in the upper income groups pay no income taxes and only nominal property taxes. Their standard of living is extremely frugal in the light of comparable absolute and relative income levels in other countries, and their consumption expenditures are on the whole low in relation to current income and accumulated wealth.

The Nicaraguan tax system is highly regressive not only because that part of income which is saved is not taxed, but because the weight of consumption taxes is heaviest on the articles of current, ordinary consumption rather than on luxury goods. Luxury products are subject to relatively lower import duties than articles of mass consumption. The yield of specific taxes falling largely on the higher income groups, such as taxes on insurance premiums or automobile license plates, is insignificant.

The peon who, in addition to food, receives a cash wage amounting to three to five cordobas (43-72 U.S. ¢) a day, spends the bulk of his income on heavily taxed articles.

The sugar tax alone, the most of which is collected from the poorer groups, yields 15 times as much as real estate taxes paid by all home owners. To make another comparison, the match monopoly yields, net, 15 times as much as real estate taxes on owner-occupied homes. Fiscal revenue from matches and sugar combined was almost as large as total tax revenue from all personal and business property, real and movable.

The incidence of taxation depends to a large part on the structure of the customs tariff. While the mission has not reviewed the tariff in detail, some examples of inequities can be cited.

Imported textiles are among the most important articles of prime necessity, although the poorest groups of the population also buy domestic cotton goods. Most rayon goods are imported. Of total imports other than capital goods (iron and steel products, chemicals and machinery, the latter being duty free) amounting in 1950 to $17.1 million, cotton goods accounted for $3.1 million and rayon goods for an additional million dollars. Thus consumer expenditures for clothing and household textiles (sheets, towels, etc.) bear a disproportionately heavy share of total import duties and taxes.

Most cotton goods are subject to specific duties which could not be analyzed in detail in the short time available, but a few examples will suffice to illustrate the heavy burden on consumers:

1. Women's, men's and children's cotton clothing is subject to a 68.75% ad valorem tax (tariff Nos. 512 and 515).

2. Rayon underwear and outerwear (dresses) are subject to an ad valorem duty of 150% (tariff No. 624).

3. Rayon hose (tariff No. 621a) is subject to an ad valorem duty of 112.5%.

To these duties must be added the 5% consular fees on the f.o.b. price, the 5% general ad valorem import tax and a 5% "basic" import tax. There are, furthermore, two taxes on the weight of imports and various minor customs and port charges falling on all imports. This, in the case of textiles and textile goods all import levies combined add to as much as twice the f.o.b. price.

In contrast, duties on gold and matches are only 20.625% (tariff No. 146) and on photographic cameras 27.5% ad valorem. The import duty on refrigerators, a luxury item in Nicaragua, is about 100 cordobas (less than $13) for an eight cubic foot unit, or about 5% of the c.i.f. value. The import duty on a grand piano is less than $75. There is no duty on the import of automobiles.

The contrast between heavy import taxes on consumption goods and relatively light duties on luxury goods is striking. It might be added that most duties on articles of mass consumption are ad valorem, thus automatically increasing with the rise of the price level, while those on many luxury items are specific duties, fixed in gold cordobas and converted at the rate of five cordobas to one gold cordoba.

CHAPTER TWENTY-ONE

The Tax Administration

I. *COLLECTION OF GOVERNMENT REVENUE*

The revenue administration reflects the heavy reliance on import duties and on taxes levied on imports and exports. Nearly half of the government revenue is collected by the Customs Administration, including certain taxes which are classified as internal revenue but which are collected at the point of entrance or exit. During the fiscal year 1950-51, more than 43% of the cash receipts of the government were deposited at the National Bank by the Customs Administration after deduction of its own administrative expenses and the service on the 1909 Ethelburga loan.[1] Since the bulk of foreign trade moves through the port of Corinto, the customs house there is one of the most important collectors of government revenue in the country.[2]

More than 10% of total government revenues are collected directly by the National Bank acting as fiscal agent. Among the principal types of revenue thus collected are the bulk of consular fees, the export tax on coffee and the profits of government-owned enterprises. Part of this revenue is collected in foreign exchange. Contrary to the practice of the Customs Administration, the Na-

---

[1] According to a table prepared by the Tribunal de Cuentas, *Movimiento de los Fondos disponibles del Gobierno en el Banco Nacional de Nicaragua durante el ano fiscal de 1950-51.* The budget table on government revenue distinguishes between customs and internal revenue. Within the second category, all revenues are grouped according to the collecting agency: Revenue Administration, National Bank and Customs Administration.

[2] In the calendar year 1950, of the 43.3 million cordobas (gross) collected by the Customs Administration, 26.9 million were collected in Corinto alone (*Memoria . . .* 1950, Estado No. 6).

tional Bank credits the government account immediately with the full amount of funds collected and does not accumulate any reserves.

The Revenue Administration

Most internal revenue is collected by the Revenue Administration, *Direccion de Rentas,* subsequently referred to as Direccion, a major division of the Ministry of Finance. In amount, however, this is less than half of the total government revenue.

Taxes on liquor and tobacco represent more than half of the total revenue collected by the Direccion. Other excise taxes on sugar, matches, soft drinks, beer and the slaughter tax account for another 10%. The only other important receipts of the Direccion are from the sale of fiscal stamps (another 10%) and from property and property transfer taxes (nearly 10%). All other taxes, or groups of taxes and fees, yield less than 100,000 cordobas a year each. About 2 million cordobas collected by the communications service in fees and by the sale of postage stamps are also shown as receipts.

The field organization of the Direccion consists of 15 district offices, *Administradores de Rentas,* subsequently referred to as Rentas, and of fiscal agencies in various parts of the country. With a few exceptions a district office covers the territory of a department. It combines the functions of a revenue collecting and disbursing office. Funds for government expenditures made outside Managua are transferred to the local Rentas offices and are disbursed by them.

Fiscal agents are usually local merchants or other persons who receive a relatively modest compensation for their services (in many small localities, only 70 cordobas, or $10 a month). Their number varies with the size of the department; in the largest— Zelaya—there are 14 fiscal agents.

Fiscal stamps and paper are sold by about 120 agents (mostly stores) who have secured a special "patent." They receive an 8% discount on the proceeds of fiscal stamps and paper sold.

The Rentas office of Managua collects more than 75% of the total internal revenue. In particular, since most excise taxes fall on products manufactured by a relatively small number of firms domiciled in the capital, these taxes are collected by the Managua office. Actually, all other local Rentas offices collect only property and property transfer and inheritance taxes, transfer taxes, the slaughter tax and some minor taxes and fees. Receipts of the 14 offices outside Managua ranged in 1950-51 from 1.65 million cordobas (Granada) down to only 78,000 cordobas in Madriz. Indeed, six Rentas offices collected less than 200,000 cordobas (or less than $30,000 a year).

Two units in the Revenue Administration in Managua are in charge of the collection of excise taxes. One deals with taxes on alcoholic beverages, the other with those on meat, beer, and sugar. The entire staff of the latter section, which is also in charge of administering several other taxes consists of one chief, three inspectors, a typist and a porter. The entire staff of the Revenue Administration, excluding typists, porters and departmental inspectors, numbers 12.

Among the excise taxes, only the bulk of the slaughter tax is collected by the local revenue offices rather than in Managua. In view of the relatively small number of producers of sugar, alcoholic beverages, and tobacco products, collection of excise taxes on these products involves few problems besides those of efficient control to determine quantities produced or marketed.

Assessment and Collection of the Property Tax

It is generally conceded that the property tax, the only direct tax payable regularly, is assessed on only part of the existing property and that assessments are considerably below their real market value. In view of the procedures used, this is not surprising.

The collection of the property tax is based on self-assessment. All property owners file annual tax declarations (*manifiestos*) with a local office or directly with the Direccion in Managua. The declaration is supposed to contain a complete listing of all real estate and other property, owned by the taxpayer, as valued by him. As the tax is payable on the net worth, liabilities as well as assets are to be listed. In order to facilitate detection of undeclared property, each declaration contains the names of owners of the property adjoining the taxpayer's property, north, west, south and east.

Taxpayers may file either in the local office or directly with the Direccion. When taxpayers file directly in Managua, the local office has no means of verifying the assessment of property located in its district. It is not even in a position to ascertain at what amount it has been assessed or whether a given piece of property has been listed at all. It is worth noting that even those foreign firms whose operations are located in other departments file directly in Managua.

There is no general cadaster, apparently not even in the larger cities. Recording of property is voluntary and many property owners record only when they sell it. Recording offices exist only in the larger cities. Much of the property changes hands, not only in outlying areas but even in or close to the principal cities, without the benefit of a recorded deed. Since property bought cannot be assessed for less than the sales price, sales contracts are frequently, by mutual understanding between the seller and the buyer, made out for only a fraction of the actual sales price. This also saves on transfer taxes which amount to one-half of one per cent of the sales price, as well as stamp taxes and lawyers' fees.

Tax returns are reviewed by the local assessment boards (*Junta de Informacion y Detalle*) which consist of three officials, including the Collector of Revenue, and are forwarded to the Direccion. The local boards have little latitude in reviewing the self-assessment made by property owners; they can only recommend a revision of the valuation of the property declared by the taxpayer. They cannot assess any property not declared by the taxpayer, unless they possess a documentary proof of ownership such as a sales contract to which a fiscal stamp has been affixed and which has been filed at the Rentas office. Thus by not declaring certain houses, farm land or other real estate, property owners can evade the tax, particularly where they are leased.

Furthermore, the local Rentas office can only make recommendations concerning the value declared by new taxpayers and for taxpayers who have filed in previous years, only for additional property reported for the first time. The final decision rests with the Direccion in Managua which makes the final assessment on all returns. It prepares a tax roll, *Cuadro B,* for each department and sends it to the local Rentas office. The names of the taxpayers are listed alphabetically, together with the amount of assessed property and the amount of tax due. Copies of the original declaration of taxpayers, with all the revisions made, are also attached.

Once the assessment of property has been approved by the Direccion and the tax roll is prepared, the local Rentas office can increase the total assessment of a taxpayer in subsequent years only if he lists additional property. Valuations of property already assessed in previous years cannot be increased. If the owner values a piece of property at a lower figure than in the previous year, the board may reinstate the previous year's evaluation but may not go above it.

Tax bills are sent out by the local assessment boards under the signature of the Administrator de Rentas in his capacity as a member of this board. All accounting is concentrated at the Direccion in Managua.

Taxpayers are frequently delinquent for several years. To collect overdue taxes the Ministry of Finance sends letters to delinquents. While fines may be imposed for delinquency no foreclosure of property is provided for. The only means of enforcing payment is the requirement that, to sell property or to obtain a license, a legal document or a passport, a taxpayer must prove that he has paid property taxes due.

The Customs Administration

The Customs Administration, the other important collector of government revenue, enjoys a semi-independent status. This situation has its origin in obligations assumed by the government at the time of the Ethelburga loan of 1909. It is understood that legislation placing the Customs Administration under the Ministry of Finance is being prepared and that the existing contractual obligations toward the foreign bondholders do not preclude this step.

The Collector of Customs (*Recaudador General de Aduanas*) collects all customs revenues as well as a number of import and export taxes, port charges and some miscellaneous municipal revenue in the main ports (including revenue that is transferred to autonomous local funds). The Collector is also in charge of the maintenance and policing of ports and the construction and the maintenance of customs houses, lighthouses and other structures.

The Customs Administration meets its own payroll and other expenses from customs receipts (although since 1949-50 they are included in the *gastos administrativos directos* of the general budget). The sums remaining after payment of all costs of the Customs Administration and of the interest and amortization on the Ethelburga loan are paid into the general fund, unless the Customs Collector is specifically instructed to make other payments directly. However, payments into the general fund are made at the discretion of the Collector. The Collector retains such reserves as are required, in his judgment, against depreciation of customs buildings, for contingencies, for the purchase in the free market of Ethelburga bonds and for unspecified purposes.

The cash balance of the Customs Administration is divided among till cash, deposits at the National Bank in both cordobas and dollars, and deposits in dollars and pounds sterling abroad (for the purchase below par of Ethelburga bonds that might be offered). Some part of reserve balances is invested in United

States Government securities. Not all of these reserves are shown in the Annual Reports of the Collector.

In addition to its own cash balances and reserve accounts, the Customs Administration is the custodian of sizable escrow accounts (*depositos de ganancia*) arising from deposits by importers and exporters, pending the determination of exact amount of duties due and decisions on customs litigation cases. No separate accounts at the National Bank are maintained for escrow accounts which are merged with general receipt of the Customs Administration.

In recent years, several types of taxes on imports have been imposed which are most conveniently collected by the Customs Administration. In some cases, these were import and export duties disguised as taxes (impuestos), presumably to place their proceeds in the hands of the Revenue Administration rather than in those of the Customs Administration. The Customs Administration thus became the collecting agent of the Revenue Administration. It has, however, escaped any close supervision by the Ministry of Finance, even of that part of its activities which represent fiscal agency functions.

The Customs Administration does not maintain a separate account at the National Bank for taxes collected as agent of the Revenue Administration. It does not automatically put into the general fund all such tax receipts and therefore accumulates reserve balances. For instance, of the nearly 3 million cordobas held in reserve accounts by the Customs Administration at the end of 1950, about one third represented accumulated internal revenue funds. The autonomy of the Customs Administration has resulted in the co-existence of two practically separate treasuries.

In view of the recurrent deficits in the general budget, the temptation has been strong for the Minister of Finance to draw upon the reserves of the Customs Administration, either by ordering the Collector to make additional payments (which in recent years ranged between 1.1 million and 4.5 million cordobas) or to meet from customs reserve funds expenditures which normally should be made from the general fund.[3]

Because of the original legal provision specifying duties in gold cordobas which were then equivalent to dollars, in its annual report, the Customs Administration, which collects part of its revenue in dollars, adds dollars and cordobas without converting the former into cordobas. Equally, in its internal accounting, the Customs Administration treats dollars as equivalent to cordobas, although the dollar is worth five or more cordobas, depending on the applicable exchange rate.

II. *THE COST OF COLLECTION*

The costs of collecting internal revenue are high. The 1950-51 budget of the Revenue Administration provides 2.3 million cordobas to collect 32.1 millions of taxes. This is a cost ratio of 7%, even without allocating to collection expenses a proportionate share in overall expenditures of the Ministry of Finance or those of the Accounting Office. The percentage is about the same, if not higher, when the comparison is based on closed accounts of recent years rather than on the budget for 1951-52. This cost ratio of 7% compares with 2.4% in Bolivia, 5% in Guatemala and about 5.6% in San Salvador.

III. *CONTROL AND AUDITING*

The control of government revenue is vested in the Accounting Office (Tribunal de Cuentas). Because of its independent status, the Customs Administration has not so far been audited by the Tribunal de Cuentas, nor by any outside agency. Fiscal accounts of municipalities, about 120 in all, are audited by the Municipal Control Office (*Controlaria Municipal*) of the Ministry of the Interior. The auditing is conducted, at irregular intervals, by traveling auditors of the Control Office. The municipalities are

---

[3] The Annual Report of the Customs Administration does not show any breakdown of the payments to the general fund.

assessed for this service, for the benefit of the general fund of the Treasury, at 5% of their gross revenue.[4]

The Accounting Office receives every five or ten days, depending on the importance of the reporting office, an itemized telegraphic report of receipts and disbursements of the various revenue offices. Net receipts of the offices are deposited at the local or nearest branch of the National Bank.

A division of the Accounting Office (*Sala de Centralisacion de Cuentas*) checks the reports of the Revenue Offices and of the Customs Administration for internal consistency and prepares monthly summaries of receipts of individual taxes by collection office. For reasons which we were unable to determine, some types of revenue collected in Managua, such as excise taxes, are allocated to other revenue offices whose statistically recorded receipts thus appear to be much higher than actual collections. The fiscal agencies deposit their collections with one of the 15 revenue offices each of which is responsible for the operations of the agencies in its department.

The supervision of Revenue Offices is at a minimum, the telegraph being the main medium of communications between the Ministry and the local Revenue Offices. Periodically the Revenue Offices are examined by travelling inspectors of the Sala de Glosa, one of the three divisions of the Tribunal de Cuentas.

All fiscal accounting is on a cash basis. Receipts are posted when reported telegraphically, but the lag between reporting and actual deposit of funds at the head office or branches of the National Bank is relatively short.[5] Expenditures are charged when checks are issued.

---

[4] All new municipal taxes have to be approved by the Minister of the Interior who usually consults informally with the Minister of Finance; the final decision, however, rests exclusively with the Minister of the Interior.

[5] As mentioned earlier, customs receipts are available for meeting general budgetary expenditures not when actually collected, but when transferred by the Collector to the account of the Ministry of Finance.

The Constitution requires that final audited accounts be submitted to Congress not later than 30 days after the end of the fiscal year. In recent years, however, final accounts have been submitted only after a considerable delay. They are not published.

In discussing the assessment of direct taxes, we pointed out that all final decisions are reserved to the Collector of Revenue. There is no court of tax appeals to which taxpayers can appeal decisions of the tax administration.[6] There is, however, a customs court which deals with all litigation arising from the administration of the Customs Tariff.

---

[6] The "court of appeals" consisting of the Revenue Administrator, the chief of the section of the Revenue Administration in charge of the collection of the property tax, and its secretary (*Ley del Impuesto sobre Capital*, Art. 22) cannot be regarded as an independent judicial court of appeal.

CHAPTER TWENTY-TWO

Recommended Reforms of
the Fiscal System

Nicaragua's most pressing fiscal problem is the need for increasing government revenue. No comprehensive program for developing the resources of the country and for improving the health, education and welfare of its people can be erected on the narrow basis of a government budget which amounts to less than 10% of national income. The development expenditures within the budget absorb only about 2% of national income. These are small figures, particularly since Nicaragua has no administrative units endowed with separate budgets, such as provinces or departments, between the national government and municipalities. While certain welfare functions carried on by autonomous bodies are not exclusively financed by assigned or shared taxes, for all practical purposes the national budget represents the total amount of revenue available for the general administration and the economic development of the country, except for municipal revenues which are very modest by all standards.

The main objectives of the fiscal reform and the main recommendations were outlined in the Summary. In the following section, a more detailed discussion of the principal recommendations is given. In order to make the discussion as concrete as possible, we have dealt with the administrative aspects of the existing situation and of the proposed reforms as well as with their rationale.

I. THE PERSONAL AND CORPORATE INCOME TAX

The mission recommends the introduction of a progressive income tax on personal and corporate income to provide a sound foundation for a modern, equitable and elastic fiscal system.

All persons in the country, including legal persons such as corporations, should be subject to the income tax. Nonprofit religious and charitable institutions should be exempt from all taxation as they are now from the property tax.

The personal income tax should be simple and have a relatively high exemption. It should be only mildly progressive. Maximum yield should be sought through complete coverage rather than by steepness of progression. The exemption, at least in the beginning, should be generous, perhaps 20,000 cordobas for a married couple. To ease the tax burden of large families additional exemptions should be provided for dependents, for instance, for each child after the third.

A possible range of rates would be from 5% for the first bracket (20,000-50,000 cordobas) with a top of 15% for annual incomes over one million cordobas. The whole problem of exemptions and rate structure should be studied carefully after collection of the necessary basic statistical material on the income distribution in the higher brackets. When more experience has been gained, the minimum exemption and the rate structure should be reviewed.

Since very few individuals—probably less than 10,000 if the exemption is 20,000 cordobas—will actually have to pay this tax, adequate information for preparing tax rolls could be obtained from the records of the Revenue Administration, the Department of Agriculture, the Customs Administration, the National Bank, the Mortgage Bank, and from other sources.

In a country such as Nicaragua, it is practically impossible to draw a line between private and business income from agriculture. Fincas and plantations are normally operated as sole ownerships, although in some cases several members of a family have an interest in the same property. Income from farming and trade will have to be taxed under the provisions of the personal income tax (except for plantations and trade firms operated as corporations). Joint returns by husbands and wives should be required, as is now the case for the property tax, and safeguards will be needed to defeat tax evasion by splitting entrepreneurial and property income between several members of a family.

In order to channel the greatest volume of savings into productive investments, funds invested in bonds and shares of the Instituto de Fomento and its subsidiaries and possibly of other industrial enterprises might be deductible from net income. Whether an individual enterprise qualifies for this benefit should be determined by the National Economic Council, according to the contribution of the undertaking to economic development.

Similarly, in order to stimulate development and improvement of farm land, appropriate deductions might be granted corresponding to the cost of clearing, terracing and irrigating land, or for the acquisition of farm machinery.

Misuse of these provisions could be avoided by providing that deductible investments cannot exceed 50% of net taxable income, or it might be sufficient to make them subject to the first bracket tax rate only (or to a reduced first bracket rate). If the investments are liquidated within a specified period, the corresponding amounts should become taxable at the marginal rates applicable in the year when such investment is made.

Another possibility for using the income tax indirectly to foster channeling of savings into developmental expenditures would be to exclude from taxable income dividends from the Instituto de Fomento (and its subsidiaries).

Simultaneously with the introduction of the general income tax, special taxes on coffee exports, taxes on net income from coffee and cotton and on cattle exports should be revised. Special taxes on producers of the principal export crops are justified by (a) the fluctuating character of world prices of such products, combined with relatively stable production costs, and (b) the need to draw upon resources of existing industries to develop a balanced domestic economy.

Taxes on these crops should be rather modest in years of

average production and world prices. But as the margins between world prices and production costs widen they should be sharply progressive in order to siphon off a substantial part of the resulting windfall profits.

Provisions should be made for averaging farm income over several years, either by carrying back losses only or by averaging net incomes over, say, a three-to five-year period.

In making these recommendations, full account has been taken of the difficulties of administering an income tax in a country with the economic and social structure of Nicaragua. There are no illusions about the possibilities of evasion. In view of past experience with the property tax, any endeavor to obtain trustworthy and complete tax returns for the first year or two must be discounted. Within a period of three years, however, we believe, the tax can be made fully effective by insistence on adequately filled out returns and by putting on the tax rolls all persons receiving income above the exemption limit. Subsequently the number of taxpayers could be increased by lowering the exemption limit. Thus the fiscal system could gradually be made more flexible and a further shift from reliance on indirect to direct taxes would be achieved.

The Corporate Income Tax

There are relatively few corporate enterprises in Nicaragua. At the present time, the only form of taxation to which they are subject is the property tax. While there are no statistics available on the total amount of taxes paid by corporations, they are probably very small.

The corporate tax should be imposed at a rate of about 20%. It should be slightly progressive by granting an exemption for very small corporations, say those with an income of 50,000 cordobas.

Property taxes paid by the 36 foreign corporations operating in Nicaragua amounted in 1950-51 to only 218,000 cordobas, or a little over $30,000 a year. For the duration of their concessions, they are protected from new taxes. The objective of attracting additional foreign capital would be better achieved by putting foreign enterprises on an equal competitive footing with domestic capital rather than by special long-term privileges which have often been out of proportion to the benefits derived by Nicaragua. Special tax concessions may be desirable to stimulate new industries, but these should be granted to foreign and domestic corporations alike. Inflexible concessions, binding the government for extended periods, should be avoided in any event.

The law should provide for fair treatment of foreign companies taxed abroad, but in all other respects such companies, to the extent that they are not protected by existing long-term concession contracts, should be treated on a par with domestic companies. United States companies taxed in Nicaragua will be able to offset the higher United States corporate taxes by the amount of taxes paid in Nicaragua.

The principle of profit-sharing between foreign concessionaires and the Nicaraguan government should be established. This is, perhaps, the most equitable method of attracting foreign capital and technicians while permitting the country to share some of the profits, particularly if these exceed expectations. In the case of successful operations whose profits under favorable circumstances might represent a very high return on the capital invested, the government should obtain its share not through specific taxes, but by sharing profits on a sliding scale. The higher the profit above a minimum amount representing a fair return which allows for the greater risks of foreign investments as against investments at home, the higher should be the share of the government. Arrangements of this type are currently in operation in many countries with considerable mining resources. While profit sharing in lieu of income taxation is particularly applicable to mining and lumber companies, it could be applied to plantations and all types of foreign enterprises which, by the nature of their business, require special contractual arrangements with the government. Receipts from income-sharing with foreign concessions might be allocated to the Ynstituto de Fomento.

The present export taxes on gold, timber and bananas should be applied only to concessions which have not signed profit sharing agreements. Export taxes should be payable in foreign exchange.

II.   PROPERTY AND PROPERTY TRANSFER AND INHERITANCE TAXES

Instead of yielding only little more than 3% of total tax revenue, property taxes even at the present low rates, should, if properly enforced, yield at least 10%. A moderate increase in property rates is recommended.

The Property Tax

The property tax is now largely evaded, either by undervaluing property or by omitting from the annual return part of the taxable property. The property tax should be one of the pillars of the Nicaraguan tax system. Instead, as was pointed out earlier, it is largely evaded and yields only slightly over 2.8 million cordobas a year. At existing rates it should bring in at least 10 million cordobas a year and at the proposed rates approximately 20 million cordobas.

The property tax should be only mildly progressive, mainly through the provision of a minimum exemption. The rate on owner-occupied homes should be increased to at least 0.5% from the present rate of one cordoba per 1,000.[1] The rate on other property should be increased from the present 6.5 per 1,000 to 1%, with the exemption increased from 3,000 cordobas to 5,000 cordobas.

---

[1] The higher rate is amply justified by the fact that the property tax is implicitly also a tax on that part of imputed income which the owner derives from occupying a house rent-free. In many countries, for instance, the United Kingdom, taxable income of a home-owner is defined to include the estimated value of imputed rent.

1. Low property taxes encourage holding of land for prestige and speculative purposes. Accumulated wealth frequently takes the form of land holdings, which lie idle or are not used to best advantage. A continuous increase of land prices reflects primarily the abundance of capital seeking safe and painless investment. The property tax should be high enough to force owners of land to obtain a minimum economic return or to sell it to individuals who would be willing to apply enough effort and capital to obtain such a return. Alternatively a surtax on nonincome-earning real property should be considered in order to compel owners of land which is not cultivated to lease it or to cultivate it themselves. Such a surtax would accomplish two purposes:

    a. it would compensate the Treasury for the loss of tax revenue which would have been collected if the owner obtained a return on his land, and

    b. it would discourage speculative buying and holding of land which absorbs funds that should go into productive uses.

2. Drastic measures are needed to enforce a realistic appraisal of real estate and other property. To achieve a given yield, the alternative to higher rates is widening of the assessment basis to include all property that should be on the tax rolls. High rates penalize those taxpayers who honestly declare the full value of their property.

The present situation has apparently developed because:

a. By and large, taxpayers declare property at only a fraction of its true value. Even when the original tax return is drastically revised upward by the Revenue Administration, the property owner who makes an unrealistically low self-assessment is still likely to be assessed at less than the actual market value.

b. Once a property is on the tax rolls, any subsequent increase in its value, even if it results from improvements and other capital investments, does not, as a rule, lead automatically to an upward revision of the official assessment.

c. No generally established minimum appraisal rates or schedules are in use.

d. Penalties for nondeclaring or underdeclaring of property are not sufficient to enforce compliance.

e. Cooperation between the local assessment boards and the Direccion in Managua with other agencies (such as the National Bank, the Mortgage Bank, the Recorders of Real Property, the Departments of the Interior, of Public Works, and of Agriculture) which should help to obtain a complete and realistic appraisal of property is practically nonexistent.

Several measures to obtain a complete listing of taxable property and realistic assessments can be taken.

a. Minimum appraisal values for the guidance of tax assessors should be set on the most widely distributed types of property, such as urban real estate, various classes of farm and timber land, houses and other structures, tractors and other implements, cars and trucks, cattle, coffee trees (in production and not yet in production), etc. Those tables should be fairly detailed. For instance, the value of coffee trees might be graduated according to average yield; the value of automotive and farm equipment according to age, etc. They should be reviewed periodically.

b. The law on property taxes might be amended to give any person or government unit the right to bid for a property at, say, twice the value declared for tax purposes. The bid would become effective after the next filing date, thus giving the owner a chance to revise his valuation upward. Free access to, or even posting or publication of, property tax rolls would be required to enforce such a provision.

c. A complete cadaster of urban and rural property should be prepared within a reasonable time.[2] Tax assessors should have unlimited access to real estate and all related public records.

---

[2] The government is currently engaged in compiling, for the first time, an inventory of all government property. The records obtained recently during the DDT campaign could be used in preparing a cadaster of private property.

d. The National Bank and the Mortgage Bank could be instructed to base credit appraisals on property values declared for tax purposes. By existing legislation a copy of the list of individuals and firms subject to the property tax is supposed to be deposited with the National Bank; we understand, however, that this is not done at the present time and that when appraising the credit worthiness of prospective customers the National Bank does not make use of property values declared for tax purposes. Thus, the owner of a coffee finca may tell the tax authorities his net worth is 20,000 cordobas, and yet file with the National Bank a loan application giving his net worth at 100,000 cordobas.

e. All property should be reappraised periodically. A program for reappraising all types of property at least every five years should be developed.

f. All property should be assessed in the department in which it is located, in order to permit visual examination by appraisers. When individuals and business firms list properties in more than one department, the appraisals should be made locally, but computation of the tax, and billing and collection should be centralized.

g. Foreclosure for nonpayment of property taxes should be provided by law. Penalties for nonlisting of taxable property should be increased and enforced.

These measures are aimed at the preparation of complete and realistic assessment rolls. To achieve this objective, action will also be necessary to revitalize the assessment boards and to staff them adequately. In departments covering wide areas, use should be made of traveling teams of appraisers. Possibly the personnel of the fiscal agencies could be used.

Given adequate training of the personnel of the Assessment Boards, sufficient funds, and able, impartial and independent central supervision, the task of revising completely the present Cuadro B can be achieved within a three-year period. Within the first year, the value of property listed on the tax rolls should more than double the present amount of less than 550 million cordobas, and in three years it is likely to rise to somewhere between three billion and five billion cordobas.

The Property Transfer and Inheritance Tax

The rate of the transfer (sales) tax for immovable property is a flat 0.5%. The inheritance and gift tax is graduated according to the degree of parentage; for spouses and direct descendants and ascendants, it ranges between 0.5% for legacies between 500 and 3,000 cordobas ($71 to $429) to 7% for those exceeding 500,000 cordobas ($71,430). For the middle range of 50,000-100,000 cordobas ($7,143-$14,286) the rate is 2.5%. The corresponding range for the most distant relatives and strangers runs from 3% and 15%, the rate for the middle bracket being 8%.

These rates are very low. In comparison, in San Salvador the rate on property transfers is 1.5% or three times as high as in Nicaragua. The inheritance and gift taxes range in San Salvador from 1.4% to 20% for close relatives and between 12.4% and 50% for distant relatives and unrelated persons—again, three or more times the level of Nicaraguan rates.

The mission recommends raising the present rates on property transfers and gifts as well as on the inheritance tax.

1. The yield of the property transfer tax is currently reduced by the practice of drawing up sales contracts for a fraction of the actual sales price to save on taxes, stamp duties and legal fees. Also, since property transfer taxes are collected only by the Revenue Offices, transfers in smaller communities are generally not taxed. Collections could be increased if this tax were payable also at fiscal agencies.

2. The property transfer and gift tax should be modified to include features of a capital gains tax.

Successive increments in the value of real estate, both rural and urban, should be taxed at fairly heavy rates when title is transferred. To discourage land speculation, increments in value should be taxed at higher rates when the holding period is short, say, less than one year. Allowance should, of course, be made for any actual improvements.

3. The possibility of shifting from the present inheritance tax to an estate tax should be studied. An estate tax is cheaper to collect, easier to assess and can be settled much more quickly than an inheritance tax, which may involve a lengthy search to locate all heirs and determine their shares. Also, progressive rates can be made effective more easily in the case of an estate tax.

III. *BUSINESS TAXES*

There is no general business income tax. Some types of business, in particular those producing primarily for export, are subject to special taxes on the quantities or value of products exported. Domestic trade, manufacturing and—prior to the recent imposition of the tax on net income from cotton—the entire agricultural production other than coffee have remained free of even indirect taxation of income.

Other national taxes falling on business are exceedingly small. Some types of establishments are subject to special taxes or license fees, while others, in similar lines, are not. Thus, movie theaters, drug stores, producers of alcoholic and soft beverages and foreign trade houses are subject to special taxes, while all other types of manufacturing, including sugar mills, cement and textile factories, hotels and intercity transportation, are not.

Trade establishments pay a very small combined gross sales and payroll tax. This tax is payable by all retail and wholesale establishments with annual gross sales of 5,000 cordobas ($710) or more. It is levied on: (1) cash sales, (2) reduction of credit balances, and (3) total payrolls. Several types of merchandise, such as unprocessed food, are exempt. The tax rate is two per 1,000. Thus total business taxes paid by a trade establishment with annual sales of about 5 million cordobas and about 100 employees is 11,000 cordobas, or $1,500 a year.

It is generally believed that many merchants underreport their sales and that many establishments with a sales volume over the exemption limit do not pay this tax at all. In a country where bookkeeping is at best haphazard there is bound to be considerable evasion. Little or no attempt is made to enforce payment in cities in which no Revenue Offices are located. Although at least in Managua, books of the merchants are supposed to be inspected by collectors, it is by no means certain that this is done generally. The collectors are not regular employees of the Revenue Administration. They are free-lance collectors who are able to secure for a nominal fee a "patent" and who obtain their compensation from an 8% discount (*honorario*) on the amounts collected. In order to secure a patent a collector does not have to pass any examination or prove any knowledge of accounting. Under such circumstances, all sorts of arrangements between taxpayers and collectors are possible, not all of which involve actual inspection of accounting records.

This system is open to abuse; it should be replaced by direct filing of tax returns by trade establishments. The tax should be payable in cash or by check drawn to the order of the Revenue Administration, rather than by purchasing fiscal stamps and affixing them on returns, to be cancelled by collectors who frequently are also sellers of these stamps. Books should be inspected by periodic, unannounced spot checks by trained inspectors on the payroll of the Revenue Administration.

The same recommendation applies to the tax on admission tickets to movie theaters. The administration of taxes on admissions could be simplified by unifying the three taxes presently levied, one of which is payable in fiscal stamps, and unifying the bases of assessment. If necessary, the receipts from the tax on admissions could then be earmarked, according to a formula, for the various purposes for which the present taxes are levied.

Licenses

Many types of business require a license variously called a *licencia, matricula, inscripcion* and *patente.* The rationale of such licenses usually is that these particular types of manufacturing or trade establishments require special supervision, periodic examination or investigation before permission to open for business is given.

The whole system of licenses needs to be re-examined. When the output of an industry is heavily taxed, as in the case of alcoholic beverages, beer and soft drink industries, the payment of a relatively insignificant monthly "patent" fee has little justification. In general, the practice of frequently renewable licenses offers an opportunity to exact "on the side payments" from businessmen and permits other abuses.

Annual license fees are not graduated according to the size of establishment and are, therefore, regressive. They represent a relatively heavy burden for the small businessman, but are a negligible item of expense to the larger producer or trader.

With the introduction of a general income tax, the need for licenses as a means of business taxation will no longer exist. It is recommended that free registration (or a nominal fee) be substituted where maintenance of complete and up-to-date records of certain types of business is required for regulatory or inspection purposes. Compliance should continue to be enforced by fines.

Fiscal Stamps and Paper (Papel Sellado y Timbre)

Although the revenue from stamp taxes in the narrow sense (excluding such taxes as the tax on gross sales of stores and receipts of movie theaters which, properly should be collected by means other than stamps) is not reported separately, it must be very small. In 1950-51, total net income from fiscal stamps was 3.2 million cordobas.

At the present time, all sorts of documents such as bills, receipts, checks, mortgages and even academic degrees and military commissions must bear a fiscal stamp in order to be valid. As the stamp tax is proportionate to the amount involved (usually one or two cordobas per 1,000), it is common practice to draw up contracts as well as bills and receipts for only a fraction of the actual sales price, thereby reducing the amount of the property transfer tax and of legal fees. Many stamp duties are collected only spasmodically, usually when the document requiring affixing of a fiscal stamp has to be produced in court or before some government officer. Others apply to specific legal documents required in adoption, divorce, naturalization or other proceedings rather than to general business transactions.

The taxation of business transactions as such rather than of the income resulting from them is a carryover from a semifeudal economic and social system. In many cases, it obstructs the smooth and efficient flow of business transactions. At best it is a nuisance without the redeeming quality of being a lucrative or rational source of government revenue. The fact that all legal acts (*escrituras*) are onerous makes for their avoidance.

The whole system of stamp taxes should be reviewed to determine whether its preservation in a modern tax system can be justified. If it is kept at all, the list of rates should be reviewed with a view to:

(a) Eliminating from taxation those transactions on which rates amount to only a few centavos. Rates which yield very little in relation to their collection costs represent a disproportionally heavy burden on consumers.

(b) Consolidating stamp duties with other types of taxation. Thus a license, to be valid, should not require affixing of a fiscal stamp. If necessary, fees for licenses should be adjusted upward to include the equivalent of the present stamp duties.

(c) The present practice of granting an 8% discount to vendors of fiscal stamps and stamp paper lends itself to abuses. Although this discount is intended only for nongovernment vendors, apparently, government employees sometimes obtain the necessary patents and sell fiscal stamps directly to taxpayers, retaining for themselves the 8% discount.

Transportation

The future of Nicaragua depends to a large extent on the development of its transportation system. The extent to which existing taxes on various types of transportation encourage or hinder the exchange of goods and the maintenance and development of an efficient transport network deserves careful consideration.

In recent years, the largest increase in the volume of goods transported has been carried by truck. The extension of a modern highway system is now under way. With the completion of the strategic sections, in particular, those financed partly by loans from the International Bank for Reconstruction and Development, trucking will take an even more prominent position in the transport field.

Present transportation taxes include: (a) a tax on passenger tickets, (b) a railroad freight tax, (c) automobile license fees, (d) licenses for all other types of vehicles, (e) a monthly highway use tax of 1.2 cordobas and (f) sailing permits for boats. Apparently the last two taxes are not generally enforced, if at all.

It is striking that while all sorts of assigned taxes abound in Nicaragua, yet one earmarking that is common practice in many countries including the United States—the assignment of the proceeds of the gasoline tax to road construction and maintenance —is conspicuously lacking.

The mission recommends replacement of the flat 1.2 cordobas highway use tax by a graduated use tax, falling mainly on commercial trucking and intercity bus lines. Trucks used by farmers and ranchers to bring crops to the market and supplies to the farm should be subject to relatively light annual taxes.

Commercial trucks should be taxed in proportion to mileage and to loads carried. This type of taxation should be used to enforce maximum load limits without which heavy trucks and excessive payloads may damage roads not built to carry them.

The railroad freight tax falls largely on goods entering foreign trade. Relatively heavy charges for the use of the port of Corinto fall exclusively on export goods. The small tax on sailing permits is apparently not actually collected and should be abolished.

IV. EXCISE TAXES AND CUSTOMS DUTIES

The largest share of government expenditures is borne by the lower and lowest income groups, mainly in the form of heavy excise taxes and customs duties. The proportion of revenue derived from these two sources is in the neighborhood of 85%; the precise extent of regressiveness of the Nicaraguan tax system is difficult to appraise because customs duties constitute such a large proportion of government revenue. Because of the obsolete character of the Nicaraguan tariff and the deficiencies of import statistics, it was impossible to obtain a breakdown of duties by category of merchandise. This very uncertainty of the incidence of the tariff makes it desirable to de-emphasize as much as possible customs duties as a source of fiscal revenue.

As was pointed out earlier the overwhelming bulk of the disproportionally heavy duties and taxes on imports falls directly on consumers. Agricultural and other machinery is very largely imported duty free, while imports of raw materials except for fuel are negligible. As there are no excise taxes on luxury items, excise taxes fall on the broad masses of the population and are highly regressive.

Whatever the origins of the present situation, in shifting part of the burden of consumption taxes from the poorest to those able to pay, customs duties and internal excise taxes have to be considered jointly. The problem of whether to tax at the point of entrance, or on the final distribution level, is one of expediency, not of principle. In most cases, it will be more convenient to place the levy on the import stage, to minimize evasion and to reduce the cost of collection. Moreover, it is easier to control luxury imports in relation to the foreign exchange situation when the tax is levied at the time the item enters the country rather than when it is sold.

On the other hand, the upper income groups save a very large proportion of their income and a considerable proportion of their expenditures consists of items that are not easily made subject to luxury taxes. Expenditures for servants, maintenance of several homes, ownership of cars and refrigerators, and foreign travel, are some of the items which account for a relatively large proportion of expenditures of the highest income groups. While some of these forms of luxury do not lend themselves to taxation, new taxes probably could be imposed on certain other types of expenditure typical of the upper income groups.

The revision of the taxation of consumers must be two-pronged:

(a) Excise taxes on mass-consumption goods, in particular those on sugar, meat (slaughter tax), soft drinks and matches should be either replaced or drastically reduced, even at the cost of a drop in government revenue. If necessary, this could be accomplished by stages. The regulatory aspects of the slaughter tax can be achieved in other ways.

The government has already announced its intention to reduce consumption taxes. The maximum amount that would be lost to the Treasury would be less than 3.5 million cordobas (the estimated current yield of the sugar, slaughter and soft drinks taxes combined, plus the sales margin of the match monopoly). This is considerably less than the amount that could be recovered by rigorous enforcement of the property tax at present rates and would represent a slight increase in the standard of living of the bulk of the population.

Taxes on alcoholic beverages involve considerations of social and economic policy, as well as of fiscal yield. The mission therefore makes no specific recommendation in this regard, except to draw attention again to the exceedingly high proportion of government revenue which they have provided in the past. In appraising the incidence and the progressiveness of the Nicaraguan fiscal system as a whole, the heavy indirect taxation of the lower income groups via heavy taxes on alcohol (only mildly mitigated by apparently rather wide use of bootleg alcohol) should be taken into account.

(b) The customs tariff should be thoroughly revised to lower duties on articles of mass consumption and to offset, in part, these losses of revenue by raising duties on luxury goods.

V. MISCELLANEOUS TAXES AND FEES

This category, in spite of the number and variety of taxes and fees involved, yields a negligible part of total government revenue. Some of these taxes have been dealt with in the preceding section. Others such as licenses for dogs and firearms are collected mainly for regulatory purposes or, like automobile or boat registrations, represent fees which are also encountered in the most advanced countries. There are, however, several taxes on the books which are not actually collected. The whole list of such minor taxes should be reviewed.

VI. ASSIGNED AND SHARED TAXES

Although the number of assigned and shared taxes has been growing in recent years, total revenue collected by the national government and transferred to autonomous budgets amounts to not much more than 5% of total net government revenue. With the formulation of a comprehensive development program and the general increase of the fiscal resources of the government, the need for earmarking taxes for specific purposes will be removed. Since in most cases it is difficult to establish a direct relationship between revenue raised through earmarked taxes and expenditures for specific projects, all earmarking of this type should be discontinued.

In particular, earmarking of funds for welfare and similar purposes and sharing of taxes should be discontinued. The government should decide what resources are required for such purposes and make the necessary provisions either within the general budget or by transferring funds from the general government revenue to autonomous bodies, such as the Juntas de Asistencia Social.

In some cases it might be desirable to assign revenue from specific taxes to the broad purposes of capital development, such as to the Instituto de Fomento or to the road building program, rather than to specific projects. In such cases at the end of each fiscal year, as part of the liquidacion, the actual use of these revenues should be accounted for. Amounts not spent for the assigned purposes should be deposited in a segregated reserve fund.

VII. NONTAX REVENUE

Besides the match monopoly, the telephone and telegraph service is the principal business activity of the government. It should continue to be attached to the post office and operated directly by the government (see chapter 14). The operations of the communications service, including the post office, should be placed on a business accounting basis. All other business activities of the government, most of them a heritage of wartime shortages, should be liquidated, as is now being done for the most part, or transferred to the Instituto de Fomento.

The government derives surprisingly little revenue from the sale and lease of public lands. The absence of an inventory of public lands and of any office specifically in charge of evaluating government land are possibly important explanations. In any case the uniform sales price is unrealistically low—one cordoba per manzana.

Concrete plans should be developed for taking the greatest possible advantage of the opportunities for leasing public lands. In areas to be opened up by the construction of new roads, sales should be made final only upon appraisal of the real value of the land after completion of the entire road improvement and not merely of the section on or near which the parcel is located. Sales prices should be not only raised but graduated.

The main objective of this program, however, should not be

narrowly fiscal. The aim should be to raise the taxable wealth and income of the country by increasing the area under cultivation (or other productive use) and to avoid any situation whereby land speculators reap the fruits of public development expenditures.

CHAPTER TWENTY-THREE

Recommended Reforms of the Revenue Administration

Administration of the individual and corporate income taxes recommended by the mission and thorough reorganization of the administration of the property tax will require a considerable expansion of the personnel of the Ministry of Finance and development of new administrative procedures. The mission recommends the appointment of a technical advisor to the Minister of Finance to help in the development of appropriate methods and techniques, in the selection and training of the staff, and in setting up of appropriate machinery for an efficient administration of the new income taxes.

The shift in emphasis from indirect to direct taxation will require better trained officials than are now available. It is easier to collect a tax defined in terms of so many cordobas per physical unit produced or sold, or to sell fiscal stamps to those taking the initiative of buying them, than to verify income or net assets of individuals and of business firms. To administer the present tax system, honesty and knowledge of arithmetic are the two essential qualities. To administer a system based largely on income and property taxes will require in addition a knowledge of business organizations and practices, together with imagination and initiative.

Recruiting additional personnel is only the first step. The Ministry of Finance will also need to institute a comprehensive program to train officials capable of interpreting the tax laws and assisting taxpayers to prepare their returns properly. An efficient staff must be trained to audit returns and to detect under-reporting, evasion and fraud. Because this is not a task which can be accomplished overnight, it is important that the training program begin simultaneously with the introduction of fiscal reforms. At the same time appropriate units should be organized within the Revenue Administration to make the functioning of the new tax system a success from the very start. Only an impartial and efficient staff will be able to obtain the respect of taxpayers and the confidence of the public at large.

Some additional recommendations are summarized below:

(a) One of the best means of maintaining honesty and impartiality in the Revenue Administration is to pay salaries sufficient to attract high caliber personnel. Another is to have an independent inspection service. The rudiments of such an inspection service exist in the Examination Division (Sala de Glosa) of the Accounting Office. Its efficiency could be increased not only by an expansion in its staff, but also by modernization of its procedures.

(b) Local tax administrators must have at their disposal an up-to-date collection of tax laws, regulations and procedure manuals. There should be no doubt in their minds as to whether a given tax is still on the books—a situation which was found to exist even among the top officials at the Ministry itself. Likewise, the taxpayer needs to know for which taxes he is liable, and at what rates. He should be able to obtain clear, concise and authoritative information on all tax laws and regulations.

As soon as review of the tax laws can be completed, a tax manual should be prepared which would include all remaining or new tax laws, together with the relevant amendments and regulations. As tax laws are usually couched in involved legal phraseology, a simple, nontechnical, descriptive compilation of tax laws should also be prepared and made available free to taxpayers. The ordinary taxpayer should be able to determine his tax liabilities without engaging the services of a lawyer and without making a trip to Managua.

(c) Taxpayers should be protected against arbitrariness or

even incompetence in the past of officials. On the other hand, the government should be in a position to punish wilful violators of tax laws. The establishment of a tax court of appeals, whose decisions should be widely publicized (and collected for reference), will provide the ordinary taxpayer with protection and the government with a convenient means of enforcing compliance. It also will be of great educational value. In a country where only a negligible minority of the population have ever had direct contacts with officials of the tax administration, where tax consciousness is low, and where voluntary compliance with tax laws is spotty at best, a well-functioning tax court will perform the role not only of a policeman but of an educator for the taxpayer and the tax administrator.

Members of the tax court should be appointed for long terms and every effort should be made to select competent judges and to protect their independence while in office.

(d) Fraud and evasion are not discovered simply by verifying whether figures add up. The use of collateral information, and of average ratios (for example the average rental value of a dwelling or a percentage of gross receipts of various types of retail stores for estimating income, and yield per acre to check income from farming) is valuable in auditing and assessment. Membership records of professional and trade organizations, as well as records of individuals to whom various licenses and patents have been issued should be used to check compliance with tax laws.

(e) In setting up machinery for processing and auditing of income tax returns, and for billing and collecting the tax, some basic decisions must be made. The advantages of centralizing billing and collections in Managua, while decentralizing filing and auditing, should be considered. Adequate records for administering the carry-back provisions must be set up.

(f) A separation between collection and disbursing of government revenues would greatly simplify accounting and auditing.

At present revenue collectors outside Managua also perform the function of disbursing officers. While the amounts disbursed outside of Managua are relatively small—only 17%, according to the budget for 1951-52—several disbursing officers should be appointed for the departments. In most cases, one officer could handle an area covering several departments.

(g) Since checks are not widely used, and since there are no postal money orders or any other facilities for transferring funds, taxes are usually paid in cash at the collector's office. Taxpayers frequently have to travel to the departmental capital to pay their taxes, and must stand in line to await their turn. In some cases, fiscal stamps have to be purchased in one place and cancelled in another.

Banking facilities are scarce throughout the country. Even the port of Corinto, through which the bulk of the country's foreign trade passes, has no branch of the National Bank. In view of this, the institution of a limited postal checking system should be considered. Tax payment coupons of various round denominations (say, 1, 5, 20, 100 and 500 cordobas) could be sold by all post offices. The coupons should be acceptable only in payment of taxes. Alternatively, all taxes could be made payable in fiscal stamps to be sold by post offices.

With respect to the Customs Administration, it is obvious that an administration which controls half of the total tax revenue of the government should be placed under the direct control and audit of the Ministry of Finance. The present situation is unsound and should be terminated as soon as possible. The mission recommends that:

(a) All revenues collected by the Customs Administration be covered into the general fund, after payment of interest and amortization on the Ethelburga loan.

(b) All expenditures of the Customs Administration be subject to the same rules governing the budgeting, disbursement and audit of all other government departments.

(c) The customs tariff and the procedures followed in assessing values of imports and exports be reviewed and amended where necessary.

(d) The annual report of the Customs Administration be expanded to provide more information that would be useful for analyzing the impact of foreign trade, and of duties and taxes falling upon it, on the domestic economy.

CHAPTER TWENTY-FOUR

The Preparation, Organization and Execution of the National Budget

As presently organized, the Ministry of Finance is little more than a combined collection and disbursing office performing routine functions. It has no organs of policy formation or fiscal planning to meet the overall goals of the government. There is no systematic analysis of operating results and practically no inter-departmental coordination in fiscal matters. Without either a statistical office or a research department, the Ministry is not adequately equipped to appraise the impact of various types of taxation on business and the economic development of the country, to study the incidence of taxation, to prepare a budget, or to estimate properly government revenues and expenditures.

The Minister has no staff to assist him, not even a secretariat. According to the present incumbent and two previous ministers, from 60% to 80% of his office time is spent in signing checks and in receiving private citizens who come to discuss various matters, not always directly related to taxation or fiscal administration.

Unless the Minister is relieved of the duty of signing checks for all, even the smallest, government expenditures and unless discussion of minor complaints and personal problems can be delegated to a staff officer, one of the most important administrations will remain under the direction of an official whose office schedule makes adequate examination of policy and administrative problems impossible.

In addition there is a tendency not to delegate responsibilities to the heads of the various divisions. The Minister makes final decisions on matters which should be determined at a much lower level. For example, the Minister personally reviews complaints of overassessment and makes the final decision on the amount of assessment.

The present staff of the Ministry, including auditors and examiners attached to various other ministries or autonomous bodies or traveling in the departments, numbers less than 90. This small number excludes typists, porters and guards, but includes the staffs of the purchasing office (handling supplies for practically all government departments) and of the philatelic agency.

No specific educational qualifications seem to be required for any position in the Ministry. Except for some courses for accountants for which a total annual budgetary appropriation of 32,400 cordobas (less than $5,000) is provided, there is no training program for Ministry personnel.

Without a drastic reorganization of the Ministry, no real progress, either in the preparation and control of the budget or in fiscal administration, can be accomplished. Everything relating to fiscal planning and analysis and the formulation of long-range fiscal policy must be newly created.

I. *PREPARATION OF THE BUDGET*

It is difficult to overstate the importance of fiscal planning in relation to general economic planning and development. The preparation of a budget and a clear and consistent presentation of its main features are major responsibilities of the executive branch of government. At the present time, the preparation of the budget is the personal responsibility of the Minister of Finance, assisted by the President of the Accounting Office, the Director of Revenue and the chief administrative officer of the Ministry of Finance. In estimating revenue, the advice of the Collector of Customs is secured. Beyond obtaining advice from the senior officials of the Ministry, the whole burden of preparing the budget rests on the Minister himself. On the basis of past experience and his personal judgment, unsupported by formal analysis of fiscal or other data, he estimates revenue for the coming fiscal year and reviews and reconciles expenditure requirements of the various ministries.

The budgets of the individual ministries are submitted separately to the President and are reviewed by him. The budget is then presented by the Minister of Finance to Congress where it is discussed by the finance committees of the Chamber and of the Senate. In recent years, the budget was submitted so late that only a few days remained before the beginning of the fiscal year. The members of Congress had no opportunity to study the broad features and implications of the budget.

The short reports of the two chambers make no effort to evaluate the budget in terms of any specific programs or the general needs of the country. Their review is purely perfunctory. Thus, for instance, in reviewing the 1951-52 budget, the largest ever submitted, the Senate Committee on Finance and Public Debt made only one change, splitting a subsidy of 1,000 cordobas between two churches instead of assigning it to the restoration of one. The changes proposed by the corresponding committee of the lower chamber were somewhat more numerous, but not more significant.

The budgetary powers of Congress, as defined by the Constitution, are limited by the provision that only the executive can propose an increase in the total amount of expenditures or make changes in estimated revenue. Congress cannot make any change in "fixed expenditures" such as contractual obligations, public debt service or contributions to international organizations, but it can transfer funds between "variable expenditures," provided no increase in total budgetary appropriations beyond the figure submitted by the executive results.

Once the budget is approved, there is no agency or official other than the Minister of Finance to survey the execution of the budget. A section of the Tribunal de Cuentas verifies that each check is prepared in conformity with the credits available for the given purpose, and that payments made are charged against the appropriate credits. But there the controls end. Fiscal programs are not reviewed during the year in the light of changing circumstances or actual collection experience. Appropriations voted are disbursed to the extent that funds are available, salary payments having an absolute priority. The only flexibility seems to consist in generous underestimation of revenue, the willingness to reduce payments for public debt service below budgetary appropriations, and to ask for supplemental appropriations. In each year since the end of the war, with the exception of 1947-48, an extraordinary budget has been voted; in 1949-50 it took the form of a loan from the National Bank, out of which expenditures were made without any formal extraordinary budget (see Table 1).

The supplemental credits of recent years were voted without any detail or breakdown. The following example involving a supplemental credit of 9 million cordobas (or nearly 15% of the original appropriation for 1948-49) is typical. "The extraordinary supplementary credit referred to in the preceding Article will be used to meet the pending extraordinary expenditures resulting from the further progress in completing public works and for meeting of

TABLE 1

ORDINARY AND EXTRAORDINARY BUDGETED EXPENDITURES
FISCAL YEARS 1944-45—1950-51
(million cordobas)

	1944-45	1945-46	1946-47	1947-48	1948-49	1949-50	1950-51
Ordinary budget	38.5	51.3	56.2	52.1	62.8	54.5	66.1
Extraordinary budget	3.0	3.0	14.0	—	9.0	6.4*	2.7
Total	41.5	54.3	70.2	52.1	71.8	60.9	68.8

* Officially treated as a loan from the National Bank and not as an extraordinary budget.

other expenditures which are indispensable, to cover future costs of the said needs and to pay any debts which the government should incur for emergency expenditures in cases when budgetary credits are not available to meet the said expenditures, or when budgetary appropriations are insufficient to meet such expenditures." [1]

Estimates of government revenue are extremely uncertain and consistently tend to underestimate. During each of the fiscal years 1944-45 to 1949-50 government receipts (excluding autonomous bodies and services) have exceeded budget estimates by 20-43%. This was, of course, partly due to the general inflationary developments during the period, and also to the increase in revenues due to introduction of new taxes or increases in rates. Nevertheless, it is obvious that if the budget presented to and approved by Congress is to be a realistic projection of governmental fiscal activities during the coming year, estimates of the fiscal resources (as well as of expenditures) have to be placed on firmer ground. Table 2 compares actual receipts with budget estimates for the last few years.

TABLE 2

ESTIMATED AND ACTUAL GOVERNMENT REVENUE*
(million cordobas)

	Estimated	Actual	% of Actual to Estimated
1944-45	29.9	42.8	143
1945-46	40.0	50.5	126
1946-47	47.6	58.4	123
1947-48	52.7	63.1	120
1948-49	56.7	68.8	121
1949-50	51.4	64.0	124
1950-51	63.7	83.0	130

* Current revenue only. Excluding reimbursements, loans and estimated surplus available from the previous fiscal year.
[1] *Gaceta,* April 19, 1949, p. 755.

Budget estimates of government expenditures during the last seven years have also been consistently far below actual expenditures, even after allowance for supplementary (extraordinary) budgets. In each year except the last, actual expenditures exceeded ordinary budgetary appropriations; even more, except in 1946-47, they exceeded total appropriations including supplementary appropriations. In 1946-47, however, less than four months before the end of the fiscal year, budget appropriations were increased by 25%. Even so, actual expenditures fell only 1.6 million short of appropriations. This is equivalent to only about one tenth of the supplemented appropriation which, apparently, could not be spent quickly enough. In the following year, the only one in the period covered without a supplementary budget, nearly 19 million cordobas (or 36%) more were spent than authorized in the budget.

Under such circumstances, the budget, as enacted, does not give even an approximate guide to the expected fiscal performance during the coming year.

II. *ORGANIZATION OF THE BUDGET*

In its present form, the budget is essentially a list of salaries to be paid by the government, grouped by departments and bureaus. All jobs, including minor and presumably part-time positions carrying an annual salary of as little as 720 cordobas (a little over $100) are listed individually. Some jobs held concurrently by the same individuals are listed separately. Thus, the tax receiver (Administrador de Rentas) is also a member of the local tax assessment board (Junta de Investigacion y Detalle) and as such draws an additional salary. Salaries listed in the budget thus do not give a clear indication of the salaries received by individual officials, but merely of the compensation attached to various functions. No uniform principle governs the detail given on non-salary expenditures. In some cases they are given in superabundant detail, while in others relatively large items, mainly for the purchase of goods and services, are not broken down.

In spite of its bulk and detail, the budget is of extremely limited analytical value. Total expenditures are not broken down between salary, capital, and other categories of expenditures. It is impossible to appraise from the budget either the actual cost of the various functions of government or the profitability of the various quasi-business activities of the government. There is no summary of expenditures for specific programs. Until recently the budget did not contain any general statements on the objectives of government fiscal activities (except to balance the budget) or any review of past fiscal activities of the government. It is submitted without any substantial discussion of the economic outlook for the fiscal year to which it applies, or of the results for the year which is drawing to an end. In 1949-50 and 1950-51, for instance, the Finance Minister's message to Congress accompanying the budget was the only explanatory statement offered; it was limited to four pages of large print. The most recent message of four and a half pages was not much more illuminating.

The summary tables attached to the Minister's message show only a comparison, for each department, with the proposed budget of the previous year, rather than a comparison with either the actual receipts and expenditures of the last fiscal year, for which final accounts are available, or with the preliminary estimates of the actual results of the current years. Obviously, the organization and presentation of the budget is one of the principal areas where important progress can be rapidly achieved.

The national budget should provide a complete and clear picture of the fiscal activities of the government.

1. It should give to the legislator and to the interested citizen an estimate of the cost both of governmental administration and of economic development, and a comparison with the actual expenditures in the preceding year.

2. It should be complete and include all revenues, whatever their source and ultimate use, including assigned and shared revenues (the *rentas pignoradas* transferred to autonomous bodies

and special funds). On the income side it should include only income that is actually available to the government. Gross receipts from the various quasi-business activities that are offset by corresponding expenditures should be excluded.

3. Estimates of all receipts as well as expenditures should be realistic. Adequate provision for contingencies that are likely to arise should be made.

4. Any difference between projected revenue and expenditures should be reconciled by showing the disposition of the surplus or the way in which it is proposed to meet the deficit, if any.

5. A reclassification of receipts and expenditures is necessary to achieve budgetary clarity. Receipts should be grouped by type of taxation and other sources of income or by their fiscal and economic characteristics, rather than by the collecting agency.

For administrative convenience, it is the usual practice to group expenditures by departments which actually disburse the funds. In such a case, a summary by function or purpose should be provided as an appendix. Within each government department, however, it should be feasible to break down expenditures between those for general administration and for construction. If so, capital expenditures should be broken down between those for economic development and those which serve other purposes (such as construction of government buildings, barracks, monuments, etc.).

In order to meet the objectives outlined, it is proposed:

1. To make the classification of expenditures within each department uniform and consistent. All expenditures within each department should be grouped under the following headings:

(a) current administrative expenditures, broken down between: salaries, supplies and maintenance, and other expenditures;
(b) development expenditures;
(c) other capital expenditures.

2. To include in the budget all taxes levied by the national

government, including the rentas pignoradas, in order to show the entire national tax burden borne by the country. In the last two budgets revenue transferred to autonomous funds has been excluded from the general budget. The principle of budgetary unity is not observed when segregated funds are administered outside the budget.

3. To include in the budget only the net, rather than the gross, amount of government services and monopolies, in accordance with practices in most other countries. This calls for a partial change in the present presentation which includes net income only of government enterprises and institutions, but gross income from the match monopoly and from the post and other communications services.

In the case of government services which may be classified as commercial activities, receipts represent charges for specific services rather than taxes to meet the cost of general government. Similarly, expenditures for the purchase of items for resale by fiscal monopolies or government stores and the corresponding receipts from sales are now included in the budget. Only the profits (or deficits) of such quasi-business activities should be included in the general budget. In order to appraise the profitability and efficiency of these operations, they should be detailed in separate appended budgets.

This change will follow the precedent set several years ago when receipts and expenditures of government-owned institutions (*gastos indirectos*), such as those of the National Bank and of the port of Corinto, were eliminated from the national budget, leaving in it only profits of these institutions available to the general fund.

According to the Constitution, only expenditures specifically provided for in the budget can be made legally. To avoid constitutional difficulty it might be advisable either to make the separate budgets of government services and monopolies an integral part of the budgetary document (as appended budgets) or to deduct expenditures from gross revenue (on the revenue side of the budget) in order to show net revenue.

4. To exclude fictitious items, such as dividends "paid in kind" by the government-owned railroad. The dividends paid by the government-owned Ferrocarril del Pacifico de Nicaragua represents the imputed value of services rendered by the railroad.[2] The amount of this revenue is determined by the size of the government freight and fare payments to the railroad which these "dividends" are supposed to match. This imputed item inflates the income and expenditure sides of the budget by an identical amount.

5. To group all expenditures for the National Guard under Defense (*Ramo de Guerra, Marina y Aviacion*). In the last budget some military units, such as the Managua city police (carried in Gobernacion, Cap. IX and X, and financial guards carried in Hacienda, Cap. XIV), were included in the budgets of other ministries. These two items alone equal one third, of the appropriations of the Defense Department. It is recognized that certain services which are nominally under national guard status (such as the Customs Administration and the Radio Nacional) perform functions that are not primarily military. All guard units, however, which are not clearly performing civilian functions, should be carried in the military budget.

6. To show the public debt transactions (as distinct from payment of interest on the public debt) as a balancing item and not under Finance, even though the latter department is responsible for the management of the public debt.

Showing of the budgetary surplus as a balancing item represents a radical departure from the present practice prescribed by the Constitution. Article 260 specifies that "The surplus remaining after the closing of accounts of a fiscal year should be incorporated as revenue in the budget of the following year." Con-

---

[2] The railroad transports government passengers and freight at half rates. The other 50% are supposed to represent payment of dividends in kind.

versely, "when a fiscal year results in a deficit, this deficit should appear as an item of expenditure in the budget of the following year."

Taking advantage of this provision, in recent years Treasury cash balances expected to be available (at the National Bank and in the Customs Administration) at the beginning of the year have been included under estimated budgetary receipts under the title of "fiscal reserves." As a matter of fact, this item was placed at the head of the estimate of government revenue (Title I). In the current year (1951-52) budget, this title alone amounted to nearly 12.6 million cordobas, or to more than 17% of estimated total gross government revenues.

It is generally difficult to estimate several months ahead the level of excess Treasury balances at the end of the current fiscal year. In 1950-51, for instance, when "fiscal reserves" of the general fund were estimated at 2 million cordobas and those of the Customs Administration at 1 million, the actual receipts under this title were exactly zero, according to the liquidacion supplied by the Tribunal de Cuentas.

TABLE 3

PROPOSED FORM OF NATIONAL BUDGET[1]
(million cordobas)

Expenditures		Receipts	
1. Development expenditures 50		1. Taxes	
2. Other capital expenditures 10		a. Direct taxes	
3. Administrative expenditures		1. Income taxes	
a. Legislative	5	2. Property taxes	
b. Executive[2]	43	3. Property transfer and inheritance taxes	
c. Judicial	2	4. Other direct taxes	
Subtotal	50	Subtotal	55

4. Transfer payments to
   autonomous bodies[3]   20

5. Surplus   5

   Total government ex-
   penditures   135

   Public debt transac-
   tions: retirement
   $(+)$ or increase $(-)$

   a. Internal   — 5
   b. External   +10
           —

       Subtotal   5
   Change in Treasury
   balance   0
           —
   Total   140
           =

b. Indirect taxes
   1. Import duties
      and taxes .
   2. Export duties
      and taxes
   3. Excise taxes   ∴
   4. Fiscal stamps
      and paper
   5. Licenses and
      patents
   6. Other indirect
      taxes
      Subtotal   70

2. Revenue of the com-
   munications service[4]   3

3. Revenue from quasi-
   business activities[4]   4

4. Dividends of govern-
   ment enterprises and
   institutions[4]   3

5. Other regular income   1

6. Reimbursements
   a. From abroad   2
   b. Domestic   2
           —
       Subtotal   4
   Total   140
           =

---

[1] Figures for illustrative purposes only.

[2] Expenditures by departments should be shown separately under this heading; interest on public debt to be included under Ministry of Finance.

[3] Now called earmarked revenue (rentas pignoradas).

[4] This item may be negative and appears under expenditures in the form of a subsidy.

It appears, therefore, entirely unrealistic to include in the budget any surpluses from the immediately preceding year. The full amount of the expected deficit for the given budget year should be shown. The budget for a given year should show the expected net result of fiscal operations during that period alone, not the accumulated fiscal results of that year and all preceding years. Ways should be found to make this change consistent with constitutional requirements.

The proposed changes in the organization and presentation of the national budget can be best shown by means of a summary table corresponding to the one placed at the head of the first part of the 1951-52 budget. This table should be accompanied by a comparison, item by item, of the proposed appropriations and anticipated revenues with the actual fiscal results of the last year for which final accounts are available and with preliminary estimates for the current year.

On the revenue side, the proposed summary table includes, in addition to revenue of the general fund, all assigned and shared taxes (transferred revenue—*rentas transferidas*—seems to be a better term than assigned revenue—rentas pignoradas). This arrangement follows the earlier Nicaraguan practice, but is in contrast to the most recent budgets (since 1950-51) in which such taxes are excluded from the budget.   No meaningful analysis of the tax burden and of its composition is possible unless all taxes levied by the national government are included under revenue. Assigned or shared taxes are shown under expenditure as "transfer payments" (item 3).

All tax collections (including import and export duties) are grouped by type under two subheadings, direct and indirect taxes. The following three items represent the net contribution of the communications department (item 2), of government monopolies and quasi-business activities (item 3), and of government-owned enterprises, such as the National Bank (item 4). The gross transactions of these three sources of revenue should form an integral part of the budgetary document and are discussed below.

TABLE 4

PROPOSED FORM OF DEVELOPMENT EXPENDITURES BUDGET

Expenditures	Receipts

1. Instituto de Fomento
 	
  a. Capitalization
  b. Administrative expenditures
  c. Construction, e.g. grain storage plant
	1. From assigned budget revenues
	  a. Coffee export taxes
	  b. Special taxes on net coffee and cotton incomes
	  c. Exchange surcharges
	  d. Funds from the 5% special import tax
	  e. Profits of the National Bank
	  f. Profits of state enterprises

2. Road construction
  a. Rama road
  b. Inter-American Highway
  c. Other main roads
  d. Local and feeder roads
	2. From other budget revenue*

3. General construction
  a. Health centers and hospitals
  b. Public schools and training centers
  c. Communications
  d. Ports
  e. Railways
  f. Electric power
  g. Agricultural school
	3. From foreign sources
	  a. Grants
	  b. Loans

4. Special projects
  a. Literacy campaign
  b. DDT campaign
  c. General agricultural and power surveys	

* May include funds allocated from general revenues, budget surplus of previous fiscal year, and increases of revenues during fiscal year over estimated revenues.

All other regular government income (such as fees, fines, proceeds of the sales of government property, etc.) is lumped together in item 5. It might not be possible, however, to segregate,
in all cases, fines from taxes to which they relate. The word
"regular" is used to denote the contrast to nonrecurrent reimbursements shown in the following item. Actually, item 5 may include
some items that are not current (or recurrent); if the amounts
involved are substantial, it might be desirable to create a separate
heading for such items. Also, if income from the sale or lease of
government land becomes important, such revenues should be
shown separately.

The last item, reimbursements, is self-explanatory; it includes
mainly:

(a) those from the United States for the construction of the
Inter-American Highway, and other reimbursements received from abroad; and

(b) those received by the highway department for work per-
formed for private citizens and similar domestic reimbursements.

On the expenditure side, the proposed form lists the legislative,
the judicial, and all departments of the executive branch of government. For each branch or department, salary, maintenance and
all other current expenditures including interest on the public debt
to be shown as such under the Ministry of Finance, should be
shown separately. All construction expenditure should be broken
down between development and other capital expenditures such
as expenditures for military installations and monuments (items
1 and 2).

The balancing item of the budget might be either positive when
there is a surplus or negative when there is a deficit. The disposition of any surplus to retire public debt or to add to the Treasury
cash balance should be indicated. Conversely, a deficit will be reflected by an increase in the public debt or a decrease in the
Treasury balance. In the summary table, it might be sufficient to

show these changes under two headings only, domestic and foreign debt. More detail should be provided in appendix tables.

It is believed that the recommended rearrangement of the summary table will greatly increase the value of the budget for the legislator and the administrator, as well as for all interested citizens.[3] The usefulness of the budgetary document itself and the analysis of budgetary appropriations would also be facilitated if recurrent items were numbered and titled consistently. At the present time, chapter headings are not consistent from year to year, so that comparisons of appropriations are difficult to make.[4]

A development budget (along the lines of Table 4) might be made part of the budgetary document.

III. *EXECUTION OF THE BUDGET*

Proper execution of a budget requires not only that expenditures remain within the bounds of appropriations made, but also that funds be spent for the purposes for which they have been appropriated. Otherwise, some appropriations can be rightly characterized as having been budgeted for window dressing purposes only.

There is a persistent tendency not only to exceed budgetary appropriations, but also to make expenditures for purposes not provided for in the budget and at the same time to curtail expenditures for which appropriations were made. The year 1949-50, when a serious effort was made to balance the budget, serves to illustrate the point.

Of the total cash expenditure of 62.3 million codobas (exclud-

---

[3] No suggestions have been made as to the reduction of the bulk of the budget document. As there is no civil service and no established table of organization of the various departments and services, the detailed salary listing in the budgetary document apparently serves to establish, for the coming year at least, the administrative organization.

[4] In addition to the recommendations discussed in this chapter, at the time of its visit the mission gave detailed suggestions to the government for each part of the budget. Since they were of considerable length and of a technical nature, they have been omitted from the published report.

ing the imputed payment to the railroad, amounting to 1.7 million cordobas), only 50.7 million cordobas represented funds spent as appropriated in that year. Another 9.3 million cordobas (or nearly 15% of total cash expenditures) represented holdover appropriations from previous years, while 1.6 million cordobas represented expenditures from funds transferred from one title to another within the same department, at the discretion of the Minister of Finance. (The remaining 700,000 cordobas represented miscellaneous transactions.)

Similar information for the fiscal years 1944-45 through 1950-51 is given in Table 5 below. A more detailed breakdown would show that in most years only a minor part of the appropriations made for retirement of public debt was actually spent for this purpose.

TABLE 5

GOVERNMENT EXPENDITURES

Classified by type of appropriation, fiscal years 1944-45—1950-51*
(million cordobas)

Category	1944-1945	1945-1946	1946-1947	1947-1948	1948-1949	1949-1950	1950-1951
1. Funds spent as appropriated in the budget (including extraordinary budgets)	39.0	49.7	51.2	49.4	57.0	50.7	60.8
2. Appropriations transferred within a department	4.4	6.7	8.7	10.8	15.4	1.6	1.9

3. Holdover appropriations from previous year	1.4	0.5	—	6.7	6.3	9.3	5.4
4. Automatic expenditures	—	—	4.7	—	0.4	—	2.4
5. Others	0.4	0.7	0.9	3.0	2.2	0.7	5.0
Subtotal	45.2	57.6	65.5	69.9	81.3	62.3	75.5
6. Imputed payments to the railroad	1.9	2.3	3.1	1.3	1.5	1.7	1.0
Total	47.1	59.9	68.6	71.2	82.9	64.0	76.5

* Based on closed accounts.

In any given year, the Minister of Finance can authorize, within a given ministry, expenditures to be charged to any of the three following accounts:

1. Actual budgetary appropriations for the current year (under title and chapter under which such specific expenditure was authorized);

2. appropriations transferred within the same department;

3. appropriations for a given department made in any of the previous years, but not actually spent (holdover).

Holdover accounts obscure the actual fiscal results of the current year. The handling of holdover accounts is based on a provision of the "Dispositions on the execution and liquidation of the budget" appended as "part III" to budgets of recent years. It provides for the transfer each month of all unspent funds (all salary and most other appropriations being on a monthly basis) to a "remainder account" (*Remanentes de Administracion Publica*). This cumulative account is at the "exclusive disposal of the

Minister of Finance, to be used preferably within each Department for payment of salaries for which no appropriations have been made, and for urgent and indispensible expenditures."

At the end of the year, all the balance in this account after some minor adjustments becomes, through an order of the Minister of Finance, a carryover appropriation. It is added to the cumulated holdover appropriations of previous years and becomes available for expenditure in the next fiscal year.

Since holdover appropriations never expire, in most departments substantial credits are usually available against which expenditures not provided for in the budget for the current year can be charged.

In recent years, budgetary deficits were covered by borrowing from the National Bank. Under the pretext that payments made from credits opened by the National Bank were not charged against regular revenue, they were not always included in accounts of the budgetary situation made to the public. Thus, the books showed a budgetary surplus when in fact it was more than offset by overdrafts at the National Bank which were either not publicized or not yet legalized by Congressional action.

Expenditures for which no budgetary appropriations existed were made until recently by means of *ministeriales*. These are orders to pay which are not posted as are all other checks on ledger cards showing the credit balance for each title, chapter and item of the budget. They ran into substantial sums and were subsequently legalized by supplemental appropriations. In the meantime, neither the minister nor the public knew the exact cash position of the Treasury, since no total of ministeriales was published and ministeriales might be charged against a specific credit voted several years before and still open; a call to the National Bank seems to have been the only way a minister could ascertain the actual balance.

The practice of ministeriales, which until very recently made much of the current reporting on the budgetary position largely fictitious, is now rarely used. All outstanding ministeriales have been properly legalized and liquidated, and currently ministeriales are used only to make small, urgent expenditures, such as advances for travel to officials which cannot wait for the time consuming procedures involved in securing a regular warrant.

With the practical abolition of ministeriales, the Minister of Finance is now in a better position to follow the cash position of the Treasury. The regular daily reporting by the National Bank to the Ministry of Finance of Treasury cash balances is, however, a relatively recent innovation. Even at the present time, no consolidated daily statement of Treasury cash position is being prepared, since the Customs Administration reports its balance only monthly.[5]

Lacking both budget officers and expense accounting, the individual ministries have no systematic nor uniform control for their current expenditures. While it is understood that improvement have been achieved along these lines, and that the individual departments now keep up to date records of open credits available to them, the Ministry of Finance still frequently receives inquiries from other departments on the credit balance available under some given chapter or item. Occasionally, the Ministry of Finance receives requests for payment which have to be returned because no more credits are available under the title against which the order is drawn. The department involved can then try to find another chapter to which the expense can be charged or wait until the next month when its balance is replenished. Occasionally, a department tries several times before it finds an open credit.

IV. RECOMMENDATIONS

The preparation of the budget is one of the most complicated and time-consuming responsibilities in the field of government

---

[5] An analysis of Treasury cash flow (*Movimiento de Caja*) was inaugurated only this year (covering the entire fiscal year 1950-51, not current operations), but no reconciliation between Treasury cash balance at the end of the year and the surplus shown in the liquidacion has been attempted.

finance. In order to make realistic estimates of probable revenue during a coming fiscal year, it is necessary to analyze scientifically the factors determining the yield of the principal sources of government revenue. It is, moreover, necessary to review systematically the differences between expected and actual revenues during recent fiscal periods and to study the reasons for such differences. Finally, as need arises, the probable effects on government revenue of any tax legislation or changes in rates and tariffs under consideration should be studied in the light of past experience.

When preparing the expenditure side of the budget, the requests of the various departments for funds must be reviewed in relation to the general fiscal and development policy of the government. The budgetary requirements of the various government departments must be scrutinized closely. The efficiency of their operations must be appraised.

Much of the material needed for the development of improved procedures for the preparation of the budget has become available in recent years or is likely to become available before long. In a country like Nicaragua, where the national income, and, consequently, government revenues depend to a large extent on the level of exports, the volume and value projection of exports is an important first step in the preparation of the budget. Another more general basis for estimating budgetary receipts are projections of national income and of its composition.

In order to make the national budget a complete and comprehensive financial plan for the year, its preparation should be made the major, permanent responsibility of a high government official. In many countries, this responsibility is delegated to a special bureau, either attached to the Ministry of Finance or responsible directly to the Executive.[6] The mission recommends the appointment of a director of the budget within the Ministry of

---

[6] The Bureau of the Budget of the United States, originally part of the Treasury Department, is now part of the Executive Office of the President.

Finance. He should be assisted by a technical staff of high professional competence.

The mission suggests that, in the long run, the placing of the Bureau of the Budget outside the Ministry of Finance and in the Executive Department would have definite advantages in a country which is embarking on a comprehensive, long-range development program. It will permit the Minister of Finance to devote his entire energies to the reorganization of the Ministry required by the recommended changes in the fiscal system; to the integration of the Customs Administration in the Ministry of Finance; to the management of the public debt; to development of an efficient system of auditing and inspection; to the supervision of the preparation of new, and codification of old, tax legislation; to the institution of the needed personnel training program and to the modernization and mechanization of office procedures. The Bureau of the Budget, not being like the Ministry of Finance one of the largest claimants on government revenue, will be in a better position to review impartially the appropriation requests of the various departments and to resolve the conflicting claims. However, the most important task for the government is the organization of an efficient budget bureau, whether it is placed within or outside the Ministry of Finance.

The Bureau of the Budget should be concerned not only with the coming year's budget but also with long-range fiscal problems. This will require close cooperation with the National Economic Council and the various departments represented therein, with the Instituto de Fomento, and with the National Bank.

Ways will also need to be worked out to enable the Director of the Budget to discharge effectively his responsibilities for reviewing and controlling current expenditures with a view to adjusting them to changing economic conditions. This is a function separate and distinct from the accounting controls of the Tribunal de Cuentas. Close cooperation between the Bureau of the Budget and the Tribunal of Cuentas should be established, but the Bureau should be given powers of review beyond those presently exercised by the Tribunal.

Regular and continuous cooperation between the Bureau of the Budget and the ministries can best be maintained through the appointment of a budget officer in each ministry. These officers would act to:

a. assist the Minister in the preparation of the departmental budget;

b. control the execution of the departmental budget;

c. control the utilization of individual credits and open appropriation balances;

d. analyze fiscal needs of the department with respect to personnel, maintenance and capital expenditures;

e. set standards of performance:

f. cooperate with the Bureau of the Budget in coordinating the government fiscal activities.

Recommendations with respect to the execution of the budget can be summarized as follows:

a. The Bureau of the Budget should obtain statutory powers to supervise disbursement of funds appropriated to assure that the intention of the executive branch, as approved by the legislature, is actually carried out.

b. Final accounts should be submitted in a form permitting appraisal of the overall results of the fiscal year.

The final accounts now submitted to Congress are divided into two parts. One contains a detailed breakdown of internal revenue but only a single figure for all customs receipts, the other a summary of expenditures by title and chapter, with some detail as to type of appropriations (ordinary or extraordinary, holdover appropriations, etc.). The two parts of the liquidacion are not tied together. Without considerable rearrangement and analysis of data, it is not possible to determine the size of the surplus or deficit incurred in the year. Thus, the liquidacion of ordinary expenditures for 1950-51 adds up to a total of 71.5 million cordobas. Since total liquidated receipts amounted to 85.5 million cordobas (excluding rentas pignoradas), the fiscal year seems to have resulted in a surplus of 14.0 million cordobas. Actually, an additional 1.6 million cordobas were expended without congressional authorization, and 1.5 million cordobas of "other expenditures" were made. The actual surplus thus amounted to 10.9 million cordobas (a figure which does not appear in the liquidacion), while the increase in the Treasury cash balance amounted to 9.0 million cordobas, as 1.9 million cordobas were used for additional debt retirement.

c. The liquidacion should include a clear statement of the surplus and of its disposition. If a deficit is incurred, detail should be given regarding the way in which it was met. The liquidacion should be accompanied by a statement on the public debt, and on the Treasury cash balance.

d. All authorizations for salaries and supplies not spent during a given year should lapse automatically at the end of the fiscal year. This will permit an accurate accounting and an exact appraisal of the extent to which the intention of the legislature has been realized.[7] In some cases, such as public works and other capital expenditures, it may be desirable to permit holding over appropriations for one fiscal year. The budget should, however, specifically provide for the holdover and expenditures charged to the carryovers should be shown separately in the liquidaciones, as are the present remanentes accounts. They should not be cumulative but should lapse automatically at the end of the second fiscal year.

---

[7] There is the danger of padding of expenditures, i.e., to spend during the last month all remaining appropriations. Administrative measures should be taken to avoid abuses.

Index

Abaca: 153, 290

Administrative system: proposed changes in, 12-15; of Empresa de Luz y Fuerza Electrica, 183 f.; railroad, 204-206; roads, 228-30; port facilities, 242-44; communications, 255-59; fiscal system, 328-29, 356-57, 385-89; customs, 360-62

African oil palm: 56, 108, 131, 136, 290; program for, 37-38

Agriculture: xxii-xxiii; technical assistance for, 12; proposed program for, 29-54; first priorities in, 31-45; second priorities in, 45-46; investment programs, 32-33, 35-36, 37, 38, 39-40, 41, 42, 43-44, 48; machinery in, 41-42; extension services, 47; role of Ministry in, 47-49; relation to industry, 109, 278-318; value of exports, 294; value of production, 295; estimated production, west coast selected crops, 296-97; major problems, 306-308; special problems, 309-17; see also Individual crops and Ministry of Agriculture

Airfields: 64, 248-49; proposals for, 73

Bananas: 290, 301-302

Banks: credit role of, xxvi; lack of facilities in some areas, xxvi; proposed reorganization, 12; credit and industry, 116; credit and construction, 163; credit and agriculture, 311-12; see also National Bank and International Bank

Beans: 280, 281, 290

Black Wattle: 150, 288

Budget: National for 1949-50 and 1950-51, xxv; deficits, xxv, 6; recommendations for, 80-81, 401-13; proposed form of, 401-403; proposed development expenditure budget, 403; preparation of, 390-95; organization of, 395-405; execution of, 405; director of, 410, 411, 412

Cacao: 108, 302-303

Candy: 170

Canning: 172

Capital: 116-17, 125, 168, 171, 261 f.; proposal to encourage investment of in industry, 123

Carazo: 281, 282

Cartels: 120

Cattle: expansion of production, 12, 109, 121, 303, 309; program for, 34-36; importance of grain facilities to, 46; need of slaughterhouse facilities, 55; markets for, 55-56; live exports of, 143-44; hides, 145; imports of, 145; opportunities for meat processing, 165-66; supplemental feeding, 166; see also Hides and Leather

Cement: production and demand for, 57, 120, 160-62; imports of, 110; private use of, 160; pro-